War Diaries

from

Inside Hitler's Headquarters

Edited by THOMAS FENSCH

New Century Books

For my brother Tim

....

Copyright 2015 Thomas Fensch

Trade Paperback ISBN
978-0-9963154-9-4

Hardcover ISBN
978-0-9972288-0-9

e-book ISBN
978-0-9963154-8-7

New Century Books
8821 Rockdale Rd.
N. Chesterfield, VA, 23236-2150
e-mail: newcentbks@gmail.com

CONTENTS

Introduction by Tom Fensch i

1) GREINER DIARY NOTES, 12 Aug 1942–12 Mar 1943 11

    Preliminary Matter.................... xii

    Greiner Diary Notes 1

2) OPERATION BARBAROSSA 213

    Preliminary Matter.................... i

    Operation Barbarossa 1

About the editor 369

Introduction ...

by Thomas Fensch

*The world will hold its breath
when Operation Barbarossa is executed."
—Adolf Hitler*

Operation Barbarossa was the code name for the Germany's invasion of Soviet Russia.

"The whole world will hold its breath—"

Thus Nazi historian Helmuth Greiner quoted Hitler. Greiner served as Custodian of the War Diary in Hitler's Headquarters August, 1939 until April, 1943, when he was dismissed. He was born 30 April, 1892 in Leipzig, Saxony.

The biographical material about Greiner states (names are in all capitals in original documents):

Helmuth GREINER joined the Army in December 1913, entering the 132d Prussian infantry Regiment as an officer candidate, and in July 1914 was promoted lieutenant with commission dated 23 June 1912. In World War 1 he served at the various fronts from the outbreak of war to June 1917, with two brief breaks to recover from wounds. In June 1917 he was detached to serve as military attaché on the staff of the German Embassy in Bern, Switzerland, from which he transferred to the Historical Division of the Army General Staff, Berlin, in January, 1919, remaining there until he was discharged from the Army in 1920, with a rank of captain. Less than a month later GREINER was appointed archivist in the Military History section of the Historical Branch of the Reichs Archives at Potsdam. He remained in his service until 1935, and it was during this period that he continued his studies in national economy and history at the Berlin University 1921-1924. Also during this period he did a great deal of writing on the German official history of World War 1 and was prompted Archivist.

On 1 April 1935 GREINER was re-called for service in the Wehrmacht, promoted Regierungsrat (equivalent to major in rank) and attached to the re-organized Historical Division of the Reichs Archives, a branch of the Military History Research Institute of the army. On 18 August, 1939, he was transferred to the National Defense Branch, which later was re-designated Wehrmacht Operations Staff (Wehrmachsfuehrungssteb), in Hitler's headquarters, as keeper of the War Diary. Promoted Oberregierungsrat on 1 May 1936 and Ministerialrat in 1 October 1940, GREINER was removed from his post on 22 April 1943 because of his own antinationalsocialiast sentiments. Following this he was detached to the Office of the German General attached to Italian Armed Forces Headquarters in Rome for a brief spell, 15 June–31 July 1943.

From that date to the end of the War GREINER was not employed being considered politically unreliable. He was captured by US forces at Oberhof, Thuringia on 4 April 1945.

(Note: it cannot now be determined if Greiner wrote this biographical profile or if it was written later by U.S. Army specialists; however, the all-capitals style of names and dates appear throughout the War Diary documents Greiner wrote. Slightly longer versions of this profile appear at the beginnings of the documents published here.)

A following page shows the series of documents Greiner wrote. Of prime importance, and included in this book, are two documents:

WAR DIARY NOTES 12 August 1942–17 MAY 1943 and OPERATION BARBAROSSA.

As Greiner states, in his Prefactory Remarks:

> The following note are based on the memoranda which I wrote in the capacity of custodian of the War Diary of the Wehrmacht Operations staff during the daily situation reports and discussions at HITLER'S headquarters from August 1942 to March 1943. The contents of the War Diary written during that time were based on these memoranda. All volumes containing the text and appendices of the War Diary were destroyed on orders of General WINTER, at that time Deputy Chief of the Wehrmacht Operations Staff, at Lake Hintersee in Upper-Bavaria on I May 1945. In the following pages I

have attempted to restore the War Diary, at least partially on the basis of the memoranda which are still in my possession. During the period from 26 June 1941 to 11 August, 1942, I personally destroyed all my handwritten memoranda, with the exception of some particularly important notes, as soon as I had used them for the writing of the War Diary. On 18 March 1943, I went on leave for an extended period of time. Upon my return on 22 April 1943, I was relived of my opposition as Custodian of the War Diary by HITLER for political reasons. Therefore, the following notes are confined to the above-mentioned period.
    (Prefactory Remarks, pp. 1)

Greiner survived the war without being sent to a death camp or shot. Apparently some of Greiner's notes were not fully reconstructed until 1949. They were translated from the German by U.S. Army language experts sometime between 1945 and 1949. (Names of the translators appear on cover pages of these documents.)

THE WAR DIARIES

Historians and military specialists may find all of the Greiner War Diary pages highly valuable, however these seem particularly interesting:

<u>21 December 1942</u>
Situation Report:
A report received from General Von MANSTEIN—that the Fourth Panzer Army is unable to advance beyond the section reached (Aksai) and that the Sixth Army cannot possible advance more than 300 kilometers—gives rise to a lengthy discussion of the situation in the southern section of the Eastern front between the Fuehrer and the Chiefs of Army and Air Force General Staff. However, again no definitive decisions have been made. It seems as if the Fuehrer is no longer able to make a clear-cut decision.
    (War Diaries, pp. 165)

Newsreel film of Hitler occasionally showed him holding one arm steady—the last film footage shot of Hitler in Berlin reveals a shaking hand, which some experts judged to be a symptom of Parkinson's disease. His perceived inability to make a decision in December 1942 may be an indication he had Parkinson's disease at that time.

10 January 1943
Situation Report:
East: The following quantities of supplies were flown to the Stalingrad area: 125 tons on 7 January, 99 tons (including 61 tons of food supplies) on 8 January, and 196.5 tons (including 101.1 tons of food supplies) on 9 January. Eight hundred wounded were flown back from the Stalingrad area on 9 January. At present, the daily food rations for the personnel of the Sixth Army consist of: 75 grams of bread, 200 grams of horse meat including bones, 12 grams of fat, 11 grams of sugar, and one cigarette. By 20 January, all horses will be slaughtered.
    (War Diaries, pp. 177)

The following entry appears deserves a full explanation:

Convoy JW 51B comprised 14 merchants ships enroute to Soviet Russia—carrying 202 tanks, 1,046 other vehicles, 87 fighters, 33 bombers, 21,880 tons of fuel and over 54,000 tons of other supplies. They were escorted by six British destroyers, two corvettes, a minesweeper and two trawlers. They sailed in the dead of winter to avoid the Nazi air force.

They were met by two Nazi heavy cruisers and six destroyers on 31 December 1942 in the Barents Sea, north of New Cape, Norway.

The battle took place in the dead of night in the artic winter; neither side knew much of the locations of their opponents, or even how many ships were in action. It became known as the Battle of the Barents Sea. (See: Wikipedia—the Battle of the Barents Sea.)

The ultimate outcome: one British destroyer sunk, the Bramble, one destroyer damaged, the Achates, one minesweeper sunk and 250 killed.

The German *Kriegsmarine* suffered one destroyer, the Eckholdt sunk, one cruiser, the Admiral Hipper, damaged and 330 killed.

In the confusion of battle, both sides broke off the engagement almost simultaneously.

Apparently Hitler was first informed it was a victory for the Nazi *Kriegsmarine*; subsequent reports indicated no better than a draw; in fact, it was a strategic victory for the British. All 14 merchant ships reached their destinations with all cargo intact.

Hitler became enraged at the inefficiency of the *Kriegsmarine,* which he thought was the superior force in the battle; and he *seriously considered scrapping the entire German Navy,* despite earlier successes with his U-Boat fleet.

This brought a vehement rebuttal dated 10 January, 1943 by *Kriegsmaine* Admiral Erich Raeder (the name is misspelled in the Greiner file):

By scrapping the nucleus of the Navy, we would relinquish an area which far from having become obsolete and thus superfluous, as a result of the progress made in the technique of warfare, is most vitally influencing the over-all war situation, particularly however the all-important war at sea. The enemy is utterly afraid of our reinforcing this arm. He knows his own weaknesses best and is aware of the potentialities which the German battle fleet has. The German battle fleet will be able to take advantage if these potentialities if it can operate and fight with the support of air forces without which no navy can achieve success today.
Moreover, nobody is able to foresee today where and how soon was developments might demand the commitment of sea power in decisive operations. If we should lack the large naval units at the moment when they are needed, then it will be too late as a result of our own action.
I firmly believe that the insignificant gains in personnel and material are out of proportion to the grave military and political disadvantages which the loss of the German battle fleet would entail. I am convinced that, without the battle fleet, the Navy would be unable to fulfill the offense and defensive tasks assigned to it in the battle for the freedom of Greater Germany.

READER
(War Diaries, pp. 183)

Raeder then submitted his resignation to Hitler, who apparently accepted it reluctantly. Raeder was replaced by Admiral Karl Doenitz, who held the position through the rest of the war and became German head of state briefly after Hitler's suicide.
In an entry dated 23 January, 1943, Greiner reports the following:

According to an account of the Russian losses prepared by the commander of the Russian replacement training army, which has fallen into German hands, the Russians have lost 11,.2 million men, either killed, captured or wounded and unable to return to the front. Reportedly, the Russian manpower potential is almost exhausted and large numbers of women are being employed at the front.
(War Dairies, pp. 188)

And, in an entry dated 16 February, 1943, Greiner summarizes a report by General Walter Warlimont, who visited Tunisia and Italy and also visited Erwin Rommel's African campaign. Greiner writes:

The enemy is building a road leading from Bou Arada to Madjez el Bab. He seems to concentrate strong forces in the area opposite the northern sector of the Fifth Panzer army. Batteries up to 330 mm. caliber are also emplaced in that area. Reconnaissance in the enemy rear area is not possible because the Air Force is unable to penetrated the enemy defense and because the terrain renders observation very difficult. In the southern sector, the enemy is evacuating his forward positions. American forces are employed there, and their personnel is of excellent fighting caliber, but utterly inexperienced. The British and French call them "their Italians."
(War Diaries, pp. 193)

This was, presumably, before General George S. Patton entered the African theater.

Greiner also reports on Allied air offensives:

12 March 1943
Last night a heavy air attack was carried out on Stuttgart. According to final reports on results of the air attack on Berlin during the might of 1-2 March 1943, 649 persons were killed,. 1,570 wounded—369 of them seriously—, 62 persons are missing, 35,000 homeless, 20,000 buildings destroyed or damaged, and 1,600 major fires, 500 fires of medium dimensions, and thousands of minor fires occurred. During the air attack on Essen the night of 5-6 March, 304 persons were killed, 1,440 wounded and 93 are missing; 396 mines and heavy demolition bombs,119,000 incendiary bombs, and 15,000 phosphorus bombs were dropped; 3,016 buildings were destroyed, 2,050 were heavily damaged, substantial damage was inflicted on 3,000 buildings, and 18,000 were slightly damaged.
(War Dairies, pp. 208)

THE BARBAROSSA FILE

In the first Barbarossa entry, Greiner expresses "astonishment and consternation" among all top Nazi officers at Hitler's decisions to invade Soviet Russia. He writes:

On the afternoon of 29 July 1940, General of Artillery JODL, the Chief of Armed Forces Operations Office, appeared at the special train of the Department for National Defense which was being held at Bad Reichenhall during HITLER's stay at the Berghoff. Under seal of strictest secrecy, he informed Colonel WARLIMONT, the Department Chief, as well as the chiefs of the operations divisions of the Army, Navy, and Air Force, Lieutenant Colonel von LOSZBERG, Lieutenant Commander JUNGE, and Major von FALKENSTEIN, that the Fuehrer had decided to conquer the Soviet Union by force of arms.

His move aroused extreme astonishment and consternation among the above mentioned officers Indeed, had not HITLER, while addressing his generals at the Berghoff on 2 August 1939, and in his Reichstag speech of 1 September, Declared emphatically that the nonaggression pact signed by Germany and the U.S.S.R. on 23 August signified a complete reversal of German foreign policy and for all time precluded the possibility of hostilities between the two nations! Furthermore, had not HITLER concluded this pact principally to insure that Germany would not again become involved in a two-front war as it did during World War 1! In addition, the Soviet Union thus far has fulfilled the terms of the treaty in every respect, and the German-Russian credit agreement of 189 August 1939 and the highly important commercial treaty of 11 February 1940 had resulted in remarkable benefits for Germany. Moreover, immediately after the fall of France, HITLER had issued the first instructions for a partial demobilization of the Army, particularly with regard to the discharge of the older age classes and especially technicians, and has ordered that there be a shift of armaments in favor of the air force and navy. These instructions indicated that he no longer anticipated any large-scale ground operations but was concerned only with war against England Also, on 16 July, 1940 he had actually ordered in his "Fuehrer Directive # 10" that preparations be made for landing operations in England, then in spite of this, HITLER suddenly announced his intention to attack Soviet Russia, the reasons which induced him to take this step could only be surmised.

(OPERATION BARBAROSSA, pp. 1-2)

The Operation Barbarossa file is one long, 126-page document, with few major section breaks.

On page 32, total manpower of the Wehrmaht is specified:

The Wehrmacht thus gained additional strength, bringing the total to 6,763,000 men, of which 4,900,000 men (72.5%) were assigned to the Army, 298,000 men (4.4) %) to the Navy, 1,485,000 men (22%) to the Air Force and 80,000 (1.1 % to the Waffen-SS.

Pages 54-58 constitute:

Directive # 21
Operation Barbarossa

Including: 1).OVER-ALL OBJECTIVE; 2). PROSPECTIVE ALLIES AND THEIR MISSIONS; 3). THE CONDUCTION OF OPERATIONS, including Army, Air Force and Navy. The end of this document was signed: Adolf HITLER.

The OPERATION BARBAROSSA document also says:

<u>America</u>, even if she participates in the war, does not represent any great danger. The giant block <u>Russia</u> is much more dangerous. Although Germany has concluded very advantageous political and economic agreements with the Soviet Union, it is better to rely on our power.
 (pp. 75)

Specific instructions for 14 major Army Groups, including: Army Group South; The Twelfth Army; the First Panzer Army and others are detailed on pages 77-80.

The OPERATION BARBAROSSA file also contained this directive from Hitler:

This war should not be fought according to general military rules: it is a clash of two opposed ideologies which require relentless hard-heartedness. Consequently, the Wehrmacht should discard completely all the traditional conceptions and standards. The thing that matters is the eradication of bolshevism,. The political functionaries and the commissars in the armed

forces are the exponents of the bolshevistic idea. The latter cannot be regarded as soldiers and consequently, if the occasion arises, also cannot be treated as prisoners of war. These commissars, same as the political functionaries, should be separated from the other prisoners of war immediately upon capture and placed under the control of the special task detachments (Einsatzgruppen) of the SD (Security Service) who, under the command of the Reich Fuehrer SS, will accompany the German troops to Russia. Wherever the combat situation makes it impossible to turn them over to the SD (Security Service) the functionaires and commissars should be shot by the troops.
    (OPERATION BARBAROSSA, pp. 100-101)

At the end of the Operation Barbarossa file, Greiner wrote the following:

During his conferences with the Commander in Chief of Army High Command and the Chief of the General Staff held on 9 January and 3 February respectively, HITLER has stated that Europe, and even the world, would hold its breath when Operation BARBAROSSA should be executed. However, in reality
It was probably true that the world felt relieved when HITLER, through the attack on the Soviet Union, unnecessarily burdened himself with a new enemy and thus, at the same, with a two-front war, which he had certainly always wanted to avoid. Besides, this was an enemy whose population was more than twice as large as that of Germany and whose country was huge in size and had mineral resources in enormous quantities. This colossus, which had never been really conquered, HITLER seriously believed he would be able to completely defeat and make submissive to his will in a blitz campaign lasting three, or at the utmost, four months.

… and, Greiner also writes:

He was so firmly convinced of his success that even before the start of the eastern campaign, he hatched adventurous plans which aimed still higher. As early as the middle of February, HITLER had designed General JODL to have the Department for National Defense draw up a plan concerning the assembly of troops in Afghanistan for an attack on India. In this respect too, he followed in the footsteps of NAPOLEON I.
    (OPERATION BARBAROSSA, pp. 124)

* * *

Note: In the interest of authenticity, pages in this book are reprinted from the post-World War Two U.S. Army translations of the Greiner documents. Since Greiner was relieved of his post in 1943, for his anti-national socialist sentiments or beliefs, and survived the war without being sent to a death camp or shot, readers can judge for themselves how truthful or perhaps how self-serving Greiner's comments are, toward the last pages of the Operation Barbarossa file, or if he wrote them during the post-war years, in relative safety.

Suggested readings ...

Shirer, William L.. *The Ride and Fall of the Third Reich: A History of Nazi Germany,* pub. 1960.

Speer, Albert. *Inside the Third Reich,* pub. 1969.

Warlimont, Walter. *Inside Hitler's Headquarters, 1939-1945,* pub. 1962.

GREINER DIARY NOTES

12 August 1942 to 17 March 1943

Ministerialrat
Custodian of the War Diary
In HITLER'S Headquarters
(August 1939 - April 1943)

NOTES

On the Situation Reports and Discussions at HITLER'S Headquarters

From 12 August 1942 to 17 March 1943

Translator: Werner MEYER
Editor: LUCAS
Reviewer: Lt. Col. VERNON

MS # C-065 a

FOREWORD

This manuscript is part of a narrative history of events in the German Armed Forces Supreme Command Headquarters during World War II. The writer, Hellmuth GREINER, was charged with writing the War Diary at that headquarters from August 1939 to April 22, 1943. He has based his work on notes taken at various conferences, copies of final drafts for entry in the War Diary, copies of HITLER'S directives, orders and documents he was able to save from destruction at great personal risk.

With the aid of these sources and the trained mind and memory of a professional historian, he has presented a vivid picture of HITLER'S method of command as well as his reaction to reverses and success and the various other factors which influenced decisions in both the military and the political spheres.

In addition to a general description of procedures in the supreme headquarters it includes details of organization and the composition of HITLER'S immediate staff. Brief graphic descriptions are also included of the outstanding characteristics of its chief members who served HITLER in his capacity as Supreme Commander of the Armed Forces and Commander in Chief of the Army.

The completed work to date is divided into a number of manuscripts. For easy reference the manuscripts have been listed chronologically for inclusion in the English copies.

LOUIS M. NAWROCKY
Lt Colonel, Armor
Chief, Foreign Military
Studies Branch

MS # C-065 a

Author

Helmuth GREINER
Ministerialrat im OKW*
Born: 30 April 1892
      Leipzig, Saxony.

Helmuth GREINER joined the Army in December 1913, entering the 132d Prussian Infantry Regiment as an officer candidate, and in July 1914 was promoted lieutenant with commission dated 23 June 1912. In World War I he served at the various fronts from the outbreak of war to June 1917, with two brief breaks to recover from wounds. In June 1917 he was detached to serve as military attache on the staff of the German Embassy in Bern, Switzerland, from which he was transferred to the Historical Division of Army General Staff, Berlin, in January 1919, remaining there until discharged from the Army in March 1920, with rank of captain. Less than a month later GREINER was appointed archivist in the Military History Section of the Historical Branch of the Reichs Archives at Potsdam. He remained in this service until 1935, and it was during this period that he continued his studies in national economy and history at the Berlin university from 1921-24. Also during this period he did a great deal of writing on the German official history of World War I and was promoted Archivrat.

On 1 April 1935 GREINER was re-called for service in the Wehrmacht, promoted Regierungsrat (equivalent to major in rank) and attached to the re-organized Historical Division of the Reichs Archives, a branch of the Military History Research Institute of the Army. On 18 August 1939, he was transferred to the National Defense Branch, which

---

* Administrative official attached to Wehrmacht Command, equivalent in rank to a colonel.

MS # C-065 a

later was re-designated Wehrmacht Operations Staff (Wehrmachtsfuehrungsstab), in Hitler's headquarters, as Keeper of the War Diary. Promoted Oberregierungsrat on 1 May 1936 and Ministerialrat on 1 October 1940, GREINER was removed from his post on 22 April 1943, because of his known antinationalsocialist sentiments. Following this he was detached to the Office of the German General Attached to Italian Armed Forces Headquarters in Rome for a brief spell, 15 June - 31 July 1943.

From that date to the end of the War, GREINER was not employed, being considered politically unreliable. He was captured by US forces at Oberhof, Thuringia on 4 April 1945.

In addition to his career in the civil service and the Wehrmacht, GREINER is a well-known writer on military subjects in the historical vein, his published works including, VETERANS OF WORLD WAR I, a collection of essays by soldiers of that War; THE 1916 CAMPAIGN IN RUMANIA, written for the Swedish General Staff; THE 1916 INVASION OF BELGIUM AND THE FIRST MAJOR BATTLES; THE FRENCH MOBILIZATION IN 1914; THE AMERICAN WAR OF SECESSION; GUERILLA WARFARE IN 1870-71 and FRENCH MOBILIZATION PLANS, 1885-1914, some of which were written specifically as instruction manuals for use in training.

MS # C-065 a

GREINER SERIES

OKW, WORLD WAR II	MS # C-065 b
WAR DIARY WEHRMACHT OPERATIONS STAFF, Aug-Nov 40	MS # C-065 j
SHEETS OF WAR DIARY OF THE DEFENSE BRANCH OF THE WEHRMACHT OPERATIONS STAFF	MS # C-065 m
RECORDS OF SITUATION EVALUATIONS OF THE NATIONAL DEFENSE BRANCH 8 Aug 40 - 25 Jun 41	MS # C-065 l
WAR DIARY WEHRMACHT OPERATIONS STAFF, Dec - Mar 1941	MS # C-065 k
WAR DIARY NOTES 12 Aug 42 - 17 May 1943	MS # C-065 a
POLAND 1939 (I)	MS # C-065 c
WESTERN AND NORTHERN EUROPE 1940 (II)	MS # C-065 d
Operation FELIX (IV)	MS # C-065 h
ITALY, WINTER 1940-41 (V)	MS # C-065 e
AFRICA 1941 (VI)	MS # C-065 f
BALKANS 1941 (VII)	MS # C-065 g
Operation BARBAROSSA (VIII)	MS # C-065 i
Operation SEELOEWE (III)	MS # C-059

MS # C-065a

Helmuth GREINER

-1-

Notes on the Situation Reports and Discussions at HITLER's
Headquarters from 12 August 1942 to 17 March 1943

Prefatory Remarks

The following notes are based on the memoranda which I wrote in the capacity of Custodian of the War Diary of the Wehrmacht Operations Staff during the daily situation reports and discussions at HITLER's headquarters from August 1942 to March 1943. The contents of the War Diary written during that time were based on these memoranda. All volumes containing the text and appendices of the War Diary were destroyed on orders of General WINTER, at that time Deputy Chief of the Wehrmacht Operations Staff, at Lake Hintersee in Upper-Bavaria on 1 May 1945. In the following pages, I have attempted to restore the War Diary, at least partially on the basis of the memoranda which are still in my possession. During the period from 26 June 1941 to 11 August 1942, I personally destroyed all my handwritten memoranda, with the exception of some particularly important notes, as soon as I had used them for the writing of the War Diary. On 18 March 1943, I went on leave for an extended period of time. Upon my return, on 22 April 1943, I was relieved of my position as Custodian of the War Diary by HITLER for political reasons. Therefore, the following notes are confined to the above-mentioned period.

MS # P-065a   -2-

On 16 July 1942, HITLER's headquarters were established in the Ukraine, in a small triangular area of woodland, 15 kilometers north-northeast of Winniza at the highway to Shitomir near the village of Strishawka *. HITLER and his most intimate advisers and his military staff, the field echelons of the Wehrmacht Operations Staff, were quartered there in log cabins and prefabricated barracks respectively. The camp had been given the code name "Wehrwolf." Headquarters of the Army High Command was located in Winniza after 16 July 1942.

On 12 August 1942, the first day covered by these notes, the situation on the Eastern Front was as follows:

On 28 June 1942 the great summer offensive of Army Group South, the so-called Operation BLAU, had been launched with the drive of the Second Army on Woronesh. In the course of this offensive, the German attack forces, composed of the Second Army, Sixth Army, Fourth Panzer Army, First Panzer Army and Seventeenth Army, had reached the Don in the area below Woronesh and had taken Rostov on 24 July 1942. In the course of the following days, Generalfeldmarschall LIST's Army Group A, which had been formed on 7 July 1942 by combining Armeegruppe Ruoff ** (comprising the Seventeenth Army and Rumanian Third Army) and First Panzer Army, crossed the lower Don for a thrust into the Caucasus. On 11 August 1942, Army Group A had reached the lower Kuban with the Rumanian Third Army at Slawjanskaja, with the

---

* See German Operations Map Russia 1 : 1 000 000, sheet 2.
** Not a standard organization, usually consisted of an Army plus a number of Corps or Divisions under an army type staff (Translator).

Seventeenth Army on both sides of Krasnodar and with elements of the First Panzer Army in the area around Maikop. Mountain troops of this army had advanced in the upper valleys of the Kuban and its tributaries into the High Caucasus, while its motorized forces, advancing toward the Caucasian oil fields, had taken Pjatigorsk on 9 August 1942.

In the sector of Army Group B, (Commander in Chief Generaloberst Freiherr Von Weichs) which also had been formed from Army Group South, the Fourth Panzer Army had crossed the Don at Zymljanskaja, and, in a drive toward the Northeast, had reached the southern edge of Stalingrad, while the Sixth Army had occupied the great loop of the Don north of Kalatsch from 7 to 12 August 1942. The Italian Eighth Army and the Hungarian Second Army were holding covering positions along the sector of the middle Don. The bridgehead and cornerstone of Woronesh and Army Group's northern flank between Woronesh and Liwny were held by the Second Army.

In the sectors of Army Group Center and Army Group North, no major changes in the front line established at the conclusion of the fierce defensive battles of the preceding winter had occurred. The line extended from a point adjacent to the Second Army roughly through Liwny-Orel-Ssuchinitschi-Juchnoff-Subzoff-Rshew, then turning sharply in a south-westerly direction, forming a wide salient toward the south, via Belyj-Demidoff-Welish-Welikije Luki-Cholm. It then extended along the Lowat from the so-called land bridge leading to the enclave of Demjansk, which had been held during the winter campaign, then north of Lake Ilmen along the western bank of the Wolchow up to Kirischi and from that cornerstone, turned in a westerly direction, via Malukssa and Putilowo to Lake Ladoga, and, finally, from Schluesburg in a southern semicircle around Leningrad up to the Gulf of Finland. Because of its peculiar shape, the narrow passage south of Lake Ladoga with Mga as its center was called the "bottleneck" by the Germans. The focal point of the battle in the sector of Army Group Center was the front due east of Subzoff and due north of Rshew in the Ninth Army's sector, where the Russians attacked with strong infantry and armored forces on 30 July 1942 and, by 4 August 1942, had effected wide and deep penetrations. At the most dangerous points of penetration, due east of Subzoff and east of Ssytschewka, the XXXIX Corps, comprising the 1st, 2nd, and 5th Panzer Divisions and the 102nd Infantry Division, had been committed to halt the Russian attack.

Distribution of Forces along the Eastern Front on 12 August 1942

Army Group A: Commander in Chief: Generalfeldmarschall LIST
               Chief of Staff: Generalleutnant Von GREIFFENBERG

               Armeegruppe Ruoff (Headquarters of Seventeenth Army):
               Commander in Chief: Generaloberst RUOFF
               Seventeenth Army and Rumanian Third Army

               First Panzer Army: Commander in Chief: Generaloberst Von KLEIST

Army Group B: Commander in Chief: Generaloberst Freiherr Von WEICHS
               Chief of Staff: Generalleutnant Von SODENSTERN

               Fourth Panzer Army: Commander in Chief: Generaloberst HOTH
               Sixth Army: Commander in Chief: Generaloberst PAULUS
               Italian Eighth Army: Commander in Chief: General GARIBOLDI
               Hungarian Second Army: Commander in Chief: unknown
               Second Army: Commander in Chief: Generaloberst Von SALMUTH

Army Group Center: Commander in Chief: Generalfeldmarschall Von KLUGE
               Chief of Staff: Generalmajor WOEHLER

               Fourth Army: Commander in Chief: Generaloberst HEINRICI
               Second Panzer Army: Commander in Chief: Generaloberst SCHMIDT

MS # C-065a

        Third Panzer Army: Commander in Chief: Generaloberst REINHARDT

        Ninth Army: Commander in Chief: Generaloberst MODEL

Army Group North: Commander in Chief: Generalfeldmarschall Von KUECHLER
        Chief of Staff: Generalmajor HASSE

        Sixteenth Army: Commander in Chief: Generaloberst BUSCH

        Eighteenth Army: Commander in Chief: Generaloberst LINDEMANN

Directly assigned to the Army High Command for carrying out Operation NORDLICHT, attack on Leningrad, and assembled in the area of Army Group North:

    Eleventh Army: Commander in Chief: Generalfeldmarschall Von MANSTEIN.

12 August 1942

Situation Report:

The Chief of the Armed Forces Operations Staff advises the Fuehrer that the Commander in Chief of the Air Force intends to transfer an antiaircraft division from the First Panzer Army to the Fourth Panzer Army. The Chief of Army General Staff points out that the First Panzer Army needs strong antiaircraft protection in the Caucasus and that the transfer of the entire antiaircraft division would therefore be inadvisable. General JODL will discuss the matter with the Reichsmarschall once more.

General HALDER reports that, according to statements made by captured Russian officers, the Russian Caucasus Army is gradually disintegrating. The thrust of the advanced detachment of the 1st Mountain Division into the High Caucasus does not meet with the Fuehrer's approval. The Fuehrer considers such action a scattering of the forces. He points out that the Division, if it should encounter stronger enemy forces, would not be able to overcome their resistance, but would suffer reverses, while at the same time it would be needed at another point of greater operational importance. However, the Fuehrer fails to order the withdrawal of the Division from the High Caucasus. He wants the fuel supplies available to Army Group A to be allocated primarily to Army Group's right wing in order to enable that wing to effect a breakthrough to the coast of the Black Sea as speedily as possible. After the capture of Novorossisk, the fuel supplies will be shipped across the Black Sea by the Navy.

The Fuehrer, furthermore, requests the immediate moving up of German medium artillery and antitank defense weapons, as well as the transfer of a corps headquarters staff with two divisions to the area behind the covering position of the Hungarians along the Don in the sector of Army Group B. The Chief of Army General Staff states that the 168th Infantry Division is being moved up from the north and the 336th Infantry Division from the south to reinforce the sector held by the Hungarians. Besides, one corps of the Sixth Army will be transferred to the west after the capture of Stalingrad. At that time, HITLER was constantly worried by the thought that the western Allies might attempt to land in France in order to relieve some of the pressure on their Russian ally by establishing the "Second Front" which was requested by the Soviet Union with increasing urgency. As early as 30 July 1942, HITLER, therefore, gave the order to halt the "Grossdeutschland" motorized Division, which had been advancing into the Caucasus as a unit of the First Panzer Army, and to withdraw this division to the northern bank of the Don for an early shipment to the West.

On 11 August 1942, Operation WIRBELWIND is started in the sector of Army Group Center. This operation is an attack launched by the Second Panzer Army at Ssuchinitschi in a north-northwesterly direction in order to pinch off the Russian salient protruding sharply to the west between Ssuchinitschi and Juchnoff. The Fuehrer is under the impression that in this operation the Second Panzer Army concentrates its effort too much on its outer wing, namely its right or eastern flank, instead of annihilating the enemy forces which are fighting along the front to the west by launching a thrust in the general direction west-north-west. HITLER, therefore, instructs the Chief of Army General Staff to give the order to Army Group Center to concentrate its forces solely in the direction of the main attack. The situation in the large penetration area in the sector of the Ninth Army at Ssytschewka, Subzoff, and Rshew continues to be very critical. The Fuehrer takes the withdrawal of the German forces from the cornerstone position Rshew-Subzoff into consideration, but does not announce a decision yet. The Air Force will assign additional forces to this sector.

In the sector of Army Group North, signs of an impending enemy attack against the "bottleneck" are increasing. The Fuehrer considers it desirable to make adequate reserves available to the Eighteenth Army in order to avoid the necessity for the Army Group to commit, in case of a major enemy attack, the forces intended for employment in Operation NORDLICHT. He suggests, therefore, that the Chief of Army General Staff assign to the Eighteenth Army four jaeger battalions which had just been activated at the troop training grounds at Arys in East Prussia. However, General HALDER states that the suggested assignments could not be made because he needs the battalions for other tasks.

13 August 1942

Distribution of the Flying Formations of the Air Force along the Eastern Front

Fourth Air Force: 14 bomber groups   7 1/3 airbomber groups   8 1/3 fighter groups   2 long-range fighter groups

	bomber groups	dive bomber group	fighter group	
Don Air Forces Headquarters	2	1	1	
Eastern Air Forces Headquarters	8 " 1 "	2 " – "	4 1/3 " 1 "	(in Second Panzer Army's sector) 1/3 close-support group 1/3 tank destroyer group (in Ninth Army's sector)
First Air Force	1/3 "	– "	2 "	
Northern Air Force Command	2 "	1 "	2 "	1 2/3 aerial torpedo groups

Total: 27 1/3 bomber groups, 11 1/3 dive bomber groups, 18 2/3 fighter groups,
2 long-range fighter groups, 1/3 close-support group,
1/3 tank destroyer group and 1 2/3 aerial torpedo groups,
each group comprising an average of 20 planes ready to take off,
totaling 61 2/3 groups, comprising about 1,234 planes.

The fourth Air Force and Don Air Forces Headquarters * are employed in the sectors of Army Group A and B, Eastern Air Forces Headquarters in the area of Army Group Center in the sectors of the Second Panzer Army and Ninth Army; First Air Force is employed in the sector of Army Group North and Northern Air Force Commander in Finland.

---

* On 10 August 1942, the designation of I Air Force Corps was changed to Don Air Forces Headquarters.

Situation Report:

The Chief of Army Supply and Administration reports to the Fuehrer that XXXX Panzer Corps, committed at the eastern wing of the First Panzer Army, has received fuel in a quantity sufficient to cover a distance of 100 kilometers and that this corps is therefore ready for commitment in new operations. It has been ascertained through air reconnaissance that the northern section of the railroad Astrachan-Baku between Astrachan and Machatsch Kala is still under construction. Reports have been received from the Seventeenth Army to the effect that the oil refineries in the Krasnodar area are essentially undestroyed. The Reichsmarschall reports to the Fuehrer that, according to an intercepted Russian radio message, the coastal road leading to Tuapse is completely blocked. The Chief of Army General Staff reports that the northern wing of the Sixth Army will be ready to cross the Don for the attack on Stalingrad on 15 August 1942.

In the sector of Army Group Center, agent reports have been received to the effect that new Russian armored units are being activated in the Tula area. Thus far, Operation WIRBELWIND has not resulted in a decisive success, but the beginning of a favorable development seems to be indicated by the latest reports. According to a report by the Chief of Army General Staff, the Second Panzer Army resumed its attack at its right, eastern wing early this morning, but with a limited objective only, namely an advance of 8 kilometers. Upon reaching this objective, the attack wing will turn to the west in accordance with instructions given by the Fuehrer. Meanwhile, the 9th Panzer Division arrived at the Second Panzer Army's right wing behind the sector of the 11th Panzer Division; elements of the 4th Panzer Division are also in that sector.

This morning, the expected enemy attack against the front of the Third Panzer Army was launched at Juchnoff. Thus far, the enemy achieved only local penetrations. At the front sectors at Subzoff and Rshew, the fiercest defensive fighting to date took place yesterday, according to a report received from the Ninth Army. Today, the Russians resumed their attacks at Ssytschewka and Subzoff. For the time being, the Fuehrer has abandoned the idea of withdrawing the 14th Motorized Infantry Division from the cornerstone position at Rshew to a tendon position, because it seems as if the enemy has ceased moving up reinforcements.

In the sector of Army Group North, the Russian preparations for an attack at Pogostje and, especially, at the "bottleneck" are becoming increasingly evident. The Fuehrer wants the 12th Panzer Division, which was to be committed by Army Group North in the Leningrad sector, to remain at the eastern front of the "bottleneck" to ward off the expected enemy attack.

In the Mediterranean Sea, an Anglo-American convoy was intercepted yesterday by the German Air Force north of Tunis. This morning, the convoy was attacked again near the island of Pantelleria. However, it continued its voyage through the Strait of Sicily in the direction of Malta.

Last night, the British air force carried out a very severe air attack on Mainz, where fires caused by an attack by the RAF during the night

MS # C-065a   -13-

of 11 - 12 August were not yet completely under control. A great number of aerial mines was dropped. Two-thirds of the inner city are almost completely destroyed. Twenty-three heavy, and fourteen light anti-aircraft batteries are employed in the Mainz area.

14 August 1942

Situation Report:

In the sector of Army Group A, XXXX Panzer Corps, committed at the First Panzer Army's eastern wing, has taken Georgijewskaja. Since strong enemy forces seem to assemble at Machatsch Kala for the defense of Baku, the Fuehrer gives the order to move up the 13th Panzer Division and the 16th Motorized Infantry Division to support XXXX Panzer Corps. At the right wing of Armeegruppe Ruoff, the Rumanian Third Army is to advance with the units which will cross the Kerch Strait as speedily as possible, and with the Rumanian Cavalry Corps along the coastal road. Two divisions will be withdrawn from V Infantry Corps, which is advancing on Novorossisk from the northeast in the Seventeenth Army's sector. The two divisions are to join the western group of the First Panzer Army in the advance on Tuapse. Among the units of this western group is XXXXIV Jaeger Corps. The group is to be further reinforced by transferring the 298th Infantry Division from the Seventeenth Army. The XLIX Mountain Corps, composed of the 1st and 4th Mountain Division, is to advance either on Suchum or along the "Grusinische" highway, i.e. the road from Ordschonikidse via Krestowski Pass to Tiflis.

In the sector of Army Group B the regrouping of the Sixth Army for the attack is completed, and the attack will be launched tomorrow. The 22nd Panzer Division will be moved behind the Italian Eighth Army for bolstering purposes. The shipment of the motorized "Grossdeutschland" Division to the Western Front * started yesterday. The Division will be moved into the area southwest of Amiens.

In the sector of Army Group Center, Operation WIRBELWIND has made little progress in the face of very strong enemy resistance and in difficult fortified wooded terrain. However, General HALDER hopes to gain freedom of action today. In the sector of the Third Panzer Army, the enemy achieved a wide and deep penetration. The situation at Rshew is regarded as very unfavorable on the basis of the reports received from the Ninth Army. The order is given, therefore, to withdraw the 14th Motorized Division and the 256th Infantry Division to a tendon ** position. Army Group's communication lines are frequently disrupted by partisans; at present, all railroad lines in Army Group Center's communication zone, except one, are disrupted. In order to combat the partisans, troops will be moved up from the Government General.

In the evening, shortly after 2000 hours, General Von KLUGE, Commander in Chief of Army Group Center, reports that he is no longer able to hold the positions in the sectors of the Third Panzer Army and Ninth Army with the forces at his disposal. Thereupon the order is given to shift the 72nd Infantry Division, which is on its way to the Eleventh Army in the sector

---

* See under 12 August 1942.
** A comparatively linear position to which the front in a bulge is withdrawn in order to reduce frontage.

MS # C-065a

of Army Group North, to Army Group Center. In addition, the Fuehrer gives the order to halt the shipment of the "Grossdeutschland" Division to the Western Front and to move that division up to the sector of the Ninth Army. For the time being, however, the Fuehrer reserves for himself further decision concerning the commitment of this division.

The following American forces are stationed in Britain: Three infantry divisions and one armored division. Two to three U.S. divisions, reportedly, are being shipped to Egypt or the Near East by water around the Cape of Good Hope.

In the Mediterranean Sea, approximately one-third of the Anglo-American convoy, four merchantmen, arrived at Malta under strong escort yesterday afternoon. The U.S. aircraft carrier WASP is lying ablaze north of Bizerta; apparently, it is difficult to put her under water. The north-south traffic between Italy and Africa is still interrupted.

15 August 1942

Number of the Russian Army units including those employed in Finland, the Caucasus, Iran and the Far East:

(Compiled by the East Foreign Armies Branch of the Army General Staff)

407 infantry divisions	representing the combat strength of	287 normal units
178 infantry brigades	" " " " "	142 " "
39 cavalry divisions	" " " " "	33 " "
165 tank brigades	" " " " "	131 " "
789 units	representing the combat strength of	593 normal units

These units are distributed as follows:

At the Eastern Front			In reserve	At other fronts
254 infantry combat strength divisions	134		73 infantry divisions	80 infantry divisions
83 infantry brigades	"	" 47	66 infantry brigades	29 infantry brigades
13 cavalry divisions	"	" 7	20 cavalry divisions	6 cavalry divisions
68 tank brigades	"	" 34	86 tank brigades	11 tank brigades
418 units, combat strength:	222		245 units	126 units

Total: 593 units

Eastern Front: 418; reserves: 245 other fronts: 126 Total: **789 units**

In the Mediterranean Sea, the north-south traffic between Italy and Africa has been resumed. One battleship and the aircraft carrier ILLUSTRIOUS, both belonging to the escort of the Anglo-American convoy which had arrived at Malta, entered the harbor of Gibraltar where the aircraft carrier FURIOUS left her dock to make room for the ILLUSTRIOUS. The whereabouts of two battleships are unknown. The British Admiralty admitted the loss of the light cruiser MANCHESTER. The Italian heavy cruiser BOLZANO was hit by a torpedo near Messina and subsequently beached.

16 August 1942

Situation Report:

The operations of Army Group A in the Caucasus are progressing well. Battle casualties are comparatively light; however, Army Group is losing a considerable number of men due to marching injuries and sickness. Contrary to the view held by the Chief of Army General Staff, the Fuehrer is of the opinion that the 298th Infantry Division is no longer needed by the western group of the First Panzer Army *. The Fuehrer therefore gives the order to withdraw that division to Millerowo or Stalino for shipment to another assignment. The units which will become free in the sector of the Seventeenth Army following the crossing of the Kuban are to be moved up to the eastern group of the First Panzer Army because the enemy is expected to put up stubborn resistance at the Terek. XLIX Mountain Corps is now committed in an attack on Suchum. The Corps is advancing along the Suchum road, which leads from Mikojanschachar in the Teberda Valley to Dombai Pass, and in the high mountain valleys west of the Suchum road toward the south, and the Fuehrer hopes that Corps' two mountain divisions will be able to advance speedily.

In the sector of Army Group B, the Sixth Army successfully continues the attack launched yesterday aiming at the occupation of the large northeast loop of the Don bend north of Kalatsch and at the establishment of bridgeheads on the eastern bank of the Don. The Fourth Panzer Army will launch the attack on Stalingrad tomorrow if it receives adequate supplies

---
* See under 14 August 1942.

in time. According to agent reports, great numbers of tanks supplied by the United States are assembled in the Stalingrad area. It is not clear whether these are new tank units or tank reserves. To cover Astrachan, the enemy has established a flanking position south of Stalingrad. The Fuehrer is worried about the possibility that Stalin might repeat the Russian "Standard Attack" of 1920, i.e. an attack across the Don in the area around and above Serafimowitsch in the direction of Rostov, which was successfully carried out by the Bolshevists against the White Russian army of General Wrangel in 1920. The Fuehrer fears that the Italian Eighth Army, which is employed along that section of the Don, would not effectively resist such attack, and therefore urgently demands the speedy transfer of the 22nd Panzer Division into the area behind the Italian Eighth Army to bolster up the defense there.

In the sector of Army Group Center, Operation WIRBELWIND has been progressing very slowly and the attack forces have sustained heavy losses. General Von KLUGE, in a report submitted by telephone, states that the attack cannot succeed because behind every Russian position taken in the forests at Ssuchinitschi another position is encountered and because the passage between these forests is completely blocked by mines. The Second Panzer Army intends therefore to attack in an easterly direction. General Von KLUGE regards the situation of the Third Panzer Army as very difficult. He therefore requests, in addition to the 72nd Infantry Division, the assignment of another division to reinforce the Third Panzer Army. The situation at Rshew also continues to be critical. However, the Fuehrer refuses to withdraw the front in that sector again because of the losses in material which such action would involve. Moreover, the Fuehrer is of the opinion that the Russian power to attack in this sector will not last longer than another four to five days.

The Fuehrer is very angry over the fact that in the sector of Army Group North, against his express order, (referred to under 13 August), the 12th Panzer Division was not left in the "bottleneck", but moved behind the Leningrad front. He gives the order to retransfer that division at once to the "bottleneck".

17 August 1942

Distribution of the Flying Formations of the Air Force along the Eastern Front

Fourth Air Force:	13 bomber groups	7 1/3 dive bomber groups	6 1/3 fighter groups	2 long-range fighter groups
Don Air Force Headquarters:	2 "	— "	1 "	
Eastern Air Force Headquarters:	11 "	3 "	5 1/3 "	1/3 close-support group 1/3 tank destroyer group
First Air Force	1/3 "	— "	1 "	
Second Northern Air Force Command:	2 "	1 "	2 "	1 1/3 aerial torpedo groups

Total: 28 1/3 bomber groups, 11 1/3 dive bomber groups, 15 2/3 fighter groups, 2 long-range fighter groups, 1/3 close-support group, 1/3 tank destroyer group, 1 1/3 aerial torpedo groups, each group comprising an average of 20 planes ready to take off, totaling 59 1/3 groups, comprising about 1,187 planes.

18 August 1942

Situation Report:

In the sector of Army Group A, the western group of the First Panzer Army has reached the mountain ridge, the eastern group has made little progress against stiffening enemy resistance.

In the sector of Army Group B, the Fourth Panzer Army launched the attack toward the north yesterday. Only remnants of the enemy forces are left in the large Don loop north of Kalatsch. The Sixth Army suffered only light casualties in the fighting of the last few days. The Fuehrer intends to establish a Rumanian army group composed of the Rumanian Third Army and an additional Rumanian army, and to employ that army group under the nominal command of Marshal ANTONESCU at the Don and at the Volga. The proposed chief of staff of that army group is General HAUFFE, Chief of the German Military Mission in Rumania. Discussions with General HAUFFE are scheduled to take place at the Army High Command today.

In the sector of Army Group Center, Operation WIRBELWIND is bogged down. The enemy launched a counterattack against the eastern flank of the 11th Panzer Division which could be repelled. In the sectors of the Third Panzer Army and Ninth Army, the enemy has discontinued his offensive actions, perhaps owing to the extremely unfavorable weather prevailing in that area. The 14th Motorized Infantry Division sustained very heavy losses. The "Grossdeutschland" Motorized Division is being detrained at Jarzewo, 40 kilometers northeast of Smolensk.

On 17 August 1942, 299 railroad trains were unloaded along the Eastern Front. Among them were seventy-one troop trains. A new record has thus been established.

Approximately 3,260 Russian planes are based in the Caucasus area. Among them are 2,500 training planes, 500 combat planes, and 260 Anglo-American planes, 80 of the latter employed in the protection of Baku. An additional 100 planes of foreign types, reportedly, are being assembled in the Tiflis area.

Furthermore the Air Force assumes that Anglo-American combat planes are distributed as follows: 350 in the Middle East, 1,000 in Egypt, and 600 in India.

19 August 1942

Situation Report:

In the sector of Army Group A, enemy resistance in front of the Seventeenth Army and the Rumanian Third Army has considerably stiffened. Furthermore, it appears doubtful whether XLIX Mountain Corps is strong enough to thrust forward as far as Suchum. In the sector of the eastern group of the First Panzer Army, III and XXIII Panzer Corps are subjected to harrassing strafing attacks by the enemy air forces.

In the sector of Army Group B, the Fourth Panzer Army will resume the attack tomorrow if the needed fuel supplies arrive in time. The Sixth Army, the regrouping of which is not yet completed, will resume the offensive operations the day after tomorrow. Sixth Army was able to enlarge the bridgehead established on the eastern bank of the Don northwest of Stalingrad.

In the sector of Army Group Center, the situation of the Third Panzer Army and Ninth Army, according to a report by General Von KLUGE, is very critical, and the combat efficiency and the combat strengths of the units have greatly decreased. General Von KLUGE describes Operation WIRBELWIND as unpromising because adequate forces are not available to him, and because the moving up of reinforcements has become impossible since the railroad will be engaged to its full capacity in the shipment of the "Grossdeutschland" Division and the 72nd Infantry Division until the beginning of September. Yet, General MODEL, Commander in Chief of Ninth Army, requests the assignment of two fresh divisions to bolster his front. The Fuehrer declares that, if he had forces available, those forces would have to be committed in Operation WIRBELWIND; The "Grossdeutschland" Division would belong there too. The Third Panzer Army and Ninth Army have to hold their fronts without further reinforcements. The Fuehrer gives the order to move up the 298th Infantry

MS # C-065a   -23-

Division * to the sector of Army Group Center immediately after the shipment of the "Grossdeutschland" Division has been carried out.

West: This morning at 0600 hours, British troops landed at Dieppe. Yesterday's enemy air activity in no way indicated his intention to effect a landing. The landing took place along a 30 kilometers wide front. At Dieppe proper, British tanks have been put ashore, but the local heights are firmly in our hands. The "ADOLF HITLER" SS-Division and the 10th Panzer Division have been placed at the disposal of the commander of the local sector, General KUNTZEN, Commanding General of LXXXI Infantry Corps. The Fuehrer takes the transfer of the "Grossdeutschland" Division to the Western Front into consideration again. However, he drops that idea because OB West (Commander in Chief in the West) reports that there is reason to hope that the landed British forces will be disposed of by tonight.

20 August 1942

Situation Report:

In the course of yesterday's landing operation at Dieppe, which was completely smashed before the day had ended by the available German forces, unaided by the two motorized units which had been placed at the disposal of the local sector commander, the RAF committed 800 fighters and 100 bombers, while the German Air Force employed 610 fighters and 50 bombers. One hundred and twelve British planes were shot down, the German losses in planes amount to thirty-five. Twenty-five British radio messages in clear were intercepted in the course of the landing operation. The British operations order, com-

---
* See under 16 August 1942.

MS # C-065a   -24-

prising 121 pages, fell into German hands when a Canadian brigade staff was captured.

The Fuehrer comments on the operation as follows: On the occasion of their recent discussions in Moscow, STALIN obviously brought particularly strong pressure to bear on CHURCHILL with regard to the immediate establishment of a "Second Front." For that reason, CHURCHILL, upon his return to England, ordered the execution of this very inadequately prepared operation. The objective of the British forces, apparently, was the capture of Dieppe in order to advance either in a northern direction toward the rear of the German Channel fortifications or in a south-western direction toward Le Havre. The Fuehrer orders the Wehrmacht High Command (OKW) to compile a comprehensive report on Dieppe in which the contrast between the British plans and the actual outcome of the operation is to be clearly shown. The report was published in the press on 29 August 1942.

21 August 1942

Situation Report:

The operations of Army Group A in the Caucasus are considerably hampered by heavy rain and snowfalls. The Fuehrer is angry because of the slow progress made in the crossing of the Caucasus and refers to the importance of a rigid concentration of the forces, with special reference to XLIX Mountain Corps. In order to clarify the situation at XLIX Mountain Corps, Captain Von HARBOU, of the Operations Division (Army) of the Armed

Forces Operations Staff, is dispatched to that corps on a special mission by order of General JODL. The northern section of the railroad line Astrachan-Machatsch Kala was completed on 7 August. This was ascertained by air reconnaissance, and the report of 13 August, which seems to contradict this report, is probably based on reconnaissance carried out prior to 7 August. Railroad ferries are operating at the four major rivers which must be crossed between Astrachan and Machatsch Kala. The Fuehrer approves Army Group's plan to commit two motorized divisions in an attack on Astrachan. In the course of the advance toward Astrachan, the town of Elista was occupied on 12 August 1942.

In the sector of Army Group B, the Fourth Panzer Army resumed the attack yesterday. From the Don front, considerable enemy activity is reported.

In the sector of Army Group Center, the impression prevails that the enemy forces opposite the Second and Third Panzer Armies are being reinforced. The forces committed in Operation WIRBELWIND still have not been able to gain freedom of action. The attack is greatly hampered by the swampy and woody terrain. The German striking power has considerably decreased, and the tank units sustained heavy losses. General Von KLUGE reported yesterday that the attack no longer appears promising unless the attack forces are reinforced by two additional divisions. However, the Fuehrer insists on the continuation of the operation and requests General Von KLUGE to appear at his headquarters tomorrow for a discussion of measures to be taken. At Rshew, the enemy was able to achieve another deep penetration in the sector of the 256th Infantry Division. The Rshew airdrome was lost.

MS # C-065a   -26-

In the sector of Army Group North, a major enemy attack against the Wolchow front is expected. There is heavy railroad traffic on the Russian side. General Von KUECHLER, Commander in Chief of Army Group North, is scheduled to report to the Fuehrer on the planned execution of Operation NORDLICHT, i.e. an attack on Leningrad, on 23 August. The task of directing this operation has been assigned to General Von MANSTEIN, Commander in Chief of the Eleventh Army. Von MANSTEIN has been ordered to appear at HITLER's headquarters on 24 August for a briefing on his task.

22 August 1942

Situation Report:

At the western wing of Army Group A, the German forces seem to have lost the necessary contact with each other. To correct the situation, the 125th Infantry Division will be committed at the sector boundary between the Rumanian Third Army, which took Kurtschenskaja in the Kuban depression, 18 kilometers southeast of Temrjuk, on 21 August, and the Seventeenth Army, which, advancing from Krasnodar, took Krymskaja on 20 August. In the wooded mountains of the Caucasus, to the southeast, the 97th Infantry Division and one other division will be concentrated on the two roads leading to Tuapse. Time and again, the Fuehrer emphasizes the importance of our reaching the coast as speedily as possible so that the supplying of the forces can be carried out via the Black Sea at once. A mountaineer detail of the 1st Mountain Division hoisted the German War Flag on the 5,633 meters high Elbrus Mountain yesterday.

In the sector of Army Group B, the eastern wing of the Fourth Panzer Army was able to make some progress and will now turn to the west. The Fuehrer fears that the enemy might launch an attack against the eastern flank of the Fourth Panzer Army from the direction of Astrachan. He therefore wants the 16th Motorized Infantry Division to be committed in that area, i.e. around Elista and to the north of that town. General HALDER would prefer to leave that division in the south with the eastern group of the First Panzer Army for the time being, but he failed to persuade the Fuehrer to change his mind. Despite very strong enemy resistance, the Sixth Army was able to gain two bridgeheads on the eastern bank of the Don at Peskowatka and Wertjatschij. It resumed the attack this morning in order to take possession of the land bridge between the Don and the Volga, north of the railroad line Kalatsch-Stalingrad, and to capture Stalingrad from the northwest. The enemy applies strong pressure in the Don loop northwest of Sitotinskaja, which he is still holding. For that reason, the bulk of the 22nd Panzer Division remains there, although its Grenadier Brigade has been moved into the area behind the Italian Eighth Army. However, the Fuehrer once more gives the order to employ the entire 22nd Panzer Division behind the front sector held by the Italians. As far as possible, German units are also to be used in the front sector held by the Hungarian Second Army.

Army Group Center: The enemy, obviously, attaches great importance to the German attack at Ssuchinitschi and moves up reinforcements constantly. This morning he launched a counterattack against the right flank of the Second Panzer Army. The Third Panzer Army and Ninth Army sustained heavy losses during the recent fighting, and the latter lost 750 officers and 22,000 men. Unfortunately, the period during which these losses occurred is not specified in my notes. Presumably, they occurred after 30 July 1942. Army Group North: The enemy seems to have observed the strategic concentration of the Eleventh Army for Operation NORDLICHT, i.e. the attack on Leningrad. This is no surprise in view of the influx of the rural population into Leningrad which is still going on. This also explains perhaps the heavy railroad traffic on the Russian side. The Fuehrer wants the medium artillery in the "bottleneck" to be reinforced.

Today's discussion between the Fuehrer and General Von KLUGE had the following result:

Operation WIRBELWIND will be discontinued because a decisive success can no longer be expected in view of the difficult terrain and the strength of the enemy forces. However, the continuation of the attack in this front sector is to be simulated in order to tie down the Russian forces and to prevent their employment in attacks against the other thinly manned front sectors. However, no reinforcements are assigned to the Second Panzer Army for this task. On the contrary, the 9th and 11th Panzer Divisions will be withdrawn and regrouped in the area north of Kirow in order to launch an attack together with the "Grossdeutschland" Division in a general south-southeasterly direction, and to attempt to accomplish on a smaller scale the original objective of Operation WIRBELWIND.

Distribution of the Flying Formations of the Air Force along the Eastern Front

Fourth Air Force	11 2/3 bomber groups	6 1/3 dive bomber groups	6 1/3 fighter groups	2 long-range fighter groups
Don Air Force Headquarters	1 "	– "	1 "	
Eastern Air Force Headquarters	11 1/3 "	3 1/3 "	2/3 * "	1/3 close-support group
First Air Force	– "	– "	1 "	
Northern Air Force Command	2 "	1 "	2 1/3 "	1 1/3 aerial torpedo groups

Total: 27 bomber groups, 10 2/3 dive bomber groups, 11 1/3 fighter groups, 2 long-range fighter groups, 1/3 close-support group, 1 1/3 aerial torpedo groups, each group comprising an average of 20 planes ready to take off,

totaling 52 2/3 groups, comprising about 1,054 planes.

23 Agust 1942

Situation Report:

In the sector of Army Group B, the Fourth Panzer Army has made little progress because of the lack of fuel and ammunition, which can be brought up on the inadequate roads only slowly. The Fuehrer is worried about the

---
* This is probably a mistake made in writing my notes; compare the charts of 13 and 17 August.

gap between the Fourth Panzer Army and the Sixth Army. However, there seems to be no reason for further apprehension in view of the successes achieved by the Sixth Army. This army crossed the Don at Peskowatka and Wertjatschij yesterday and is now driving toward the Volga due north of Stalingrad with XIV Panzer Corps, at the same time providing covering forces against the north.

In the sector of Army Group Center, the enemy has been attacking the eastern flank of the Second Panzer Army with strong forces, including a large number of tanks, on a 50 kilometers-wide front since yesterday morning. An extension of the attack front toward the north is expected. However, the decision to withdraw the 9th and 11th Panzer Divisions (referred to under 22 August 1942) will be carried out. Extremely heavy enemy attacks, launched by very strong forces, have again been directed against the weak front sector of the Ninth Army at Subzoff and Rshew since 22 August. The Subzoff bridgehead had to be evacuated and, at Rshew, the 14th Motorized Infantry Division had to be withdrawn behind the Volga. The Fuehrer also watches with anxiety the indications pointing to formation of an enemy focal point opposite the thinly manned western front sector of the Ninth Army. The "Grossdeutschland" Division will be committed here if the situation becomes critical. Furthermore, the Fuehrer fears that, as a result of the continuous fierce defensive fighting in the sectors of Army Group Center and Army Group North, the development of winter positions to which he attaches particular importance is neglected.

MS # C-065a   -31-

Today's discussion between the Fuehrer and General Von KUECHLER had the following result:

14 September 1942 is tentatively set as the date for the launching of Operation NORDLICHT. The Air Force is to start its preparatory attacks on Leningrad as early as 4 or 6 September. However, Generaloberst JESCHONNEK, Chief of Air Force General Staff, who is present at the discussion, regards this as too early, because the air formations employed in such drawnout preparatory missions would lack the necessary striking power at the time of the launching of the attack. Finally, 10 or 11 September was agreed upon as the date for the start of the air attacks. The air formations employed in the operation will be placed under the command of Generaloberst Freiherr Von RICHTHOFEN.

General Von KUECHLER wants to launch the attack from the southwestern front in a northeasterly direction toward the Newa, then to cross the Newa and to join forces with the Finns, while at the same time encircling Leningrad tightly, and to take possession of the city only thereafter. General HALDER disagrees, he considers it imperative to capture Leningrad in the first phase of the attack. However, he fails to gain the Fuehrer's support. The artillery available for the operation comprises 200 batteries with 800 guns. The bulk of it will be employed along the main attack front and a strong artillery group in the "bottleneck" to ward off enemy attacks which are expected to be launched against the "bottleneck" from the east. The task of warding of those attacks is assigned to General LINDEMANN, Commander in Chief of the Eighteenth Army.

Twenty-two rifle divisions, eighteen rifle brigades, one cavalry division, and seven tank brigades were newly committed by the enemy during the period from 1 - 22 August 1942.

24 August 1942

Situation Report:

In the Sector of Army Group A, the Seventeenth Army made some local progress in the advance on Novorossisk. Otherwise the situation in the Caucasus is unchanged.

In the sector of Army Group B, a difference of opinion exists between Army Group Headquarters and the Fourth Panzer Army concerning the manner in which the attack should be carried on. After having defeated the opposing enemy forces during the preceding days, the army wants to mop up the terrain ahead of its front first. However, Army Group insists upon the immediate continuation of the attack in a northern direction. This order will be carried out tomorrow. In the sector of the Sixth Army, XIV Panzer Corps reached the Volga north of Stalingrad yesterday and took Bynok, the northernmost suburb of Stalingrad.

In the sector of Army Group Center, the Second Panzer Army, Third Panzer Army, and Ninth Army again had to ward off very heavy enemy attacks yesterday. The Fuehrer comments on the situation as follows: "The severity of the Russian attacks and the limited possibilities to ward them off any longer are reminiscent of the past winter. As then, so it is now the duty of every man of Army Group to hold out at his post wherever he is stationed. The Fuehrer rejects any withdrawal for operational reasons and declares that every thought of evasion has to be eradicated from the minds of the troops." Referring to the report received from General MODEL, according to which the assigned replacements are inadequate, the Fuehrer points to the fact that the training period of Russian replacements is even shorter than that of German replacements. Eight weeks of training, the Fuehrer goes on to state, must be sufficient for a soldier to accomplish a purely defensive task. The enemy is attacking also at the western front sector of the Ninth Army at Bjeloj. The elements of the "Grossdeutschland" Division which have arrived in the meantime are released for employment as reserves in this front sector.

General Von MANSTEIN, Commander in Chief of the Eleventh Army, who is present at HITLER's headquarters, receives the following instruction for the execution of Operation NORDLICHT:

The Fuehrer explains first that Operation NORDLICHT is to serve exclusively the purpose of freeing the Baltic Sea and to occupy the Karelian Isthmus. The operation constitutes an independent task which must not be connected with the defensive fighting in the "bottleneck." General Von MANSTEIN is given only general information on Army Group North's plan of attack; otherwise, he is given full freedom of action. The following mission has been assigned: Phase 1: Encirclement of Leningrad and establishment of contact with the Finns. Phase 2: Occupation of Leningrad and razing the city to the ground. Through the assignment of artillery, the Finns are to be enabled to take demonstrative action. Details will be discussed with General HEINRICHS, Finnish Chief of Staff tomorrow; General HEINRICHS arrived at Headquarters of OKH today. The Fuehrer points to the fact that the working class of Leningrad is undoubtedly organized in a military manner and will rush to the trenches the moment the battle begins. The Air Force is instructed to bring up the ammunition for the artillery and the bomber formations until 10 September, so that the three-day Air Force preparation can start on 11 September. General Von MANSTEIN is of the opinion that the possibilities for an effective employment of the artillery are less favorable than they were at Sevastopol. Furthermore, he regards the infantry forces available for the continuation of the attack on the Karelian Isthmus as rather weak. The infantry will be reinforced by transfers from other sectors of the front in the course of the attack.

25 August 1942

Situation Report:

The situation is generally unchanged. The plan to withdraw the 9th and 11th Panzer Division from the Ssuchinitschi sector has not been abandoned. However, the question as to whether these divisions will be committed north of Kirow remains undecided for the moment. In accordance with the request of Army Group Center the "Grossdeutschland" Division will now be committed in a counterthrust at Ssytschewka, in the eastern front sector of the Ninth Army, but the strength of Division must not be expended in defensive action. Thus, yesterday's plan to commit this division in the western front sector of the Ninth Army is superseded by today's decision.

Following the discussion of the situation, Generalleutnant WAGNER, Chief of Army Supply and Administration, reports on the supply situation at the Eastern Front. He has to be told by the Fuehrer that the lack of fuel prohibits the bringing up of the supplies for Army Group A and Army Group B on heavy motor trucks from the railroad terminal stations which are located far back in the rear area, and that, instead, the undamaged or restored sections of the railroad lines must be utilized and a motor truck shuttle service organized between these points.

At today's discussion with General HEINRICHS, Finnish Chief of Staff, the following has been agreed upon: The Finnish forces employed at the Karelian Isthmus will simulate an attack by heavy artillery fire and pursue the retiring enemy. General HEINRICHS expressed his desire that, following the capture of Leningrad, Army Group North establish contact with the Finnish Forces employed at the Swir and that the Finnish forces advancing toward the Murman Railroad, upon reaching their objective, be reinforced by German units to enable them to hold the position.

26 August 1942

Situation Report:

In the sector of Army Group A, the situation is unchanged. The Fuehrer gives an order prohibiting an advance into the High Caucasus and directs the forces to block, only the two highways leading from Algir and Ordshonikidse to Kutais and Tiflis, especially since the roads will be blocked by snow as early as the middle of September. XXXX Panzer Corps will launch a thrust toward Grossnji, primarily to take possession of the railroads there.

In the sector of Army Group B, the enemy is putting up stubborn resistance by launching strong counterattacks. Since the Fourth Panzer Army fails to make progress in its present grouping, it will regroup its forces by shifting IV Infantry Corps to its right wing and the tank units to the left wing, and launch an attack with the tank forces in a northeasterly direction on 28 August 1942. In the sector of the Sixth Army, the 71st Infantry Division crossed the Don at Kalatsch on 24 August 1942, and is swiftly advancing along the Karpowka valley toward the southern section of Stalingrad. At the right * wing of the Italian Eighth Army, the enemy achieved a deep penetration. XVII Infantry Corps, employed at the Sixth Army's left wing, extended its front sector to the left in order to relieve the Italians of some of the pressure. Again, the Fuehrer demands urgently the immediate shifting of the entire 22nd Panzer Division into the area behind the front sector held by the Italians.

Very calmly, but with deep indignation, the Fuehrer receives the report of the Chief of Army General Staff to the effect that, in the sector of Army Group Center, the Second Panzer Army had withdrawn its front line at Ssuchinitschi on its own initiative. The enemy has thus been relieved of pressure at this point, but no German forces have been freed by this action.

In the sector of Army Group North, signs are increasing that a Russian

---

* Eastern

attack on the "bottleneck" is imminent. The Fuehrer wants SS-Totenkopf *
Division to be transferred to the west as soon as possible, and to be replaced by of four newly activated jaeger battalions assigned to the
Eighteenth Army **. The next four jaeger battalions, the activation of
which will be completed toward the end of August, will be employed in the
communications zone to combat partisans.

27 August 1942

Situation Report:

In the sector of Army Group A, sufficient fuel has been procured for
XXXX Panzer Corps to enable it to launch a thrust toward Grossnji on
28 August and to continue the advance toward Machatsch Kala on or after
3 September 1942.

In the sector of Army Group B, the situation at Stalingrad has developed favorably. However, a shortage of fuel exists. The Fourth Panzer
Army will attempt to establish contact with the Sixth Army by launching a
thrust in a northern direction, and will penetrate toward the northeast into
the cordon of forts only if the crossing of the river course between Iwanowka
and Karpowka is possible. The blocking position of the Sixth Army between
the Volga and the Don will be advanced in a northeasterly direction. The
Fuehrer regards the sector held by the Italian Eighth Army as the critical
point of the front. The Italians will now be reinforced by the transfer

---

* Death's Head
** Referred to under 12 August 1942.

of two German divisions. It is intended to shift the 298th * and 294th Infantry Divisions by air and Italian motor trucks to the sector of the Italian Eighth Army. Furthermore, the moving up of the Italian Alpine Corps, which is on its way to the front, will be accelerated.

In the sector of Army Group North, the enemy attack against the "bottleneck," which had been expected for some time, was launched this morning. The Reichsmarschall, who, together with the Chief of Air Force General Staff, is present at the discussion, suggests to the Fuehrer the transfer of bomber and fighter formations from the Eastern Air Force Headquarters to the First Air Force, and his suggestion is approved. The first four Tiger tanks, which are arriving in the sector of Army Group North today, will be committed in the "bottleneck" to ward off the Russian attack there. The next six Tigers, which will be shipped from the ZI to the Eastern Front during the next few days, shall also be employed in the "bottleneck." Furthermore, the 12th Panzer Division, which, despite repeated Fuehrer orders, is still behind the Leningrad front, will be transferred into the "bottleneck" at once.

During a discussion of the food situation which followed the situation report, the Reichsmarschall demands that the elements of the Wehrmacht which are stationed in the occupied territories should obtain their entire subsistence from those territories.

---

* Referred to under 16 August 1942.

28 August 1942

Situation Report:

The Reichsmarschall reports to the Fuehrer that General Freiherr Von RICHTHOFEN, Commander in Chief of VIII Air Force Corps of the Air Force, personally reconnointered the situation in the Stalingrad area and held discussions with the commander in chief of the Fourth Panzer Army and the Sixth Army. He ascertained that there were definitely no strong enemy forces employed in that area. During reconnaissance flights carried out in a northern direction, it had been difficult for the Air Force to discover any enemy forces in that coverless terrain. General Von RICHTHOFEN, the Reichsmarschall goes on to report, is under the impression that a unified command is lacking. After a discussion with General HALDER, the Fuehrer gives the order to set up an operations staff of Army Group B in an advance position and to move up infantry replacements to the Sixth Army by air. The Chief of Army General Staff reports that two Russian divisions have been transferred from Woronesh to Stalingrad and six tank brigades to Ssuchinitschi. He suggests that one division be withdrawn from the Woronesh bridgehead because it appears unlikely that an attack will be launched there in the near future. The Fuehrer agrees.

In the sector of Army Group Center, a Russian order has been captured stating that Moscow is the objective of the German attack at Ssuchinitschi, and that the Germans must be driven back into their jump-off positions. In the sector of the Ninth Army, it has been ascertained that the Russian forces which are now attacking at Subzoff have been transferred from the area north of Rshew, and it is concluded that the enemy no longer has any forces available in the depth of the area at this front sector. Headquarters of Army Group Center suggested that the commitment of the "Grossdeutschland" Division in an attack against the Russian bridgehead at Rshew be authorized, because that bridgehead position constitutes a threat for the railroad line leading from Rshew to Wjasma. The Fuehrer rejects this suggestion since this division will be committed only in extremely critical situations as an entire unit, and then be placed back at the Supreme Command's disposal as soon as possible.

In the evening, Army Group North reports that the enemy has penetrated into the "bottleneck" and that the situation there is critical. The Fuehrer therefore gives the order to shift the 3rd Mountain Division, which is being shipped by water from Norway to Finland, to Reval and to move the division up to the sector of the Eighteenth Army. Two bomber groups, one dive bomber group, and one fighter group have been transferred from Eastern Air Force Headquarters to the First Air Force.

29 August 1942

Situation Report:

The Fuehrer expresses anger over the standstill in the operations in the sector of Army Group A, for which he holds Army Group's command responsible. He gives the order to move up the 3rd Rumanian Mountain Division, which is still in the Crimea, to the sector of Rumanian Third Army by land rather than via the Strait of Kertsch.

In the sector of Army Group B, the three motorized units of the Fourth Panzer Army launched their attack this morning following a regrouping at Army's left wing, and report good progress.

In the sector of Army Group North, the 170th Infantry Division, which belongs to the Eleventh Army and is assembled for Operation NORDLICHT, will be committed in the "bottleneck" in a counterattack to be launched against the Russian penetration area from the north and south. The Division will be supported by the three Tiger tanks which are available at present, as one of the four Tigers is already out of action. In order to accelerate the shipment of the 3rd Mountain Division to Reval by water, additional shipping space is made available. At the Wolchow front too, a Russian attack seems to be imminent. Therefore, one tank group shall be assembled at the Wolchow, north of Lake Ilmen, and another one at Tschudowo.

In view of the air attacks which were carried out on Nuremberg and Munich last night, a strengthening of the antiaircraft defense is discussed. The Fuehrer wants the employment of the 88 mm antiaircraft gun as the principal weapon. He anticipates air attacks on Linz and Vienna too and states that no effective defense weapon exists against high-flying aircraft.

30 August 1942

Situation Report:

Contrary to the order which he gave yesterday, the Fuehrer urgently demands today that the Rumanian 3rd Mountain Division immediately starts the crossing of the Kertsch Strait, for which preparations had been made since 10 August. Thus far, the crossing could not be carried out because of high seas and the lack of support by the Air Force. Oberst Freiherr TREUSCH Von BUTTLAR-BRANDENFELS, First General Staff Officer (Army) in the Armed Forces Operations Staff, and Kapitaen JUNGE, Navy Staff Officer in the Armed Forces Operations Staff, are dispatched to the Commander in Chief of the Crimean Area and to the naval operations staff stationed there to insure that the Rumanian 3rd Mountain Division effects the crossing now, regardless of the weather and, if necessary, without support by the Air Force. If the crossing in daytime should appear too difficult, it will be made at night. If high seas should render the crossing of the Kertsch Strait impossible, the shipment of the division to Jeisk via the Sea of Azov will be taken into consideration. The two officers of the Armed Forces Operations Staff also are to ascertain the exact number of suitable vessels which are available for the crossing at Kertsch.

The Fuehrer is highly dissatisfied with the development of the situation in the sector of Army Group A and wants to see General LIST at headquarters tomorrow. The Fuehrer blames Army Group A, not for the manner in which the forces were originally committed, but for its failure to regroup the forces in time after it became evident that no progress could be made with the forces in their original grouping. The Fuehrer regards the situation at the road to Tuapse as particularly unpromising. He rejects the idea of withdrawing XLIX Mountain Corps from its sector at the Suchum road in order to commit it, too, in the attack on Tuapse. The First Panzer Army will force a crossing of the Terek at the Terek bend at Prokladnenski with the arriving infantry divisions and cross the Terek with the tank units in order to envelop the enemy forces employed there. The Fuehrer designates Machatsch Kala and Astrachan as the objectives of the operations to be carried out by the First Panzer Army before the end of the current year. The capture of Baku will be postponed until next year if such postponement becomes necessary.

In the sector of Army Group B, the Fourth Panzer Army has made further progress south of Stalingrad. The 298th Infantry Division will be committed with XVII Infantry Corps. The 22nd Panzer Division, which is still tied down at Serafimowitsch for the time being, will be committed in a counterattack in the sector of the Italian Eighth Army later on.

In the sector of Army Group Center, the situation at Subzoff and Rshew, where the enemy has renewed his fierce attacks, has become very critical again. The Fuehrer therefore approves the moving up of the "Grossdeutschland" Division to the Rshew area; but he still does not authorize the commitment of this division.

In the area of Army Group North, the situation in the eastern sector of the "bottleneck" has developed unfavorably. The enemy penetrated the front through a gap in the lines of the 227th Infantry Division which is employed there and gained ground toward the north. Here, the 5th Mountain Division will be committed in a counterattack. The two Tiger tanks still available for action are unable to advance on the corduroy roads owing to their enormous weight and are left behind at bridges of which the load capacity is too low. Thus far, one bomber wing and one fighter group have been transferred from the Eastern Air Force Headquarters to the First Air Force.

In the afternoon, Army Group Center reports that sixty enemy tanks achieved a deep penetration at Subzoff. Now, the Fuehrer authorizes the commitment of the "Grossdeutschland" Division.

31 August 1942

Situation Report:

In the sector of Army Group A, Armeegruppe Ruoff has made good progress at Anapa and Noworossisk. The Fuehrer wants the two German divisions employed in the Crimea to be withdrawn as soon as the situation along the coast of the Black Sea is cleared up. These divisions will be replaced by replacement training divisions which are to be reorganized into fortress divisions. The First Panzer Army is engaged in fierce fighting at the Terek.

In the sector of Army Group B, the Fourth Panzer Army has penetrated the inner cordon of forts south of Stalingrad; the distance from the point of penetration to the edge of the town is 25 kilometers. The Fuehrer requests the transfer of one motorized unit from the divisions committed at Stalingrad as soon as the situation permits. That unit is to be employed as flank protection in the Don loop northwest of Sirotinskaja.

At noon, General LIST, Commander in Chief of Army Group A, reports to the Fuehrer on his operational plans. His plans are generally approved. They provide for a continuation of the offensive in the western Caucasus at three points, namely:

1. At Anapa and Novorossisk; following the capture of these localities, the advance is to be continued along the coastal road. Here the Rumanian 3rd Mountain Division will be employed, and must effect the crossing of the Kertsch Strait as soon as possible. *

2. On both sides of the road to Tuapse; sufficient forces have to be made available for this operation to make sure that the attack will not loss its momentum.

3. Along the Suchum road where the main forces of XLIX Mountain Corps are to be concentrated while the occupation of the remaining mountain passes farther to the east will be left to weaker covering parties.

The main task of the First Panzer Army is still the annihilation of enemy forces in the Terek bend and the thrust into the oil area.

1 September 1942

Situation Report:

In the sector of Army Group A, the right wing of Armeegruppe Ruoff ** took Anapa and Natuchajakaja, 18 kilometers east of Anapa, yesterday. Otherwise, the situation is unchanged.

---

* Operation Bluecher II.
** A reinforced army with an army type headquarters.

General Von KLUGE, Commander in Chief of Army Group Center, has informed us that he will report to the Fuehrer on his further plans today. During the discussion, which takes place at noon, the decision is made, in accordance with the Fuehrer's desire as repeatedly expressed by him during daily situation reports, to free the 9th and 11th Panzer Division in the sector south of Ssuchinitschi and to transfer the 95th Infantry Division, at present employed northwest of Woronesh, to the Ninth Army. As far as the commitment of the "Grossdeutschland" Division is concerned, the directives issued on 28 and 30 August 1942 remain unchanged. The Fuehrer rejects General Von KLUGE's suggestion to reorganize the Ninth Army's front slantwise, and instead gives the order to accelerate the development of rearward positions in the sector of Army Group Center.

In North Africa, the German-Italian Panzer Army, Commander in Chief Generalfeldmarschall ROMMEL, which has been facing the El Alamein position since 30 June 1942, has launched the attack on its southern wing yesterday.

2 September 1942

Situation Report:

In the sector of Army Group A, Operation BLUECHER II, the crossing of the Kertsch Strait, was started last night. German and Rumanian troops gained a foothold on the Taman peninsula and took Tamanskaja. In the sector of the First Panzer Army, the 111th and 370th Infantry Division launched the attack across the Terek. The Chief of Army General Staff reports that

Army Group does not expect to encounter strong enemy resistance once the Terek is crossed, until the edge of the mountains is reached. According to an order issued by the Fuehrer, the 16th Motorized Division is to base its further operations on Elista.

In the sector of Army Group B, the fighting for Stalingrad continues to develop favorably. There are no enemy forces left west of the city. The Fuehrer gives the order to remove * the entire male population upon entering the city because Stalingrad with its one million communist inhabitants is a particularly dangerous place.

In the sector of Army Group Center, a strong enemy attack against the position of the Third Panzer Army was launched this morning. However, according to a report by the Chief of Army General Staff, Army Group does not regard the situation as serious. At Rshew, a detouring railroad line will be built.

According to an order by the Fuehrer, the method employed on 21 March 1918 ** is to be employed again in the artillery preparation for Operation NORDLICHT. This method provides for the concentration of the strongest artillery forces in the smallest area, effective fire being restricted to a short period immediately preceding the attack.

In North Africa, lack of fuel forced the German-Italian Panzer Army to discontinue its attack and to go over to the defense. The required fuel consumption units are available, but great difficulties are encountered in bringing up the fuel to the front line.

---
* The German term "beseitigt" is used, which can also mean eliminate. (Transl.)
** The day of the launching of the great spring offensive in France.

MS # C-065a   -48-

3 September 1942

During the situation report, the Chief of Army General Staff reports that the commander in chief of Army Group A, after a discussion of the matter with the commanding generals of Armeegruppe Ruoff, suggested the withdrawal of XLIX Mountain Corps from the central part of the Caucasus for commitment at Tuapse. The Fuehrer rejects this suggestion and demands that the attacks in the direction of Tuapse as well as toward Suchum be continued.

Furthermore, the Fuehrer rejects a suggestion to issue Directive No. 47 for the carrying out of Operation NORDLICHT prior to General Von MANSTEIN's report on his plans; General Von MANSTEIN will report on 5 September 1942.

In the evening the OB West reports by telephone that a British airborne division has been transferred from England proper to the Isle of Wight and that attempts to land on the Normandy peninsula are planned by the British. The Fuehrer therefore gives the order to shift the 7th Parachute Division, which is stationed in Normandy, farther to the north. Following a report of the Chief of OKW several days ago, the Fuehrer had given the order to transfer seven replacement training divisions from the ZI to the west.

4 September 1942

Situation Report:

Sector of Army Group A. The Fuehrer renewed his instructions to the effect that the 1st Mountain Division is to leave only weak covering parties at the occupied mountain passes, while the bulk of the Division is to be committed in the area of the 4th Mountain Division in a drive toward Suchum. The assigned special mountain units, with the exception of the unit already committed in the area of XLIX Mountain Corps, are to be employed with XXXXIV Jaeger Corps at the road to Tuapse. The replacement training battalions which originally were to be employed with the mountain corps will also be committed at the road to Tuapse.

The Commander in Chief of Army Group Center plans to commit the 9th and 11th Panzer Division, which are to be withdrawn from the area south of Ssuchinitschi, not, as was originally intended, in the area north of Kirow, but to transfer these divisions to the area of the Fourth Army because of better railroad and detraining facilities. The Fuehrer will meke his final decision later. In the area of Sytschewka, at the eastern front sector of the Ninth Army, the slackening of the enemy attacks made it possible to withdraw elements of the 1st and 5th Panzer Divisions from the front.

In the sector of Army Group North, the enemy has pierced the eastern front of the "bottleneck" in the area of XXVI Infantry Corps again and has covered half the distance to the Newa. According to a report by the Chief of Army General Staff, it had become necessary to commit the advance regiment of the 24th Infantry Division in this area, in addition to the 170th Infantry Division, 5th Mountain Division, and 86th Jaeger Division. Angry over the enemy success and the useless commitment of no less than four divisions which were assembled for Operation NORDLICHT in defensive action, the Fuehrer states that the measures taken in this connection demonstrate a complete lack of determined leadership and points out that, despite the commitment of these additional forces, the 224th Infantry Division continues to be in danger of being cut off and that, as a result of the drawing away of forces, the carrying out of Operation NORDLICHT would become impossible. The Fuehrer considers the commitment of battalions belonging to the group of General MEINDL in the "bottleneck," but he abandons this idea after the Chief of Armed Forces Operations Staff pointed out the fact that the strength of the forces available in the "bottleneck" would be sufficient and that only a determined leadership would be needed. The Fuehrer makes the following decision: With the forces made available to him, which will include the GHQ reserves General Von MANSTEIN will immediately take over the northern sector of the Eighteenth Army, acting independently of Army Group North. Von MANSTEIN's report which was scheduled for tomorrow is therefore cancelled. The Fuehrer decides that Directive No. 47 (Operation NORDLICHT), which is to be issued at a later date, shall be phrased in such manner that it can be forwarded to Army Group North by the Army General Staff without any additions.

The Shifting of the 7th Parachute Division toward the north, which the Fuehrer demanded yesterday, has been ordered by OB West in the meantime. Today the Fuehrer mentions that the "Reich" SS-Division should be shifted

MS # C-065a   -51-

into the area thus far occupied by the 7th Parachute Division because no tanks are available as tactical reserves: "General Goering" Brigade and the 6th Panzer Division. In Normandy: The 7th Parachute Division and the "Reich" SS-Division. Farther to the East: The "Adolf Hitler" SS-Division and the 10th Panzer Division.

The Fuehrer wants the German-Italian Panzer Army to be reinforced by making available to it up-to-date antiaircraft artillery for antitank defense against the heaviest tanks and an unlimited supply of mines, and by the assignment of the 22nd Infantry (airborne) Division upon the completion of its reorganization.

5 September 1942

Situation Report:

The Reichsmarschall, who is accompanied by General JESCHONNEK, Chief of the Air Force General Staff, and General Freiherr Von RICHTHOFEN, Commanding General of VIII Air Force Corps who is to report on the employment of the Air Force in Operation NORDLICHT, reports to the Fuehrer that the fighter group now stationed on the Kertsch peninsula, where it can be spared, will be transferred to the area of the First Panzer Army to strengthen the antiaircraft defense there. The Fuehrer requests the retransfer of the 46th Infantry Division to the Crimea, where it is to be rehabilitated for assignment to another point of the Eastern Front.

Army Group B: Regarding the continuation of the Sixth Army's operations,

MS # C-065a

-52-

the Fuehrer gives the following order: Advancing north of Stalingrad, the tank group (XIV Panzer Corps) will drive, if possible, as far as the old Russian defense line and then turn to the west in order to annihilate the battered enemy forces at the Don front. According to a report by the Chief of Army General Staff, Army Group intends to withdraw the 100th Jaeger Division from its sector in the great Don loop northwest of Sirotinskaja and to shift it to the attacking wing of the Sixth Army. The Fuehrer orders that Division is to be relieved by the 298th Infantry Division, which has arrived in the area behind the Army's left wing. The Reichsmarschall reports that the Air Force units employed in the Stalingrad area are still needed there for the present. The Fuehrer requests that forces which can be spared be transferred into the area of the First Panzer Army as soon as possible. Freiherr Von RICHTHOFEN suggests that the air forces employed in the area of Army Group B be replaced by Rumanian air forces as soon as the Rumanian Army Group headquarters is established *, if possible on 1 October 1942.

General Von MANSTEIN, who is directly responsible to the Army High Command, assumed command in the northern sector of the Eighteenth Army, which extends from the railroad station of Malukssa up to the Gulf of Finland, on 4 September 1942. He suggests that our attacks on a local scale be carried out along the entire front of Army Group North in order to tie down enemy forces. In the area of his army (Eleventh Army), the following corps are committed: XXX Infantry Corps comprising the 223rd, 170th, and 24th Infantry Divisions at the southern wing; XXVI Corps

---

* Referred to under 18 August 1942.

MS # C-065a   -53-

comprising the 28th Jaeger Division, 5th Mountain Division, and 227th Infantry Division in the "bottleneck"; LIV Corps comprising SS-Police Division and the 121st Infantry Division at the southern sector of the Leningrad front; and L Corps comprising the 215th Infantry Division, 58th Infantry Division, and 225th Infantry Division at the southwestern sector of the Leningrad front and in Ingermanland. The 12th Panzer Division will be assigned to XXX Infantry Corps on 7 September, the Spanish 250th Infantry Division will take over the sector of the 121st Infantry Division on the same day. General Von MANSTEIN intends to commit the 170th Infantry Division, 24th Infantry Division, 28th Jaeger Division, and 132nd Infantry Division at the point of penetration northeast of Mga in a counterattack to be launched in a northeasterly direction.

The Chief of the Air Force General Staff reports that he intends to station replacement units of the Air Force, approximately ten thousand men, in the partisan-infested communication area of the Eastern Front. The Fuehrer agrees.

7 September 1942*

Situation Report:

In the sector of Army Group A, forces of the right wing of Armeegruppe Ruoff took Novorossisk yesterday. Otherwise, the situation is unchanged.

The Chief of Army General Staff reports that Army Group Center intends

---
* 6 September 1942: No notes available.

to commit the newly assigned forces as well as units to be freed in Army Group's own sector in an effort to restore the situation in the area of the Third Panzer Army as well as south of Rshew. The Fuehrer approves the idea of restoring the situation in the area of the Third Panzer Army, but reserves to himself the decision on launching a counterattack in the Rshew area because further enemy attacks are to be expected in that area and because the "Grossdeutschland" Division, the only reserve available to the Supreme Command, cannot be spared.

On orders of the Fuehrer, General JODL, Chief of Armed Forces Operations Staff, visited the headquarters of Army Group A in Stalino to discuss the further operations in the Caucasus with General LIST.

8 September 1942

As a result of his discussion with the Commander in Chief of Army Group A yesterday, the Chief of Armed Forces Operations Staff agreed with General LIST's opinion that XLIX Mountain Corps should be withdrawn in a northernly direction from its present sector, leaving blocking parties at the Caucasus mountain passes, and be used to reinforce units concentrated in the Maikop area for a thrust toward the coast by forces especially fit for mountain warfare.

The Fuehrer is very angry over General JODL's statement, which conflicts sharply with his own opinion. He demands to see all command data concerning the conduct of the operations of Army Group A since the crossing of the Don.

MS # C-065a   -55-

The First Panzer Army has to drive toward Ordshonikidse in order to cover its flank for the further advance on Grosnij. Two additional motorized divisions will be assigned to the Army at a later time for the continuation of the operation toward Machatsch Kala.

The Fuehrer devotes himself to a careful study of the organizational measures aiming at the rehabilitation of the armies in the east during the approaching winter months. His basic directives provide for the following measures: (1) Assembly of eight motorized units in the west for commitment in the Middle East in the spring of 1943. (2) Transfer of twelve well equipped divisions to the east and replenishment of the east divisions, to be transferred to the west in exchange, by men of age class 1924.

The Fuehrer instructs OB West to ascertain whether it is possible to move the "Reich" SS-Division or at least a combat team of this division closer to the exposed coastal sector of Normandy after the 7th Parachute Division has been shifted to the north, since the latter has no tank forces at its disposal. In addition, the Fuehrer gives the order to evacuate the British nationals living on the British Channel Islands as speedily as possible.

Prompted by the new situation created by the discontinuance of the offensive of the German-Italian Panzer Army, the Fuehrer is studying the state of defense preparedness on the Isle of Crete. In view of the possibility of British attacks on the isle, he orders reinforcement of its garrison to reach the original strength of two fortress brigades. The possibility of carrying out this measure is being thoroughly investigated.

9 September 1942

Situation Report:

The Chief of Army General Staff reports that Army Group A intends to let the enemy attack the Terek bridgeheads first and then to launch the offensive. The Fuehrer regards this plan as absolutely wrong because its execution would seriously endanger the bridgeheads, particularly in view of the fact that the enemy is steadily bringing up reinforcements to the Terek sector.

In the sector of Army Group B, the Don front is to be developed to as great a strength as possible and to be thoroughly mined. In addition, reserves are to be moved up from the Stalingrad area into the sector behind the Don front and GHQ artillery is to be employed there because the Fuehrer anticipates the launching of strong enemy attacks against the front sector of the Italian Eighth Army aiming at a break-through toward Rostov during the coming winter.

In the sector of Army Group Center, the enemy has renewed his attack west of Subzoff with strong forces this morning. The Fuehrer therefore authorizes the commitment of the "Grossdeutschland" Division in a counter-thrust.

In the sector of Army Group North, the shifting of enemy forces from the Wolchow front to the "bottleneck" has been observed. At Stalingrad, several divisions have been identified which were transferred to that area from the northern and central front sectors respectively. These transfers of forces lead the Chief of Army General Staff to the conclusion that, at the present moment, the enemy lacks operational reserves. General Von

MANSTEIN intends to launch the counterattack against the penetration area northeast of Lga on 10 September. He plans to commit the 24th Infantry Division, 121st Infantry Division, and 12th Panzer Division, supported by the available Tiger tanks in a drive toward the northeast, while, at the same time, weaker forces are to attack from the north in a southeasterly direction.

OB West is against a shifting of the "Reich" SS-Division to the north. He is of the opinion that the Division's present quartering area, northwest of Angers, is more favorably located in view of its mission as a support reserve for the submarine bases in Brittany and the areas of Brittany and Normandy, and in view of a possible commitment of the division in the Netherlands.

The Fuehrer regards the occupation of the coastal areas in southern France as inadequate, especially in view of the fact that it would not be possible, in case of an emergency, to shift the motorized units to that part of the coast swiftly enough. He, therefore, gives the order to activate five new divisions specially organized for coast defense in the area of OB West until 15 November 1942. Four-fifths of the cadre personnel for the new units, or 12,000 men, is to be furnished, by OB West and the Wehrmacht* District Commander in Norway, and one-fifth, or 3,000 men, by the Commander of the Replacement Training Army. Those divisions which, in the course of the exchange of west divisions against east divisions are to

---

* Norway was the first theater of war under Joint Armed Forces Command. (Translator).

be shifted to the east first, are to be exempted from the transfer of personnel. The rest of the personnel needed for the five new divisions is to be procured from those persons subject to the draft who were deferred as indispensable to the armament industry, and will be made available now for service with the Armed Forces on 1 November. These replacements will be trained in the ZI theater of war for four weeks and then be assigned to OB West. For the time being, the new divisions will be equipped with the captured materiel available in the area of OB West. As an additional measure, the divisions employed in the west, whose designation numbers are above 700, will be reorganized as coast defense divisions.

With reference to the exchange of divisions between the east and the west during the coming winter, the Fuehrer gives the following order:

The divisions which will become available after the capture of Leningrad and the Air Force ground units employed at the Eastern Front, which will be reorganized into brigades, will be utilized to free east divisions for the transfer to the west during the first phase of the exchange. As a rule, two east divisions will be transferred to the west for each west division which is shifted to the east in the beginning. Later on, after the rehabilitation of the east divisions, one additional division will be released in the west for each division which will have arrived there from the east. Ten divisions are available in the west for transfer to the east. The exchange of divisions will begin in early or mid-October, with two east divisions exchanged against one west division a month.

Furthermore, eight motorized divisions will be prepared in the area of OB West for commitment under tropical conditions and shifted to the east, beginning in January, to be employed in the Caucasus as the attack group for the thrust toward the Middle East. At present, six motorized divisions and the "Goering" Brigade are available in the area of OB West. This number will be augmented soon by the 26th Panzer Division, which is being newly activated, the SS-Totenkopf Division, which will be transferred from the east (Army Group North), and by the motorized "Grossdeutschland" Division. Eight of these ten divisions are to be transferred to the east and, in exchange, four motorized divisions will be transferred to the west from the Eastern Front, namely from Army Group Center and Army Group North respectively, so that six motorized divisions will be available in the west again. The motorized divisions to be transferred from the east to the west are to be replaced at the Eastern Front by motorized units of Army Group A and B.

The Armed Forces Operations Staff is to submit drafts of the necessary orders to the Fuehrer without delay.

Following yesterday's controversy with General JODL, regarding the conduct of the operations of Army Group A, the Fuehrer has decided to relieve General LIST of his command as Commander in Chief of Army Group A. The Fuehrer also considers replacing the Chief of Army General Staff because of a growing conviction, particularly during the last weeks, that General HALDER is no longer equal to the mental strain connected with his position.

In the afternoon, the Fuehrer therefore sends Generalfeldmarschall KEITEL, Chief of OKW, to General HALDER to instruct the latter to prevail

MS # C-065a   -60-

upon General LIST to resign as Commander in Chief of Army Group A. General KEITEL is to advise General HALDER, at the same time, that the Fuehrer is considering a change with respect to the Chief of Army General Staff. The Fuehrer contemplates the appointment of General ZEITZLER, at present Chief of Staff of OB West, to the position of Chief of Army General Staff.

In the evening, General LIST requests the Fuehrer to relieve him of his command. The Fuehrer grants the request. For the time being, he will personally direct the operations of Army Group A from his headquarters. General Von GREIFFENBERG, Chief of Staff, remains with Army Group's headquarters staff at headquarters in Stalino as reporting and command channeling center.

The controversy between the Fuehrer and General JODL has created a lack of confidence between the two which indicates that both General JODL and General WARLIMONT might be relieved of their positions as Chief and Deputy Chief respectively of Armed Forces Operations Staff.

With the exception of the following notes on naval affairs, no notes on situation reports and discussions at HITLER's headquarters are available for the period from 10 to 13 September 1942. This is probably due to the fact that HITLER did not make any important decisions during those days. The situation remained generally unchanged. In the sector of Army Group B, the right wing of the Fourth Panzer Army reached the Volga south of Stalingrad on 10 September. On 12 September elements of the 71st Infantry Division*,

---
* Referred to under 26 August 1942.

MS # C-065a   -61-

advancing from the west, penetrated into the southern section of Stalingrad. In the sector of Army Group North, General Von MANSTEIN's counterattack against the penetration area northeast of Mga, which was launched on 10 September, encountered fierce enemy resistance and was brought to a stop. Generaloberst Freiherr Von WEICHS, Commander in Chief of Army Group B, and Generaloberst PAULUS, Commander in Chief of the Sixth Army, reported to the Fuehrer on 12 September, and General MODEL, Commander in Chief of the Ninth Army, on 13 September, on the situation in their respective sectors. On the afternoon of 12 September, HITLER discussed with General Von GREIFFENBERG, Chief of Staff of Army Group A, how Army Group's functions should be carried on until a new commander in chief should be appointed.

11 September 1942

During the situation report, the Fuehrer discloses that as far as could be ascertained to date, only one aircraft carrier appeared to be among the escort vessels of the Archangel-bound British Convoy PQ 18. Thus, he points out, favorable conditions for the commitment of German surface forces might be created if, through the employment of submarines and air forces, we would succeed in damaging the carrier. However, the Fuehrer emphasizes once more that the commitment of the naval forces has to be approved by him first.

For the time being, the Navy Command, according to a report by Admiral KRANCKE, liaison officer of the Navy attached to HITLER's headquarters, is

MS # C-065a   -62-

still skeptical of the claim that there is only one carrier among the escort vessels. Otherwise, however, it shares the Fuehrer's operational concept. It is aware of the absolute necessity of obtaining the Fuehrer's approval prior to the commitment of surface forces, and realizes, furthermore, that according to the Fuehrer's decision, the commitment of the surface forces is justifiable only if it appears reasonably safe to assume that no major unit would be lost.

With regard to the stationing of naval forces in Norway during the winter 1942 - 43, the Fuehrer wants as many surface units as possible to be left there during the coming winter. The stationing of surface units in ports of the ZI for repairs and training will be restricted to an absolute minimum. The Commander in Chief of the Navy covered this subject also in his latest report to the Fuehrer on 25 August 1942. He shared the Fuehrer's point of view with respect to the stationing of surface units in Norway. At present, the Navy Command is studying the question of how the Fuehrer's request can be complied with by further shortening the duration of the stay of individual units in ports of the ZI. As soon as this study is completed, Admiral KRANCKE will report results to the Fuehrer.

14 September 1942

Situation Report:

General of Mountain Troops KONRAD, Commanding General of XLIX Mountain Corps, reports to the Fuehrer on the situation in the sector of his corps; no notes on his report and the Fuehrer's remarks are available.

In the sector of Army Group A, the "Wiking" SS-Division will be shifted from the Seventeenth Army to the eastern wing of the First Panzer Army, and the 46th Infantry Division, in exchange, will be transferred to Armeegruppe Ruoff.

In the sector of Army Group B, according to a report by General Freiherr Von RICHTHOFEN, the enemy resistance at Stalingrad seems to be weakening. For this reason, and because of the lively enemy activity opposite the sector of the Italian Eighth Army and the left wing of the Sixth Army, the 100th Jaeger Division* and 22nd Panzer Division ** will not be shifted to the Stalingrad area, but will remain in their present areas, i.e. behind the sector of the Italian Eighth Army and in the Don loop, northwest of Sirotinskaja, respectively.

Sector of Army Group Center: The Fuehrer wants the attack planned by Army Group for the purpose of restoring the situation east of Wjasma to be carried out by the Third Panzer Army as soon as possible. According to the attack plan submitted by the Chief of Army General Staff, a strong northern group and a weaker southern group will be formed for carrying out the attack. In the sector of the Ninth, the "Grossdeutschland" Division will be withdrawn from the front, since the enemy attacks at Subzoff have abated. No decision has been announced, thus far, on Army Group's suggestion to launch an attack aiming at restoring the situation in the Rshew area. If the attack in this area is not carried out, the withdrawal of the 72nd Infantry Division and

---
* Referred to under 5 September 1942.
** Referred to under 22 and 30 August 1942.

14th Motorized Infantry Division from the salient west of Subzoff could be contemplated.

Sector of Army Group North: In the "bottleneck," the limited attack will be launched by the 170th Infantry Division tomorrow. The main attack will be carried out by the 170th Infantry Division, 24th Infantry Division and 5th Mountain Division on 18 September 1942.

Area of OB West: On orders of the Fuehrer, the 7th Panzer Division will not be shifted farther to the south until an additional motorized division has arrived in the west. The evacuation of the British Channel Islands will begin on 16 September 1942.

Bomber formations of the 5th Air Force attacked the British Convoy PQ 18 yesterday. No detailed reports on the result are available at this moment.

In Lybia, a British attempt to effect a landing at Tobruk was frustrated yesterday.

15 September 1942

The situation at the Eastern Front is generally unchanged. In the sector of Army Group North, the limited attack by the 170th Infantry Division, originally planned for today, has been postponed until tomorrow.

On orders of the Fuehrer, the shipping space available in the Mediterranean Sea is to be allocated in the following order: First priority will be given to Crete-bound shipments, second priority to shipments destined for Africa, and third priority to shipments in the black Sea. Furthermore, the strength of the German forces in Italy will be reduced by two-thirds.

Finally, the Fuehrer decides that the Antiaircraft Training School will not be transferred to Palermo, as requested by the Air Force, but to Bordeaux.

16 September 1942

Situation Report:

In the sector of Army Group A, headquarters of the Rumanian Third Army has been transferred to Rostow.

In the sector of Army Group B, the southern wing of the Sixth Army has made good progress in Stalingrad. On orders of the Fuehrer, the forces committed in the battle for Stalingrad will be placed under the unified command of the Sixth Army. In view of enemy attacks against the sector of the Italian Eighth Army anticipated by the Fuehrer he orders the immediate transfer of the 22nd Panzer Division and 113th Infantry Division from the Sixth Army to the area behind the sector held by the Italians. The attack by the Hungarian Second Army on the Russian bridgehead at Dawjdowka, 60 kilometers south of Woronesh, will be discontinued.

17 September 1942

The situation is generally unchanged. The limited attack launched by the 170th Infantry Division in the "bottleneck" yesterday was successful. Discussion of the Chief and the Deputy Chief of the Armed Forces Operations Staff with Generaloberst LOEHR, Commander of the Southeast Military District, who had arrived at HITLER's headquarters:

General LOEHR reports that the situation created by the uprisings in Croatia has become more serious, that the units of the Croatian army are increasingly disintegrating, and that the Croatian military command displays a non-cooperative attitude toward German suggestions to take joint actions. General LOEHR suggests permeating the Croatian regiments with German officers and recommends leaving the second regiment of the Croatian division in Croatia rather than committing it at the Eastern Front. He describes the food situation in Croatia as bad. The Chief of the Armed Forces Operations Staff demands that at least the German troops stationed in Croatia receive their food supplies from that country's economy. In the course of his report to the Fuehrer, scheduled for today, General LOEHR will ask the Fuehrer for instruction as to what action should be taken in case of the collapse of the Croatian Government. This question was prompted by the fact that an order of the insurgents was intercepted by the German troops revealing that the guerilla bands are directed by a central agency of the Comintern.

The Commander of the Southeast Military District suggests providing the 714th and 717th Infantry Division in Serbia at least partially with mountain equipment. In compliance with the suggestion made by General LOEHR, the question of an extension of the Bulgarian zone of occupation will not be discussed further because such extension would have an unfavorable effect on the feelings of the Serbian population which looks upon the Bulgars with contempt because of the latter's failure to participate in the war.

With regard to the situation in Serbia, General LOEHR reports that the Serbs regard Mihailovic as a national hero. The prevailing situation, he points out, makes a unified leadership under the Commanding General and Military District Commander in Serbia imperative. Actually, however, such unified leadership is nonexistent, because, in addition to General BAADER, Consul-General NEUHAUSEN, Economic Commissioner, and President TURNER, Chief of Civil Administration, claim the right to leadership, and the Senior SS and Police Officer insists that military as well as civil administration is under his control. He has requested that the entire civil administration be placed under his control and is about to build up an administration of his own by establishing police districts. The groupwise employment of the "Prinz Eugen" SS-Division which had been deemed necessary by the military district commander in Serbia was rejected by the Senior SS and Police Officer.

With regard to the troop shipments to Crete, General LOEHR submits a transportation survey. The survey prepared by him concerning the intended distribution of forces on Crete will be discussed first with the commander on Crete. General LOEHR requests the assignment of motor trucks to the forces on Crete and the reinforcement of the Antiaircraft at Iraklion. As far as a British landing operation is concerned, he regards the southern coast at Timbakion as most endangered because the only through-road leads from that point to Iraklion and Chania.

MS # C-065a   -68-

18 September 1942

Situation Report:

In the sector of Army Group A, the first phase of the Seventeenth Army's attack is to begin at the right wing with a thrust of the Rumanian 3rd Mountain Division on 20 September. The "Wiking" SS-Division is being shifted to the First Panzer Army which was successful in warding off enemy attacks at the Terek during the last days.

In the sector of Army Group Center, the planned attack by the Third Panzer Army aimed at restoring the situation east of Wjasma, in which the 9th Panzer Division and 95th Infantry Division will be employed, has been postponed on account of the prevailing bad weather.

In the sector of Army Group North, the counterattack in the "bottleneck" which was scheduled to be launched today has also been postponed on account of bad weather.

West: The Fuehrer orders that the "Goering" Brigade and other motorized units in the area of OB West are to be equipped with tanks.

The Fuehrer has appointed General of Infantry ZEITZLER to succeed General HALDER as Chief of Army General Staff. General ZEITZLER will be succeeded as Chief of Staff of OB West by General BLUMENTRITT.

20 September 1942 *

Situation Report:

Army Group A: The next attack wave of the Seventeenth Army will jump off

---
* 19 September: No notes available.

on 22 September. The Army requested the employment of stronger forces by the Air Force. The First Panzer Army receives the order to thrust forward farther to the south on the eastern bank of the Terek in order to block the exits of the Grusinische and Ossetische Highways. A further advance of Army toward the east in the direction of Machatsch Kala cannot be contemplated for the time being.

Army Group B: At Stalingrad, the 24th Panzer Division and 94th Infantry Division will be withdrawn from their present sectors and be committed for the cleaning out of the northern section of Stalingrad on 22 September. The Air Force preparation for this operation will begin on 21 September. At Woronesh, the 27th Panzer Division will not be employed in house-to-house fighting.

On the request of the Chief of Army General Staff, the right sector boundary of Army Group Center will be moved farther to the South. On the basis of its estimate of the enemy situation, Army Group expects the enemy to continue his attacks on Rshew and to launch new attacks against the northwestern cornerstone of the Ninth Army in order to gain possession of the railroad line Nelidowo-Rshew. Army Group wants to shift the 11th Panzer Division to the area behind the northwestern front sector of the Ninth Army to serve there as tactical reserve. In this connection, the Fuehrer renews the order to withdraw the "Grossdeutschland" Division and to shift the 95th Infantry Division from the area of the Third Panzer Army to the north. In case of a major enemy attack against the northeastern and northwestern front of the Ninth Army, the planned attack by the Third Panzer Army will be cancelled if necessary to make it possible to free additional forces there for transfer to the north.

Denmark: On orders of the Fuehrer, the 416th Infantry Division will be prepared for commitment in offensive operations until 1 March 1943.

The Fuehrer, furthermore, orders shipment by air of the personnel destined for Crete to strengthen the defense of the isle, and the most urgently needed equipment will also be shipped by air.

In the afternoon General FELMY, commander of the special desert combat unit activated and trained in Greece, arrives at HITLER's headquarters to discuss with the Chief of the Armed Forces Operations Staff questions concerning the commitment of his unit at the eastern wing of Army Group A. *

21 September 1942

Situation Report:

Army Group A: *In the sector of the Seventeenth Army, the consecutive attacks of the 125th Infantry Division and the Rumanian 3rd Mountain Division have been delayed by one day and will therefore start today and on 23 September respectively. The attack by Army's center on Tuapse is scheduled for 27 September. The Fuehrer designates Ordshonikidse as the objective of the First Panzer Army's attack. In this operation, III Infantry Corps is to thrust forward toward the South on both sides of the Terek, LII Infantry Corps will cover the eastern flank of the attack forces, and XXXX Panzer

---

* The result of the discussion is referred to under 21 September 1942.

Corps will take over the general covering against the east.

Following the report of the Chief of the Armed Forces Operations Staff, the Fuehrer decides that the FELMY Special Combat Unit will be employed as a covering force at Army Group's eastern wing north of Grossnij. Only the employment of the unit as a whole is permitted, and due consideration is to be given to the fact that this unit will have to accomplish its actual task after crossing the Caucasus and that, therefore, it must not be worn down in major combat. Changes in the commitment of the unit are subject to the OKW's approval.

According to a report received from the Air Force, Operations Staff, the following air formations are committed in the task of supporting the Seventeenth Army and First Panzer Army in their operations: Three reconnaissance squadrons comprising 12 planes each, two long-range fighter squadrons comprising 20 planes, five fighter squadrons comprising 60 planes and one bomber group comprising 20 planes.

According to a report by Army Group B, the attack on the northern section of Stalingrad * cannot be carried out for the time being because of a considerable decrease in the strength of the infantry units. The Fuehrer, therefore, orders the moving up of the 100th Jaeger Division to Stalingrad **. He issues the following directive concerning the continuation of the attack on Stalingrad: First phase -- cleaning out of the northern section of Stalingrad, second phase -- mopping up of the western bank of the Volga south of

---

* See under 20 September.
** See under 14 September.

MS # C-065a   -72-

Stalingrad, third phase — launching of an attack toward the north for the purpose of establishing a firmer hold on the Volga. The Fuehrer finally orders a study of the question of whether the 11th Panzer Division can be returned to Army Group B after the enemy attacks southeast of Ssuchinitschi have abated.

In the sector of Army Group North, the Eleventh Army launched the attack aiming at the elimination of the enemy penetration northeast of Lga early this morning. General Von MANSTEIN reported that Operation NORDLICHT cannot be carried out until 15 October, that he needs an additional division for the operation, and that he intends therefore, if necessary, to withdraw 58th Infantry Division from the Oranienbaumer front sector *.

The Fuehrer approves the suggestion made by the Chief of Army General Staff to start the ordered exchange of divisions between the east and the west ** by transferring two east divisions, namely the 161st Infantry Division and 328th Infantry Division, in exchange for one west division with a unit designation number above 300. OB West is to report which division can be transferred and at what time its shipment can begin. Thereupon, the exchange of the division will begin in the west.

With the exception of the following *** brief note of 2 October, no notes are available for the period from 22 September to 4 October. This is

---

*   See under 5 September.
**   See under 9 September.
***   See p. 39.

partly due to the fact that HITLER was in Berlin from 27 September to 4 October, and during that period there were no situation reports and discussions at his headquarters. On 24 September, HITLER released General HALDER, and General ZEITZLER, the new Chief of Army General Staff, reported for duty on the same day.

No major changes in the situation at the Eastern Front occurred during the aforementioned period. In the sector of Army Group A, the attack waves of the Seventeenth Army, which jumped off on 21 and 23 September respectively * achieved only local adjustments of the front line. On 21 September, a Russian attempt to effect a landing between Anapa and Novorossisk was frustrated. The First Panzer Army took Prischipskaja, located at the Terek bend and at the railroad line to Ordshonikidse, on 23 September and captured Elchotowo and Werchnij Kurp south of the Terek on 3 October. In the sector of Army Group B, strong Russian relief attacks against the Sixth Army's blocking position between the Volga and the Don were repelled on 24 and 25 September. In the battle for Stalingrad, large Party buildings in the proximity of the bank of the Volga were captured on 25 September and the northwestern suburb of Orlowka was taken on 3 October. No major fighting took place in the sector of Army Group Center. In the area of Army Group North, the counterattack in the "bottleneck," which had been launched on 21 September, made slow progress and was halted within a few days.

5 October 1942

Situation Report:

Army Group B: The Fuehrer contemplates the evacuation of the Woronesh

---

* See under 21 September.

bridgehead in order to free the forces committed there for other tasks. He refrains, however, from making a decision at this juncture. He watches with anxiety the assembly of enemy forces in the sector opposite Army Group Center in the area around Toropez. He regards the sharp decrease in the traffic on the Russian railroads in the southern section of the Eastern Front as an indication of planned major enemy operations in the aforementioned area and assumes that about twenty Russian divisions have been shifted to that area recently. It is assumed that the Russians plan the launching of an attack either against the western front sector of the Ninth Army, or in a southern direction on Smolensk, or in a western direction on Welikije Luki. The following reserves are available to Army Group Center in the area of the Ninth Army: The "Grossdeutschland" Division, which will be relieved by the 95th Infantry Division *, 9th Panzer Division ** and local reserves. No units will be transferred from the Eleventh Army to the Ninth Army. In order to ward off an enemy attack against the front north of Smolensk, Army Group Center will make available the 328th Infantry Division, which will not be transferred to the West ***, and elements of the 11th Panzer Division ***. In order to forestall an enemy advance on Welikije Luki by offensive action through a counterthrust toward Toropez, forces will be assembled in the area around Welikije Luki. For this purpose, the first three Air Force ground divisions shall be moved up to this sector and preparations will be made, as far as transportation is concerned, for the transfer of elements of the

---

* See under 20 September.
** See under 18 September.
*** See under 21 September.

Eleventh Army to that area. The question of whether Operation NORDLICHT will still be carried out under these changed conditions remains undecided. Instead of this operation, an attack toward the southern shore of Lake Ladoga via Wolchow * is being contemplated.

In the west, a British raid was carried out on the British Channel Island of Sark. In view of the fact that the landed British commando troops handcuffed the German PW's they took, the Fuehrer announces his intention to handcuff all British PW's who were captured at Dieppe, including the officers, until an official statement is received from the British Government to the effect that no German PW's will be handcuffed in the future. The Chief of Staff of OB West is instructed to submit a sworn affidavit signed by the German engineer soldier who was captured, but managed to escape later on, in which the details of the handcuffing are stated. The handcuffing of the British PW's will depend on the contents of this affidavit.

In view of the contents of numerous reports received from agents recently, the Fuehrer again fears that the British might attempt to effect landings in the west. He therefore gives the order that the following measures be taken:

1. OB West will alert those coastal sectors which, in view of weather conditions, may be regarded as endangered. The Fuehrer anticipates that this measure will have a deterring effect because the alert is bound to become known to the British soon.

---

* See map of South Russia, Sheet 20, 1 : 4 000 000, Zyanka.

2. The 337th Infantry Division, which was scheduled to be shipped to the east some time after 10 October *, will not be shipped until further orders are received.

3. The transfer of the 7th Parachute Division, which had been sent from the west ** to the Berlin area during the last few days ***, back to the west is contemplated if such measure should appear necessary. According to a report received from the Air Force Operations Staff, three air transportation groups are always available to carry out the shipments.

On the Fuehrer's request, the Chief of the Air Force General Staff makes the following statement regarding the present strength of the air forces employed in the west: "There are 8 bomber groups, each of them comprising about 20 planes, and 6 fighter groups, each of which comprise about 40 planes. This strength can be increased by the assignment of the senior classes of training and replacement groups. In addition, it is possible to strengthen the air forces in the west by the transfer of night fighters from the zone of the Air Force Command Center."

4. OB West will report on the intended employment of the 161st Infantry Division, which will be transferred from the east ****, the time of its arrival,

---

*   See under 21 September.
**   See under 3d and 4th September.
***   The shipment was completed on 4 October.
****   See under 21 September.

MS # C-065a   -77-

its quartering and its strength in personnel, equipment and materiel *.

5. The 182nd Infantry Division will remain in the area where it is employed at present; its present organization will remain unchanged **.

6. The 67th Infantry Regiment *** will be shipped to Denmark only on special orders. At present, it is still stationed in the west.

Referring to the activation of five coast defense divisions in the west which had been ordered by the Fuehrer, Reich Minister SPEER reports that the armament industry cannot spare the requested number of 50,000 to 60,000 men and that, for this reason he cannot furnish more than 12,000 to 15,000 men. Therefore three static divisions will be activated from the number of the regular replacements for the west until 1 November. Two additional divisions will be activated at a later time. The plan to activate divisions by drafting armament workers has been abandoned; the armament workers will be added to the regular replacements ****.

Subsequent entry for 2 October 1942

According to a report by the Chief of the Armed Forces Operations Staff,

---

*   It is intended to employ the Division in the area previously occupied by the 337th Infantry Division, referred to above under item 2.
**   On the basis of my notes, it cannot be ascertained where the Division was employed at that time.
***   The Regiment belonged to the former 23rd Infantry Division which was reorganized into the 23rd Panzer Division, but only two of the Division's regiments were reorganized
**** See under 9 September.

General ROMMEL, Commander in Chief of the German-Italian Panzer Army in Africa, reporting to the Fuehrer in Berlin, gave the following account of the situation at his front: The British position at El Alamein is still very strong; one million mines are planted along a 60 kilometers wide front; the strong enemy superiority in the air is hampering the movements of the German tanks; the German fighters are unable to disperse the enemy fighters and reach the British bombers.

6 October 1942

Situation Report:

Army Group A: It is intended to reinforce the Air Force units employed in the northern Caucasus by the transfer of forces from the north. The forces of XLIX Mountain Corps will be reduced to the minimum required for the defense of the high mountain ridge. General der Flieger FELMY's special desert combat unit is covering the deep eastern flank of the First Panzer Army. The newly constructed railroad line Kisljar-Astrachan will be destroyed through air attacks. The Fuehrer no longer attaches particular importance to the operation against Astrachan *.

Army Group B considers it justifiable to abandon Operation HERBSTZEITLOSE, i.e., the attack on the northern section of Stalingrad. Owing to a temporary lack of forces and exhaustion of the troops, the continuation of the attack in Stalingrad is not possible for the time being. The mopping up of the pockets at Orlowka will be the next task. The Fuehrer attaches great

---

* See under 21 and 30 August and 2 September.

importance to the establishment if a firm hold on the Volga south of Stalingrad on a wide front. Two bomber groups of the First Air Force are assigned to VIII Air Force Corps, Commander in Chief General Freiherr Von RICHTHOFEN, which is employed in the Stalingrad area. The Rumanian Third Army will be used between the Sixth Army and the Italian Eighth Army at the Don on 10 October; The Rumanian Don Army Group will assume the command on 20 October if Stalingrad has been captured by that time.

Army Group Center: Reports have been received to the effect that the enemy is carrying out major movements, involving tanks, in the sector opposite the Second Panzer Army in the area east of Lzensk; the purpose of these movements could not be ascertained thus far. No reserves are available at that point. A decision as to the measures to be taken has not been made yet.

The purpose of the concentration of forces in the area of Toropez remains obscure. While the Chief of the Armed Forces Operations Staff considers a 2-pronged attack against the Ninth Army likely, the Fuehrer expects the Russians to launch a thrust toward Smolensk. The elements of the 11th Panzer Division assembled east of Smolensk will remain there. The forces which are to launch a counterthrust in the area of Welikije Luki in case of a Russian attack can be assembled until 23 October. For this purpose, the 12th Panzer Division and three Air Force ground divisions have already been shifted to that sector. In addition, it is intended to transfer two infantry divisions from the Eleventh Army to that area. The 337th Infantry Division * cannot be shipped from the west until 17 October because the railroads are

---
*See under 5 October.

MS # C-065a

already overtaxed. The shipment of the 161st Infantry Division * is to be carried out on schedule.

Army Group North: General Von MANSTEIN considers it possible to start Operation NORDLICHT on 1 November provided his army is reinforced by the assignment of eighteen battalions and 10,000 men replacements during October. The commitment of the 3rd Mountain Division in place of the battered 28th Jaeger Division, which was intended by the Eleventh Army, was prevented by the Fuehrer. The Russian bridgehead across the Newa will not be attacked, but only neutralized; the 170th Infantry Division will be committed there. Of its one million vacancies, the Army intends to fill 600,000 by reductions in TO's; the remaining 400,000 vacancies will be filled, on orders of the Fuehrer, by reducing the personnel and authorized strength of antiaircraft and air signal communication units. Age class 1924 will be utilized only for new activations.

7 October 1942

Situation Report:

Army Group A: The Chief of Army General Staff suggests the organization of landing parties from engineer units of V Infantry Corps under the Seventeenth Army and units of the Navy, to train and commit them between Novorossisk and Tuapse in minor operations. The Fuehrer agrees. The First Panzer Army took Malgobek, located at the oil pipe line northwest of Grossnji, yesterday.

---

* See under 21 September and 5 October.

Army Group B reports that the regrouping for the resumption of the attack in Stalingrad cannot be completed prior to 12 October. The attack will, therefore, not be resumed until 13 October. The Fuehrer is dissatisfied with the delay, and orders an increased commitment of the Air Force and the carrying out of frequent raids by assault detachments, in order to deprive the enemy of the opportunity to build up his defenses again.

In the sector of Army Group Center, major enemy movements in the area of Mzensk and the assembly of river-crossing equipment were observed yesterday. However, no enemy reinforcements have been identified thus far. The enemy's intentions in the area of Toropez remain obscure. The Chief of the Armed Forces Operations Staff still expects the enemy to launch a two-pronged attack against the Ninth Army from the east and from the west. The Fuehrer, however, is of the opinion that the Russians will launch a thrust toward Smolensk, perhaps in the course of a winter offensive.

The Fuehrer points out that, with weather conditions in the Arctic progressively deteriorating, the Navy will have to take over the reconnaissance and combat tasks of the Air Force to an increasing extent.

In view of the situation, the Operations Section (Army) of the Armed Forces Operations Staff makes the following suggestions:

1. East

In view of the fact that it is most important to clear up the situation at Stalingrad as soon as possible in order to carry out the further operations planned for the southern sector of the Eastern Front, it appears essential to relieve additional German divisions at the Don front and to commit them at

Stalingrad. However, most of the arriving Rumanian relief divisions are being directed toward the area behind the Italian Eigth Army's Eastern front sector. It appears advisable to commit those Rumanian divisions which are available first in the area south of Kremenskaja, at the northern bend of the Don loop at Sirotinskaja, and to provide for the relief of the Italians by those Rumanian divisions which are being moved up from areas farther to the rear.

2. West

According to advice received from the Chief of OKW Army Division, the plan to activate five Ruestungsdivisionen * has not been abandoned, although a different personnel policy has to be adopted. Three divisions will be activated before 1 November. In view of this situation, it appears necessary to again consider the transfer of corps headquarters from the east to the west. It is considered necessary to transfer two to three corps headquarters to the west. The transfer of one corps headquarters each from the Seventeenth and the Sixth Army appears possible.

/s/ Helmuth GREINER 29 May 1949

---

* Divisions to be organized from hitherto deferred indispensable armament workers (Translator)

MS # C-065a   -83-

9 October 1942 *

Situation Report:

The Chief of the Army General Staff states: "Thus far, the reasons for the complete lull along large sectors of the Eastern Front remain obscure. The Russians have withdrawn units from the front either for rehabilitation or for commitment at other front sectors, perhaps in the course of a winter offensive. It is therefore of particular importance to organize reserves."

In the sector of Army Group B, the Rumanian 3rd and 9th Cavalry Divisions will be committed in the sector of the Fourth Panzer Army.

Army Group North: According to an order by the Fuehrer, the planned attack from the Welikije Luki area in the direction of Toropez is to be carried out in any case, even if the enemy fails to launch his expected attack from the area around Toropez. The attack will be launched on 6 or 8 November. For the attack, the 12th Panzer Division, 3rd Mountain Division, and 337th Infantry Division are assembled in the area around Newel. The 7th Parachute Division will be moved up to the area of Smolensk. South of Lake Ilmen, the group under General MENDL will launch a thrust in an eastern direction up to the Lowat **. Operation NORDLICHT will not be carried out in the manner originally planned. However, the strong artillery concentrated in that area will be employed in the support of attacks with limited objectives which will be launched in order to advance the German lines south of Leningrad and to tighten the encirclement of that city. According to an order by the

---

*   8 October 1942: No notes available.
** Operation WINKELRIED.

Fuehrer, the Eleventh Army's next task will be the mopping up of the pocket of Pogostje. The attack will be launched, not from the two cornerstones toward the center, but from the deepest point in a northeastern direction.

West: On the basis of numerous reports, the area around Cherbourg is considered threatened again. OB West has been ordered to take the necessary measures.

Prompted by yesterday's enemy air attack on Suda Bay (Isle of Crete), the Fuehrer gives the order to strengthen the harbor defenses of Suda and Heraklion by the assignment of additional heavy antiaircraft. The shipment of the antiaircraft equipment to Crete will be given first priority. Needed personnel will be procured, if necessary, by the resumption of the former policy of relieving the German antiaircraft crews employed in the Rumanian oil district by Rumanian personnel.

No notes are available for the period from 10 - 13 October. These gaps and the following are largely explained by the fact that General ZEITZLER, newly appointed Chief of Army General Staff, usually restricted his noon reports on the situation to very brief statements and discussed all important operational questions with the Fuehrer alone during the afternoon or evening. This practice was motivated primarily by professional jealousy, the purpose being to exclude General JODL, Chief of Armed Forces Operations Staff from top level command as far as the Eastern Front was concerned.

14 October 1942

Situation Report:

Marshal Antonescu requested that the Rumanian 5th and 8th Cavalry

Divisions should not be transferred to the Fourth Panzer Army because it would no longer be possible to set up winter quarters for these divisions in time. The Fuehrer rejects the Marshal's request. The Rumanian Third Army has taken over its sector along the Don from Kletskaja up to the area near the Don bend southeast of Kasanskaja. The Sixth Army resumed the attack on Stalingrad yesterday.

In view of strong enemy concentrations in the Toropez area, it is now generally assumed that a 2-pronged attack against the Ninth Army is intended. According to the statement of a PW, such attack is scheduled to be launched tomorrow. The 7th Parachute Division is being shipped to the area of Smolensk and the 20th Panzer Division, also destined for the Smolensk area, has reached Brjansk. The First Air Force has transferred forces to the Eastern Air Forces Headquarters for the purpose of smashing the Russian concentrations in the Toropez area. The Eleventh Army will launch the attack against the 18th Labor Settlement at Leningrad tomorrow.

15 October 1942

During the situation report, the reports received in ever increasing numbers concerning intended and imminent Anglo American landings in West Africa are discussed. A suggestion, made by the Chief of Armed Forces Operations Staff, to permit the French Government to reinforce its forces in North Africa from the home country in order to enable those forces to resist possible Anglo American landings effectively is rejected by the Fuehrer out of consideration for the Italians, who view any reinforcement of the French forces in North Africa with the utmost suspicion. In view of the fact that the situation in the Mediterranean Sea is growing increasingly critical, the placing of the isle of Crete, a vital Air Force base, under the command of Generalfeldmarschall KESSELRING, OB South, is being contemplated. However, the decision is to be left to the Reichsmarschall; thus far, Crete has belonged to the area of the OB Southeast.

Vice Admiral Nomura, Chief of the Japanese Naval Delegation, during a trip to the Balkans observed rivalries between Italians and Germans everywhere. The report to this effect arouses the Fuehrer's anger, and he emphasizes once more that the Balkans are to be regarded as Italy's sphere of interest.

Admiral KRANCKE, Liaison Officer of the Navy Command attached to HITLER's Headquarters, reports to the Fuehrer that the pocket battleship ADMIRAL SCHEER, stationed in Norway, needs overhauling, and that it will be withdrawn to a ZI port as early as the beginning of November. To replace the ADMIRAL SCHEER, the heavy cruisers PRINZ EUGEN and LUETZOW will be dispatched to Norway toward the beginning of November.

17 October 1942 *

Situation Report:

The Chief of Army General Staff points to the danger of enemy landings in the area of Army Group A along the eastern coast of the Black Sea in the sector of the Rumanian 10th Infantry Division. On orders of the Fuehrer, the Air Force will be committed against the port of Poti. The center of

---

* 16 October 1942: No notes available.

the Seventeenth Army took Schaumjan, 30 kilometers northeast of Tuapse, on 16 October. In the further course of the attack on Tuapse, the 97th Jaeger Division will advance along the road; Division Lanz, i.e. the 1st Mountain Division, through the mountains; and the Slovakian motorized division in a general southeasterly direction. The First Panzer Army intends to advance at its western wing with the 13th Panzer Division in a south-southwesterly direction, with the main effort concentrated on Naltschick, and plans to start this advance on 30 October. The Fuehrer regards this as far too late. Corps Headquarters FELLY * decided to attack the opposing Russian cavalry forces in the steppe.

Army Group B: In Stalingrad, the Sixth Army took the "Dsherschinskij" tractor plant on 15 October and the "Rote Barrikade" ** gun factory on 16 October. South of the gun factory, the Russians are still holding the "Roter Oktober" *** steel works. The Soviet units encircled in the "Spartakowka" labor settlement were annihilated. Army Group intends to eliminate the penetration at the Woronesh bridgehead in the near future.

Army Groups Center and North: In the discussion of the commitment of forces north of Smolensk, the Air Force ground divisions play an important part. It is now intended to activate twenty-two of these divisions. The 197th Infantry Division is occupying a very wide sector. The question of whether the SS-Cavalry Division, which had been withdrawn from the front, or the Air Force ground divisions will be committed at this point remains undecided for the time being.

---

* A corps staff for special employment formerly referred to as Special Desert Combat Unit FELLY. (Translator)
** "Red Barricade."
*** "Red October."

The Fuehrer orders to reinforce the attack group advancing on Toropez by moving up the 337th Infantry Division to that area. Through PW statements, information has been obtained on the enemy situation in this area to the effect that the enemy was unable to complete his preparations for the attack in time and lacks mobility, owing to the fact that the muddy season has set in. In the northern sector of the Demiansk salient, II Infantry Corps will launch an attack on 19 October. In the sector of the Eighteenth Army the front line is thinly manned because of the fact that the 269th Infantry Division is being relieved by the 69th Infantry Division which is arriving from Norway.

The Air Force ground divisions were originally activated in order to relieve the first east divisions to be transferred to the west. Pointing to the fact that the Air Force is greatly overstaffed, the Army High Command had suggested the direct transfer of Air Force personnel to the Army, but in view of representations made by the Reichsmarschall, the Fuehrer rejected this suggestion. The activation of the Air Force ground divisions resulted in a disadvantage to the Army, for while the great number of its vacancies remained unfilled, it had to transfer materiel to the Air Force.

On the suggestion of the Reich Minister for Foreign Affairs, the Fuehrer decided to send Envoy NEUBACHER to Athens as his plenipotentiary to ascertain to what extent the cost of occupation can be reduced in view of the progressive deterioration of the Greek currency. General WARLIMONT, Deputy Chief of Armed Forces Operations Staff, who saw the Commander in Chief of OB Southeast in

Salonika on 10 and 11 October, found that the problem has not been created by the cost of occupation, but, on the contrary, is due to the utter derangement of the national economy in Greece. Actually the cost of occupation is insignificant.

For the period from 18 to 21 October 1942, no notes on the situation reports, but only the following notes on individual events, are available.

18 October 1942

In view of the activity of the Russian Navy in the Black Sea, especially the appearance of the battleship at Poti, the Fuehrer orders the commitment of an aerial torpedo group to destroy the battleship.

19 October 1942

On orders of the Fuehrer, the four heavy batteries which are emplaced in Norway will be protected by one infantry battalion each. In addition, special protection will be provided for the island of Andoe northwest of Narvik.

The Fuehrer is very angry over the fact that the evacuation of the British Channel Islands * has not yet been carried out and demands the acceleration of the evacuation.

The comparative strengths of the opposing forces in North Africa are as follows:

---

* Referred to under 8 and 14 September 1942.

British Eighth Army	German-Italian Panzer Army
107 - 123 battalions	62 battalions
120 - 140 light batteries	90 light batteries
12 - 20 medium batteries	28 medium batteries
800 - 900 tanks	592 tanks

20 October 1942

On the occasion of the resumption of the attacks on Malta and the sinking of Axis ships in the Mediterranean Sea, the Fuehrer referred to the value of such fortified islands and to the impossibility of capturing them. In this connection, he once more demanded the strongest possible fortification of the German occupied islands, such as the Channel Islands and the Norwegian Islands, which, once lost, could never be recaptured.

22 October 1942

Situation Report:

Area of Army Group A: Reports have been received to the effect that the Russians are moving up reinforcements in the sector opposite the extreme eastern wing of the Seventeenth Army. The Chief of Army General Staff will go to headquarters of the Seventeenth Army tomorrow to discuss the countermeasures to be taken. The First Panzer Army intends to continue its attack on 25 October.

The Fuehrer agrees with the Economy and Armament Office in the opinion that major Air Force attacks on Baku and Astrachan are of vital importance.

In the area of Army Group B, the Sixth Army will resume its attack in Stalingrad with a newly organized attack group. During the discussion of the measures taken by the Italians for the development of the Don position, reference is made to the difficult position of General of Infantry Von Tippelskirch, Liaison Officer of the OKH to the Italian Eighth Army, resulting from the arrogant attitude of the Italians on this matter.

Sector of Army Group Center: In the Toropez area, enemy attacks against Belyj and Subzoff, and possibly against Kirow are now expected. In contrast to the opinion previously expressed by him, the Fuehrer now regards the two-pronged attack against Subzoff and Belyj as most serious. As a countermeasure against the new Russian assault tactics, i.e., launching an attack on a narrow front out of the depth, the Fuehrer recommends the adoption of the defense tactics employed by the French during the great German attack on both sides of Reims in 1918, namely emplacement of the artillery far to the rear and assembly of large stocks of ammunition. The Army General Staff will issue the pertinent order.

23 October 1942

Situation Report:

Area of Army Group B: The Sixth Army resumed its attack in Stalingrad and achieved initial successes. The greater part of the steel works "Roter Oktober" was captured this morning. The Army intends to break through to the Volga on a wide front and to roll up the enemy lines toward the south and north. The Rumanian Third Army refuses to relieve the right wing of the

Italian Eighth Army * because the prerequisites of such relief have not been established. The Rumanians point out that, in addition to their own sector, they have taken over parts of the sector previously occupied by the Sixth Army's left wing and that, furthermore, the German divisions which are to be employed behind the new Rumanian right ** wing are not yet available, but still tied down in the Stalingrad area. Preparations for relieving the Italians are being made by the Rumanians, but no definite date has been set thus far. The Fuehrer decides that the intended relief is to be postponed for the time being.

Army Group North: In the sector of the Sixteenth Army, II Infantry Corps intends to launch an attack aiming at closing the gap in the northern sector of the Demiansk area. The Fuehrer refers to the heavy Russian traffic which is still going on across Lake Ladoga toward Leningrad and orders the Air Force to interfere effectively with that traffic.

As a retaliatory measure for the latest British air attack on a clearing station in North Africa, the Fuehrer orders that British PW's captured while carrying out an act of sabotage against the power plant in the Glomfjord be shot immediately.

25 October 1942 ***

Situation Report:

The Chief of Army General Staff reports on his visit to the Seventeenth

---

*   Divisions Celere and Sforzesca.
**   Should probably read "left", see under 25 October 1942.
***   24 October 1942: No notes available.

Army. He reports that the Rumanian units in particular are permeated with German signal units. This ensures that the German Command receives those reports which otherwise would not be passed on by the Rumanian command authorities. The Fuehrer wishes all allied units to be gradually permeated with German signal units. The inadequate combat performance of the Rumanian forces, particularly of the Rumanian 19th Cavalry Division, according to General ZEITZLER's report, is due, not so much to low morale among the troops, as to the bad relations between officers and enlisted men. While the officers are having plenty of everything at their quarters farther to the rear, the troops at the front line are left without the necessary food supplies. Withdrawals, which repeatedly occurred, were carried out by the troops primarily in order to obtain food in the rear area.

The Fuehrer again emphasizes that he expects an early destruction of the Russian battleship stationed at Poti by the Air Force.

Advancing on Tuapse, the Seventeenth Army took the heights southwest of Schaumjan on 23 and 24 October. The First Panzer Army launched its attack at the western wing today and achieved initial successes. Army's center will join the attacking wing on 26 October.

In Stalingrad, the Sixth Army took the remaining part of the steelworks "Roter Oktober," which was still in enemy hands, with the exception of one building. In addition, the greater part of the labor settlement Spartakowka was captured. In the sector opposite the Rumanian Third Army, the enemy is bridging the Don at several points. On orders of the Fuehrer, the development of the German positions along the Don will be supplemented by the construction of support positions. The relief of the two Italian divisions employed at the right wing of the Italian Eighth Army will be carried out in such a manner that, first, only the easternmost divisional sector will be taken over by the Rumanians, while the adjacent sector will be taken over only after adequate German forces have arrived in the area behind the wing which is to be relieved.

The Fuehrer, once more, refers to the heavy Russian traffic on Lake Ladoga. In this connection, he elaborates on the fact that, while the Army and the Navy have been utilizing large quantities of captured weapons and equipment items which are not fully adequate, the Air Force is using only first-class equipment. Like the Russian Air Force, the Air Force has to utilize older equipment, particularly planes, to a greater extent in order to carry out a greater number of missions. The Fuehrer particularly points to the fact that no attacks have been carried out on Leningrad for a considerable length of time and that the enemy thus has been afforded an opportunity to recover and to resume work in the power plant and to continue production in the armament industry, as well as to restore the streetcar service. This situation, the Fuehrer declares, cannot be tolerated any longer. He demands constant attacks on the city and the traffic on Lake Ladoga as well as on Moscow, Gorkij, Kuibyschew, Saratow, and Baku. In addition, the Fuehrer demands the early availability for commitment of the He 177 model plane. The constant tests made with this plane in order to employ it as a dive bomber prevent its commitment in action. The Fuehrer would prefer that the He 177 model planes drop large numbers of bombs in horizontal flights, and that the tests, which have delayed the commitment of the planes time and again, be discontinued.

In North Africa, the British Eighth Army launched an attack from the El Alamein position yesterday morning. General ROMMEL, who was on leave in the ZI, left for Africa with General KESSELRING this morning. In connection with the British attack, the Fuehrer regards the western Mediterranean area as greatly endangered. He requests detailed reports on the defense facilities on Corsica and contemplates the occupation of the isle by Italian forces.

26 October 1942

Situation Report:

In its attack launched yesterday, the First Panzer Army caught the enemy by surprise and, as a result, reached Naltschik, the objective of the operation, as early as 1000 hours. It is intended to continue the attack from there in an easterly direction. In view of the fierce resistance put up by the enemy, the Sixth Army does not expect the battle for Stalingrad to result in the complete capture of the city until around 10 November.

The Fuehrer again expresses fear that the Russians might launch a major attack, perhaps a winter offensive, in the sector held by the Allied armies across the Don in the direction of Rostow. The Fuehrer's anxiety is due especially to the extensive enemy movements observed in this area and to the bridging of the Don which has been carried out at numerous points. The

Fuehrer orders that the Air Force ground division be employed to bolster the front in the sectors of all three Allied armies. Thus, the German divisions employed in these sectors will be freed and, together with other units moved up to this area, available as reserves behind the front sectors occupied by the Allies.

The transfer, this winter, of five west divisions to the east, either to serve as reserves or to be committed in the Caucasus, is being contemplated in order to free motorized units there which could be committed again only after the mountains have been crossed. For this purpose, five divisions will be withdrawn from the west and rehabilitated. They will be replaced by five east divisions which will also be speedily rehabilitated and retransferred to the east as the last of the fifteen divisions which are scheduled to be shifted from the west. In addition, the transfer of the 3rd and 5th Mountain Divisions from the Eleventh Army to the Caucasus and the transfer of two jaeger divisions from there to Norway and Finland is contemplated. The details of the transfers will be further examined.

The extensive enemy movements observed in the Kirow area convey the impression that an enemy attack is imminent there. The Fuehrer orders the Air Force to carry out a major attack on Kirow as soon as the needed formations are available. The Chief of Army General Staff obtains the Fuehrer's confirmation for his order that all armored divisions stationed behind the front shall move northward by one sector as soon as the 20th Panzer Division [*] arrives in

---

[*] Referred to under 14 October.

the Smolensk area. Thus, a mobile reserve will be made available for the Kirow area.

27 October 1942

Situation Report:

The Chief of Army General Staff reports on Russian propaganda on a grand scale being disseminated about approaching large-scale operations. General ZEITZLER regards the Russian propaganda as empty talk rather than a reflection of actual intentions.

To reinforce the Seventeenth Army, the 50th Infantry Division, which is in very good condition, will be moved up as soon as it is relieved in the Crimea by an Air Force ground division. The withdrawal of additional units from the high mountain front in the Caucasus is not possible at this time because of the danger of avalanches. It is intended to continue the attack launched by the First Panzer Army in the direction of Ordshonikidse in order to block there the two highways leading across the Caucasus.

After the capture of Stalingrad, the Sixth Army will continue its attack in a southern direction. The threat of a Russian attack across the Don in the direction of Rostov is under discussion again. General ZEITZLER suggests the assembly of divisions of the greatest snow mobility behind the threatened front sector as tactical reserves. For this purpose, divisions of low combat strength, equipped with a large number of heavy weapons, will be employed. It is intended to concentrate the cadres behind the area of prospective commitment. These reserve divisions will be placed under the command of the

German generals attached to the allied high commands.

The 19th Panzer Division, which is employed in the Orel area, will be transferred to the area around Brjansk in order to have a mobile reserve available in Army Group Center's rear area. The 13th Police Regiment, which will be employed in the task of combating partisans, will be released only after all units of the 7th Parachute Division have arrived at Smolensk. According to statements made by deserters, the Russians have moved up fifteen units to the area opposite the western front of the Ninth Army, eleven of these units are said to be employed at Belyj, three opposite the southern sector of Ninth Army and one east of Welikije Luki.

The Fuehrer intends to appoint General Von MANSTEIN to the post of Commander in Chief of Army Group A. Headquarters of the Eleventh Army will be employed at Witebsk to direct a thrust into the Toropez area, if such action should become necessary. In such case, General MODEL would assume the command and General WEISS would temporarily replace General MODEL as Commander in Chief of the Ninth Army. It is no longer possible to carry out Operation NORDLICHT as originally planned for some time to come.

30 October 1942 *

Situation Report:

According to a report received from the Seventeenth Army, the conduct of operations by the Russian command in that area has become more methodical. Three battalions shall be withdrawn from Army's high mountain front to reinforce the attack groups.

---

* 28 and 29 October 1942: No notes available.

In the further course of its attack in Stalingrad, the Sixth Army will dispose of the groups resisting in the southern section of the city first and then regroup in order to mop up the northern section of the city.

Since new reports have been received to the effect that the enemy is carrying out extensive movements opposite the Second Panzer Army in the Suchinitschi area, the order is given to move up an assault gun battalion from the west which, together with a jaeger battalion, will be placed under the command of a bearer of the Knight's Cross and assembled in the area west of Suchinitschi as local reserve. In addition, the shifting of the 11th Panzer Division from the Woronesh area farther to the north is being contemplated. In the sector of the Ninth Army, the "Grossdeutschland" Division will be shifted to the south to the area east of Belyj to serve as reserve. The Fuehrer, furthermore, orders the commitment of the 7th Parachute Division in the southern front sector of the Ninth Army and to withdraw the jaeger battalions committed there and assemble them behind the front as tactical reserves.

The Eleventh Army with headquarters established at LIX Infantry Corps in Witebsk assumes the command of the operations against the Toropez area. For the launching of a counterthrust, the 12th Panzer Division and 3rd Mountain Division will be available to Army on 3 November. If the Russians should fail to attack prior to that day, the Eleventh Army will launch the planned attack on 12 November. For this operation, the 18th Motorized Infantry Division, which will be relieved by an Air Force ground division, shall also be assigned to Army if possible.

MS # C-065a

According to the statement of a captured Russian company commander, the Russians are thoroughly investigating the possibilities of bacteriological warfare, primarily in respect to the spreading of bubonic plague, anthrax, and typhoid bacteria. The Fuehrer decides that nothing similar will be done on our side.

No situation reports and discussions took place on 31 October and 1 November because, during these days, HITLER's headquarters was retransferred from Winniza to his former headquarters "Wolfsschanze," located in the Goerlitz Forest east of Rastenburg in East Prussia.

2 November 1942

Situation Report:

In view of the fact that Russian attacks are expected to be launched at several points of the Eastern Front on 7 November, the Chief of Army General Staff will issue an order, based on the Fuehrer's winter Directive, setting forth again the principles according to which operations are to be conducted. Particular emphasis is to be given to the demand that every strong point is to be defended to the last.

The western wing of the First Panzer Army took Alagir on 1 November. The Fuehrer is confident of further progress in the attack on Ordshonikidse.

To the south of the Fourth Panzer Army, the Rumanian Forth Army was committed toward the end of October. This Army has been placed under the command of Generaloberst HOTH, Commander in Chief of the Fourth Panzer Army. In the Stalingrad area, the strength of the German infantry is failing, and the

71st Infantry Division, particularly, is severely battered. The Fuehrer rejects the Sixth Army's suggestion to move up the 29th Motorized Infantry Division from the Fourth Panzer Army to Stalingrad, but he approves the suggestion, made by the Chief of Army General Staff, to withdraw engineer battalions from the divisions and commit them in Stalingrad. A third suggestion, to discontinue the attack for eight days in order to grant the troops a needed rest, is rejected. Films submitted by the Air Force show that the number of new bridges built across the Don in the sector of the Rumanian Third Army is steadily growing. The Fuehrer therefore still expects a major Russian attack across the Don in the direction of Rostow. He orders heavy air attacks on the bridge sites and assembly areas in the forests on the northern bank of the Don. The Second Army intends to eliminate the penetration at Woronesh as soon as adequate forces of the Luftwaffe are available.

The Chief of Army General Staff submits a map on which the distribution of the Russian armored forces is marked. Three focal points are noticeable: Stalingrad, Kirow, and the northeastern front of the Ninth Army. Only comparatively weak armored forces are assembled in the Toropez area. Two strong rear groups are assembled in the area around Saratow, presumably for rehabilitation. According to available information, no strong armored forces are committed at the front for the time being.

The Fuehrer decides that the Air Force ground divisions are to be committed only in defensive action until such time as they are welded together and have gained combat experience. He recalls, by way of comparison, the commitment of volunteer units in Flanders in late fall of 1914 when these units were prematurely committed in offensive action and, owing to their inadequate training, sustained disastrous losses.

On the request of General Von MANSTEIN, headquarters of XXX Infantry Corps (Eleventh Army) is transferred to Army Group A.

The heavy congestion of the railroad traffic prevailing at present has caused considerable difficulties in the bringing up of supplies at the Eastern Front. The Fuehrer orders that loaded trains which cannot be dispatched because of the congestion will not remain loaded where they are halted, but will be unloaded so that the empty trains can be returned.

The Fuehrer demands the employment of the strongest possible air forces in the western Mediterranean area in order to be able to prevent the British convoys from reaching Malta. In North Africa, only fighter-bombers will be employed at the front as far as possible because they alone are capable of achieving success, owing to the great superiority of the British Air Force. New groups of Ju 88 model planes will be shifted to the Mediterranean area. In view of the repeated British air attacks on German clearing stations in North Africa, the Fuehrer orders the Air Force to carry out air attacks on the British dressing stations.

The Fuehrer expresses his dissatisfaction with the utterly inadequate supply of ammunition to blockade runners. The blockade runners will also be supplied with Hexogen-ammunition to enable them to defend themselves against armored planes. The Fuehrer, furthermore, criticizes the fact that the

MS # C-065a
-103-

blockade runners are not provided with radio equipment to enable them to establish contact with the Air Force.

No notes are available on the events of 3 November. This is due to the following incident: On the evening of 2 November, General ROMMEL reported via teletype that the German-Italian Panzer Army was no longer able to hold its position against the heavy attacks of the far superior British Eighth Army, and that he intended to disengage the Italian infantry divisions from the enemy during the coming night and to withdraw them into the Fuka position. The motorized units would cover this withdrawal movement and then withdraw to the Fuka position. This teletype message was submitted to HITLER at once, but he failed to give any instructions. Early on the morning of 3 November the Armed Forces Operations Staff received another teletype message from General ROMMEL in which he reported that the Italian infantry divisions had disengaged themselves from the enemy during the night according to plans and started the withdrawal movement. The motorized units would follow in the course of the day. In view of the early hour (it was between 0500 and 0600 hours) and the fact that nothing new was contained in the message, which dealt merely with the execution of a measure which had already been reported, Major der Reserve Dr. BORNER, officer on duty in the Operations Section (Army) of the Armed Forces Operations Staff, did not submit the message to the Fuehrer at once, but presented it to him around 0900 hours together with the other morning reports. HITLER was utterly enraged over the failure to submit General ROMMEL's message to him at once. He claimed that he would have been able to prevent the withdrawal of the German-Italian Panzer Army, which he did not approve, if he had received General ROMMEL's second teletype message in time (actually, this would have been absolutely impossible). He ordered Major Dr. BORNER and General WARLIMONT, Deputy Chief of Armed Forces Operations Staff, to report to him and demoted the former to the rank of private after listening briefly to his explanation. Dr. BORNER was transferred to an artillery replacement training unit in Potsdam on the evening of the same day and then transferred as a private to an Army coast artillery battery in France. On a petition submitted on his behalf by General SCHMUNDT, Chief Adjutant of the Wehrmacht, HITLER reinstated Dr. BORNER three months later, at the same time forcing his retirement. In the forenoon of 3 November, HITLER did not even receive General WARLIMONT, but instructed General KEITEL to inform him that he had been relieved of his post. General WARLIMONT turned over his duties to Colonel Freiherr Treusch Von BUTTLAR-BRANDENFELS, senior general staff officer of the Armed Forces Operations Staff and left HITLER's headquarters in the evening of 4 November in order to go to Upper-Bavaria, via Berlin, to join his family. The entire incident, one of HITLER's customary arbitrary actions, embittered both officers and enlisted men of the Armed Forces Operations Staff at HITLER's headquarters, and aggravated the lack of confidence already existing since the dismissal of General LIST and the discord between HITLER and General JODL. On General SCHMUNDT's intercession, HITLER revoked the dismissal of General WARLIMONT from his post in the forenoon of 5 November because the latter obviously could not be blamed for the failure of Major Dr. BORNER to submit General ROMMEL's message at once. General SCHMUNDT telephoned General WARLIMONT in Berlin on the afternoon of the same day, and informed him of

HITLER's decision. On his request, he was granted a short leave which he spent with his family at Lake Tegernsee. It was due to this incident that no officer of the Armed Forces Operations Staff attended the noon discussion of the situation on 3 November.

Notes concerning 4 November 1942

Yesterday the Fuehrer ordered the transfer of the 6th Panzer Division, the 306th Infantry Division, and one other infantry division from the west to the sector of Army Group B in the east, to serve as tactical reserve in the area behind the sectors of the Rumanian Third Army and the Italian Eighth Army.

In accordance with his instructions as received from General ROMMEL, Ministerialdirigent BERNDT (equivalent to Brigadier General) reported that, in view of the employment of overwhelming quantities of materiel by the British Eighth Army, it appeared likely that the Fuka position and also the Mersa Matruth position would be untenable, but that General ROMMEL hoped to be able at least to hold the position along the Lybian-Egyptian border. This border position will be organized in the meantime by General NEHRING and newly arriving troops in such manner that it can take up the Africa Panzer Army. To reinforce this army, the 47th Infantry and the two battalions of the 5th Parachute Regiment, which were originally scheduled for transfer to the "Goering" Division in France, will be shifted to Africa as speedily as possible. In addition, it is contemplated, if possible, to transfer the 7th Parachute Division from the Eastern Front to Africa; a decision, however, has not been

MS # C-065a   -106-

made thus far. Three Africa replacement training battalions are the only complete units stationed in Italy at present; they, too, shall be transferred to Africa at once. Above all, the Fuehrer demands that the twelve Tiger tanks and twelve Mark III tanks which are scheduled to arrive in Italy till 15 November, namely six Tigers and six Mark III tanks till 11 November, the rest till 15 November, are forwarded together with the prefabricated naval barges by express transportation to Africa. However, the rehabilitation of the 6th Panzer Division will not be effected at the expense of the other motorized units in the west. The Eleventh Army, for the time being under the command of General Von MANSTEIN, has assumed the command in the Witebsk sector.

According to aerial observation, one battleship, two aircraft carriers, five cruisers, and twenty destroyers are assembled at Gibraltar. The assembly of naval forces in such strength in the western part of the Mediterranean Sea seems to point to an imminent naval operation, perhaps the escorting of another convoy to Malta.

5 November 1942

Ministerialdirigent * BERNDT, General ROMMEL's special missions staff officer, saw the Fuehrer last night and reported to him on the difficult situation of the German-Italian Panzer Army, in accordance with instructions received from General ROMMEL. Ministerialdirigent BERNDT, on this occasion, strongly denounced General Von RINTELEN, German General attached to the Italian

---
* Title of an official with executive functions in a Ministry.
Equivalent to military rank of a brigadier general.

Armed Forces High Command, for his failure to prevail upon the Supreme Command to comply with General ROMMEL's requests for supplies and for having thus contributed to the reverse suffered by the Africa Army. Besides General Von RINTELEN, a General for Special Assignments will now be stationed in Rome. He will be assigned directly to General ROMMEL and will be joined by the Chief of Army Supply and Administration at Rome, who, thus far, has been assigned to General Von RINTELEN. The General for Special Assignments will forward the supply requests of the Africa Panzer Army.

The Air Force will transfer two fighter groups from the east and one bomber group from Norway to Sicily and ship ten 88 mm antiaircraft Model 41's by express transportation to Salonika and southern Greece for further transfer to Africa. The transport ships in the Mediterranean Sea will be more strongly armed with antiaircraft, namely with new four-barreled guns, and will be supplied with Hexogen ammunition. At the HENSCHEL plant in Kassel 15 additional Tiger tanks will be completed during the current month.

East: General Von KUECHLER, Commander in Chief of the Eighteenth Army, and General BUSCH, Commander in Chief of the Sixteenth Army, report to the Fuehrer on the situation in their respective sectors. Both of them request the assignment of additional divisions. General Von KUECHLER expects the enemy to resume his attack against the "bottleneck" in the near future.

6 November 1942

Distribution of the Flying Formations of the Air Force along the Eastern Front

Fourth Air Force:	12 bomber groups	4 1/3 dive bomber groups	9 1/3 fighter groups	2 long-range fighter groups	1 1/3 close-support groups
	of them: (3 Rumanian)		(4 1/3 allied)		
Don Air Forces Headquarters:	1/3 bomber groups Hungarian	0 dive bomber groups	1 1/3 fighter groups (of them: 3 squadrons allied)		
Eastern Air Forces Headquarters:	7 bomber groups	2 dive bomber groups	4 2/3 fighter groups		
	(one-third of which are Spanish)				
First Air Force:	3 1/3 bomber groups	1 dive bomber group	3 fighter groups		
	(one-third of which are Croatian)				
Northern Air Force Command and Fifth Air Force	1 bomber group	1 dive bomber group	2 2/3 fighter groups	1/3 aerial torpedo groups	

Total: 23 2/3 bomber groups, 8 1/3 dive bomber groups, 21 fighter groups, 2 long-range fighter groups, 1 1/3 close-support groups and 1/3 aerial torpedo group (of them: 9 1/3 groups of the allied air forces), each group comprising an average of 20 planes ready to take off; totaling 56 2/3 groups, comprising about 1134 planes.

    The heavy cruiser Admiral Hipper, together with four destroyers, put to sea yesterday afternoon to operate against the enemy Atlantic routes.

The British naval forces which were assembled at Gibraltar left port in an eastern direction last night. Nine German U-boats are operating in the western part of the Mediterranean Sea at present. They have been committed against the British naval forces.

7 November 1942

Situation Report:

The situation of III Panzer Corps, committed at the western wing of the First Panzer Army, has become critical. Therefore, the 50th Infantry Division will be transferred from the Crimea to this sector by air. The Chief of Army General Staff reports that, according to agent reports, it has been decided at a supreme council held in Moscow on 4 November attended by all commanders in chief, to launch a major offensive either at the Don front or in the center sector before the end of the year. In the area of Army Group North, the 9th Air Force Ground Division is being committed in the western sector of the Leningrad front near Oranienbaum in order to free an Army division.

North Africa: According to a report received from General ROMMEL, the German-Italian Panzer Army is carrying out a withdrawal toward the Sollum-Halfaya position. At present, its situation is considered less critical. The British Eighth Army reportedly is composed of the following units: the 1st, 7th, and 10th British Tank Division, 1st South African Division, 2nd New Zealand Division, 9th Australian Division, 5th Indian Division, 44th (London) Division, 50th and 51st (Scotch) Divisions, one brigade of General de GAULLE's forces, and two regiments composed of Greeks and Levantines.

The British Gibraltar-based naval forces have joined a strong enemy convoy coming from the Atlantic and proceeding in an easterly direction. Opinion differs regarding the destination of the convoy, which comprises a large number of troop transports. The Fuehrer is inclined to believe that the enemy intends to carry out a major landing operation, involving about four or five divisions, at Tripoli or Bengasi. Admiral KRANCKE, Liaison Officer of the Navy Command attached to HITLER'S headquarters, is of the opinion that the strength of the enemy landing forces does not exceed two divisions. A reinforcement of the German air forces in the Mediterranean area is not possible at this moment. On orders of the Fuehrer, OB West has alerted the units destined, if necessary, to march into unoccupied France (Operation ANTON).

At 1340 hours, the Fuehrer leaves with his closest advisers (among them General KEITEL and General JODL) for Munich via Berlin to deliver his traditional annual address to his old Party comrades in the Buergerbraeukeller on the evening of 8 November. The field echelons of the Armed Forces Operations Staff, under the direction of Colonel Freiherr Treusch Von BUTTLAR-BRANDENFELS, First General Staff Officer of the Army attached to the Armed Forces Operations Staff, remain at HITLER'S headquarters, "Wolfsschanze." Due to the Fuehrer's absence, no situation reports were made during the following days, but situation orientations were given at the Armed Forces Operations Staff under the direction of Colonel Von BUTTLAR.

8 November 1942

Situation Report:

Frosty weather has set in along the entire Eastern Front. The thermometer has dropped to 23 degrees Fahrenheit in the Leningrad area and to 5 degrees in Finland. Otherwise, the situation is unchanged. **Mediterranean area:** Last night, the British Air Force carried out a heavy attack on Genoa. Approximately sixty-five planes were committed in this operation. Early this morning, American forces carried out landings at Algiers and Oran and apparently also at the western coast of Morocco at Casablanca. Reportedly, the landings at Algiers and Oran were repulsed by the French forces, while the enemy was successful in the area around Algiers. Admiral DARLAN, who went to Algiers several days ago to visit his sick son, is organizing the defense there in accordance with directives issued by the government in Vichy. A Gaullist revolt which had broken out in Casablanca was suppressed immediately. All American consuls in French North Africa and Morocco have been arrested. The German air forces committed against the convoys obviously achieved very little. Only 5 of the 20 planes committed in the first wave, and 7 of the 56 planes in the second wave were able to reach the target. On orders of the Fuehrer, OB West has started the preparatory movements for Operation ANTON, although the demarcation line must not be crossed as yet. The Italians too have finished preparations for the march into the Provence and for the occupation of Corsica. The Fuehrer, furthermore, has given the order to speed up the reinforcement of the garrison of Crete. Crete-bound transports are to be considered equally as important as Africa-bound transports. The French Generals WEYGAND and GIRAUD are to be brought to Vichy for constant surveillance. (At this time it was not yet known to the Armed Forces Operations Staff that General GIRAUD had escaped to North Africa via Gibraltar).

9 November 1942

Situation Report:

Along the western coast of Morocco, fierce fighting is taking place between French and American naval and ground forces. Detailed reports have not been received as yet. Three American divisions have been put ashore in French North Africa. Admiral DARLAN'S attitude seems to be uncertain. The negotiations with the French, the Vichy Government, have not been concluded yet. General WARLIMONT, Deputy Chief of Armed Forces Operations Staff, joined General JODL in Munich yesterday morning. General JODL had recalled him from leave because of the greatly increased workload. It is possible that General WARLIMONT will be sent to Paris (or Vichy?) as special plenipotentiary of the Fuehrer.

10 November 1942

Situation Report:

The American forces which landed along the western coast of Morocco at Safi (approximately 200 kilometers southwest of Casablanca), at Fedala (20 kilometers northeast of Casablanca), and at Port Lyautey (approximately 100 kilometers northeast of Casablanca) are engaged in fierce fighting

MS # C-065a   -113-

with the French ground troops which are apparently putting up stiff resistance. Several naval engagements took place between the French naval forces stationed at Casablanca (the battleship Jean Bart, the light cruiser Primauguet, and a number of destroyers and submarines) and the far superior forces of the U.S. Navy; the French naval units gave an excellent account of themselves. Apparently only a few French units are still offering resistance at Oran and Algiers.

11 November 1942

Situation Report:

This morning at 0700 hours, Operation ANTON began; units of the First Army and Armeegruppe Felber crossed the demarcation line and marched into unoccupied France, and apparently have not encountered any resistance. The Fuehrer sent a message to Marshal Petain. Coming from Sardinia and from the Italian mainland respectively, two Italian divisions landed on Corsica, and units of the Italian Fourth Army marched into the French Riviera. One Italian corps headquarters with two divisions will be transferred to Tunisia. One reinforced Stuka group and two fighter groups of X Air Force Corps stationed in Sicily have been committed in Tunisia. Six German E-boats being transferred to Tunis reportedly reached the entrance of the harbor this morning at 0900 hours; seven additional E-boats are to follow. Further ship concentrations (approximately seventy-five vessels) at Gibraltar were observed by the Air Force. In Lybia, differences of opinion occured between General BARBASSETTI, Italian Commander in Chief, and General ROMMEL with regard to the time required for the evacuation of Cyrenaica. General BARBASSETTI has filed a complaint with the Supreme Command against General ROMMEL.

On 12 November 1942 at noon, orders arrived from Munich to the effect that the field echelons of the Armed Forces Operations Staff were to be transferred to Salzburg. The field echelons left Goerlitz station (railroad station of HITLER'S headquarters "Wolfsschanze" in the Goerlitz forest east of Rastenburg) on their special train "Atlas" at 2155 hours. They arrived at Salzburg at 0220 hours on 14 November 1942, after a short stay in Munich on the evening of 13 November, when "Atlas" stopped beside the Fuehrer's train which was standing at the main railroad station.

The Armed Forces Operations Staff remained on the special train in the main station of Salzburg, while the Fuehrer and his closest advisers moved from Munich to the Berghof at Berchtesgaden and General KEITEL and General JODL established themsleves in the Reich Chancellery at Berchtesgaden.

On 14 November 1942 at 1800 hours, General WARLIMONT, Deputy Chief of the Armed Forces Operations Staff, returned from the Reich Chancellery in Berchtesgaden to the Armed Forces Operations Staff on the "Atlas" and resumed his duties. Immediately after his return, he advised the Custodian of the War Diary on the events of the preceding days as follows:

Following the American landings in North Africa on Sunday, 8 November, the Fuehrer believed at first that close co-operation with the French could be counted upon. The general attitude toward France was influenced, on the one hand, by the Fuehrer's desire to respect Italy's interests as far as

possible and, on the other hand, by the French antipathy toward the Italians
The Italian Foreign Minister, Count CIANO, arrived at Munich in the afternoon of 9 November, and French Minister President LAVAL, during the night of 9 - 10 November. The negotiations with the latter lasted throughout the day (10 November), but failed to produce definite results except for the fact that the carrying out of Operation ANTON could be ordered at 2030 hours. During the night of 10 - 11 November, the Fuehrer sent a message to Marshal PETAIN, who thereupon issued a directive to the French forces ordering them not to resist the advancing German forces. Simultaneously, a tentative agreement was reached with Italy regarding the demarcation line between the respective zones of occupation. The line Geneva-Lyons-Toulouse which had been envisaged was now disregarded. Contrary to expectations, the advance into unoccupied France was carried out without incident. Meanwhile, the occupation of the rest of France had receded into the background, whereas the establishment of a defensive front in Tunisia had become the primary consideration.

The present status of the German-French relations is as follows:

It remains uncertain how the political and, thus, the military relations between Germany and France will develop. Under no circumstances will Italy be offended. An attitude of watchful suspicion toward France is necessary, and a basis for the conclusion of a new treaty with her can develop only gradually along with the further development of mutual relations. The guiding principle for the military co-operation with France must be development from the lower levels up. The Fuehrer's strong suspicion of the French has been intensified as a result of the flight of the commander of the French 16th Division. First directives concerning the co-operation were issued on 12 November (teletype letter, Chief OKW, Armed Forces Operations Staff No 004205/42, top secret, dated 12 November 1942, is no longer available to me). These directives contain only basic principles and need supplementation. The first task will be a check of the loyalty of the French 16th Division. If the result of the investigation should not be satisfactory, the divisions will be disarmed.

On 14 November the Fuehrer ordered the closing of the borders of the newly occupied French territory. Furthermore, he ordered the return of the 328th Infantry Division and the SS Death's Head Division, which belong to the forces that marched into unoccupied France, to their former quartering areas. On 13 November, General WEYGAND was arrested by the SD (Security Service) and taken to Germany. Marshal PETAIN, in a letter to the Fuehrer, demanded the immediate release of the general and threatened to resign from his post if his request were not complied with. According to monitored conversations between North Africa and Vichy, Admiral DARLAN is working for the Vichy Government. He is trying to gain time in order to organize the defense of North Africa and to prevent the desertion of French troops to General GIRAUD.

As far as the demarcation line between the German and Italian forces is concerned, the Fuehrer rejected the suggestion offered by the OB West to place the entire coast of southern France under the command of OB West, and, under this condition, to permit the Italians to advance into southern France as far as they want to go. The possibility of the establishment of a German command over the German and Italian forces can therefore be disregarded. The Fuehrer probably was prompted by the anticipation that German-French co-operation will function more smoothly than the co-operation between the Italians and the French. The demarcation line, if possible, will be drawn in such manner as to leave the Rhone valley with its railways and roads, as well as the Rhone estuary, in German hands. Marseille, like Toulon, which as a fortress area will remain under French command, will be occupied by the Italians. The Italian reply has not yet been received, but the Italians agree that the coast up to Toulon will remain under German command until such time as Italian forces in sufficient strength have arrived.

The Organization of the Basis Area Tunisia (Code Name BRAUN)

The basis area is placed under the exclusive command of OB South; General der Panzer NEHRING, local Commander in Chief of the Tunisian area is assigned to OB South. According to advice received from the Duce, the Italians have no objections and will dispatch troops to Tunisia as speedily as possible. The basis area must be organized in a race with the Americans. The following major units will be transferred to Tunisia: the 10th Panzer Division (Marseille), Goering Division (Cognac), and the 334th Infantry Division (Kriemhilde Division). The activation of this Division from replacement training units in the ZI Theater of War was ordered on 8 November. The divisions will be transferred as they are ready for shipment, depending, of course, upon the availability of rolling stock. A special task detachment of the SD, in the strength of seven officers and seventeen men will also be dispatched to Tunisia.

For several weeks, General KESSELRING, Commander in Chief of OB South, has been endeavoring to clarify and reorganize the chain of command in the Italian area. Ministerialdirigent BERNDT, General ROMMEL'S special-missions staff officer, saw the Fuehrer again in the evening of 12 November in order to convey new complaints of the field marshal against General Von RINTELEN. The Deputy Chief of Armed Forces Operations Staff now suggested the appointment of OB South as the only Wehrmacht commander in the Mediterranean area. The Fuehrer approved this suggestion and gave the following instructions for the drafting of the pertinent directive:

OB South will be Commander in Chief of: (1) Second Air Force, which is employed in the Mediterranean area; (2) the basis area Tunisia; and (3) the entire coastal defense in the Mediterranean area (such is the wording of my notes. Actually, the directive probably refers to the defense of the coasts of Sicily and Tunisia only). OB South, furthermore, will represent all branches of the Wehrmacht in relations with the Supreme Command. General Von RINTELEN, German General attached to the Italian Armed Forces High Command in Rome, and all his agencies will be assigned to OB South. General Von RINTELEN retains his present Wehrmacht functions, but will again primarily represent the Army at headquarters of OB South. OB South's authority over the German naval units employed in the Mediterranean area will not be affected by this directive. General GAUSE,

Authorized General of the German-Italian Panzer Army in Rome, will be assigned to General ROMMEL, and will handle the requests and wishes of the Panzer Army in accordance with ROMMEL'S orders. However, his actions will be governed by directives issued by OB South and he will not be authorized to requisition Italian ships on his own responsibility. The Chief of Army Supply and Administration at Rome will not be assigned to him, but, as hitherto, to General Von RINTELEN.

15 November 1942

Situation Report:

German-French relations have become tense. French orders will be carried out in future only if they are approved by General Von NEUBRONN, authorized representative of OB West in Vichy. The Deputy Chief of the Armed Forces Operations Staff has instructed General BLUMENTRITT, Chief of Staff of OB West, accordingly. General BLUMENTRITT reports that the first trains carrying units of the 10th Panzer Division will be dispatched this afternoon, probably to Naples. The Fuehrer ordered the transfer of all 88 mm. Anti Aircraft Model 41's available in Italy to the German-Italian Africa Panzer Army. Tobruk was evacuated on 13 November, and Derna and Bengasi will be evacuated within the next few days.

16 November 1942

Situation Report:

East: General Von MANSTEIN is still in command of the Eleventh Army, and will assume command over Army Group A only after the attack on Toropez is carried out. The task force of the Eleventh Army is made up of the following divisions: the 12th Panzer Division, 3rd Mountain Division, 83rd Infantry Division, and 291st Infantry Division. The Fuehrer insists upon the transfer of the 3rd and 5th Mountain Divisions from the Eleventh and Eighteenth Armies respectively to Army Group A in the Caucasus area, and the transfer of two jaeger divisions of Army Group North to Finland and Norway respectively. The 1st and 9th Panzer Divisions will remain in the area west of Subzoff for the time being. Of the Air Force ground divisions which are currently available, three divisions will relieve two infantry divisions in the southwestern sector of the Leningrad front at Oranienbaum, one will relieve the 20th Motorized Infantry Division, one a division of II Infantry Corps (At Demiansk) one a division at the Don front, and one will be employed in the Crimea. Three German U-boats have arrived in the Black Sea, where they are committed against the Russian naval forces, particularly the Russian battleship stationed at Poti.

North: Reports received from Sweden during the last days unanimously agree in the opinion that the events in North Africa have deeply impressed the Swedish Government. With reference to these reports, the Fuehrer states that he attaches greater importance to the absolute security of the northern area than to a far-reaching offensive in the east in the spring of 1943. He orders the reinforcement of the 25th Panzer Division (employed in Norway) by the transfer of Panzer Battalion 40 (committed in Finland), the shipment of the 5th Jaeger Division to Norway and the 28th Jaeger Division to Finland, and the activation of an Air Force ground division in Norway for the purpose of relieving an Army division employed there.

West: According to a report received from the Chief of the Air Force General Staff, the following air forces are available to the Third Air Force, committed in the west under the command of Generalfeldmarschall SPERRLE: 9 reconnaissance squadrons, 10 2/3 bomber groups, 1/3 dive bomber group, 7 1/3 fighter groups, 1 2/3 fighter-bomber groups, 1/3 close-support group, and 1 night fighter group. OB West is instructed by teletype letter to exercise the utmost caution in co-operating with the French Armed Forces. Five of ten replacement training divisions available in the area of OB West will be stationed in the communications zone of the newly occupied French territory. Six squadrons of the Garde Mobile are transferred to Marseille because of the uncertain attitude of the city's population. Toulon, which has not been occupied by German or Italian troops, will not be occupied by French Army troops, but will be defended only by French naval forces. On orders of the Fuehrer, preparations will be made for a surprise seizure of the French naval units lying in the harbor of Toulon. These preparations, which will be carried out in agreement with the Italians, must be kept strictly secret from the French. The Armed Forces Operations Staff is given the order to draft the pertinent directive.

Mediterranean Sea: According to reports received from Spain, the British asked the Spanish Government on 12 November whether the latter would grant them the permission to occupy the isle of Minorca for a period of a few months. The Spanish General Staff is informed of these reports.

The draft of a directive concerning the reorganization of the chain of command in the Mediterranean area has not yet been submitted to the Fuehrer. The original plan, meanwhile, has been modified in respect to the position of General GAUSE. He will not be appointed Authorized General in Rome, but will serve only as the representative of General ROMMEL and General NEHRING at OB South. Strong British and American forces have crossed the Algerian-Tunisian border. French Admiral PLATON arrived in Bizerte on 15 November at 0900 hours. He has been ordered by Marshal PETAIN to clarify the situation in Tunisia, and to ascertain how the co-operation of the French division stationed there with the forces of the Axis Powers could be put into practice. Admiral PLATON has not received any definitive orders because several members of the French Cabinet refuse to support Minister President LAVAL. The attitude taken by Admiral PLATON and by the French division in Tunisia in the face of the advance of the British and American forces across the Tunisian border appears utterly obscure. The utmost vigilance there is essential. The harbor of Tunis is open, the barrier there has been removed.

General JODL is under the impression that General ROMMEL intends to withdraw the German-Italian Panzer Army beyond the Mersa el Brega position (southwest of Agedabia) to a position based on a large salt lake.

On orders of the Fuehrer, one of the Air Force ground divisions which will be activated in December will be transferred to Crete. However, the transfer will be effected only after the shipment of the 22nd (Airborne)

Division* is completed, in order to prevent the division's remaining idle in Greece. Furthermore, the Fuehrer considers it advisable to reinforce the occupation troops in the Peloponnesus.

17 November 1942

Situation Report:

West: The Commander in Chief of the Navy has suggested the fortification of the coast of the North Sea in a manner similar to the West Wall, apparently prompted by a desire to protect himself. From France, approximately one half of the units of the 6th Panzer Division have left for the east and six trains carrying elements of the Goering Division have been dispatched to Italy. The attitude of the French remains uncertain. OB West therefore ordered the withdrawal of the French troops from the Mediterranean coast. Within the Armed Forces Operation Staff, the opinion prevails that the unfavorable development in France is essentially a result of HITLER'S consideration for Italy. General Von RINTELEN, German General in Rome, reported last night that an agreement has been reached with the Italians on the demarcation line between the respective zones of occupation. The Rhone valley with its railways and roads will belong to the German zone, but the Italians have been granted the right to use the roads on the eastern bank jointly with the Germans. Additional agreements will be concluded between OB West and the Italian Fourth Army directly.

---

* As far as I can remember, this division was not transferred to North Africa, as was HITLER'S intention on 4 September (see p. 27), but from Greece to Crete; however, its shipment was not yet completed on 16 November.

Mediterranean Area: Last night, OB South received a preliminary order from HITLER concerning the chain of command in the Mediterranean area. The powers of OB South will be limited to the southern area including Crete, Greece, southern Italy, and North Africa. General GAUSE will not be the representative of General ROMMEL, but a representative of the Army for the two theaters of operations in North Africa. KAUFMANN, Reichsstatthalter (equivalent to civilian governor) of Hamburg, has been appointed Reich Commissioner with the functions of requisitioning shipping space in the Mediterranean and directing its employment according to urgency. General Von WUEHLISCH, Chairman of the Armistice Commission in Wiesbaden, reports that, according to reliable information, French Army and Air Force officers, in a treacherous manner, had paved the way for the American landings in Morocco long ago. Admiral DARLAN deserted to the Americans as early as 11 November.

General NEHRING has assumed the command in Tunisia. The code name BRAUN need not to be used any longer. The 5th Parachute Regiment (The Koch Regiment, see under 5 November) has arrived in Tunis. The German security forces are engaged in combat with British and American motorized forces 100 kilometers west of Tunis.

German U-boats in the Mediterranean: After the transfer of additional U-boats, eighteen U-boats have lately been available in the western Mediterranean. Of these, three were probably sunk during the last few days and seven were returned to ZI ports after having been damaged by depth bombs. Thus, only eight U-boats are currently committed against the enemy. Eight U-boats were employed in the eastern Mediterranean. Of these, one was sunk during the last few days. Until the end of November, the assignment of four U-boats can be expected.

18 November 1942

Situation Report:

In the Mediterranean, the 10,000-ton Italian tanker Giordano, bound for Tunis with a cargo of 4,000 tons of fuel, was sunk last night. OB South has ordered General NEHRING to clarify the attitude of the French division in Tunisia not later than today. The forces under General NEHRING will advance farther to the west today. A British convoy of thirty ships coming from the east had reached a point level with Derna this morning. In accordance with the order issued by the Commander in Chief of the Air Force, the 10th Air Force ground division is being shipped to Crete. In the Rumanian petroleum area, the command was taken over by the Rumanian Air Force on 17 November at 1200 hours. General Von GLAISE, German General in Croatia, reported last night that, according to HITLER'S decision, the Croatian Legion committed at the Eastern Front will not be returned to Croatia.

19 November 1942

Situation Report:

In the course of the day alarming reports are received from the Chief of Army General Staff, who had remained at the headquarters of the Army High Command in East Prussia, concerning the Russian offensive which had long been expected by the Fuehrer and which was launched at the Don front in the sector opposite the Romanian Third Army this morning. On orders of its chief, the Armed Forces Operations Staff will make preparations for the establishment of the Military Administration in the newly occupied French territory.

20 November 1942

Situation Report:

The Chief of Army General Staff reports that the Russians have achieved deep penetrations in the sector of the Rumanian Third Army. The situation is still somewhat obscure. In the afternoon, the Fuehrer orders the disintegration of the attack group of the Eleventh Army and the transfer of the Eleventh Army Command Staff from Witebsk to Army Group B for employment in command of Army Group Don, which will comprise the Fourth Panzer Army, Sixth Army, Rumanian Fourth Army, and Rumanian Third Army. General LOEHR, Commander in Chief of OB Southeast, reports growing disturbances throughout the Balkans. General LOEHR saw the Duce within the last few days, and the latter suggested to the Fuehrer the establishment of a joint German-Italian command for the entire Croatian area.

21 November 1942

On orders of General JODL, the field echelons of the Armed Forces Operations Staff move from Salzburg to the Jaeger-Kaserne (riflemen barracks) in Strupp near Berchtesgaden during the forenoon hours.

Distribution of the Flying Formations of the Air Force along the Eastern Front

	Bombers	Dive Bombers	Fighters	Long-range Fighters	Close Support / Other
Fourth Air Force:	9 bomber groups	4 1/3 Dive bomber groups	8 1/3 fighter groups	2 1/3 long-range fighter groups	1 1/3 close support groups
of them:	(3 Romanian)		(4 1/3 allied)		
Don Air Forces Headquarters	1/3 bomber gr. (Hungarian)	0 "	1 1/3 fighter group (1 allied)		1/3 close support group
Eastern Air Forces Headquarters	7 bomber groups	2 Dive bomber groups	4 1/3 fighter groups (1/3 allied)		
First Air Force:	3 "	1 Dive bomber group	3 fighter groups		
Northern Air Force Command and Fifth Air Force	1 "	1 "	2 2/3 " "		1/3 aerial torpedo group

Total: 20 1/3 bomber groups, 8 1/3 Dive bomber groups, 19 2/3 fighter groups, 2 1/3 long-range fighter groups, 1 2/3 close-support groups and 1/3 aerial torpedo group (of them: 9 groups of the allied air forces), each group comprising an average of 20 planes ready to take off, totaling 52 2/3 groups, comprising about 1,054 planes.

Situation Report:

The Russians were able to deepen considerably the penetration achieved by them in the sector of the Rumanian Third Army between Kletskaja and

Serafimowitsch. Toward noon on 20 November, Russian tank spearheads, advancing in the upper Liska Valley, reached the area of Gurejew and south of it. South of Stalingrad and in the Kalmuck Steppe too, the Russians, employing powerful forces including numerous tanks, launched attacks against the eastern flank of the Fourth Panzer Army and the Rumanian Fourth Army.

Last night the British Air Force carried out a heavy attack on Turin. The casualties amounted to twenty-eight killed and a great number wounded. In Lybia, the enemy took Bengasi yesterday.

In the evening the Fuehrer orders the Sixth Army, with headquarters reportedly at Kalatsch, to hold the western and southern cornerstones of its position under all circumstances. The 22nd Panzer Division, which is employed in the area behind the Rumanian Third Army, will attempt to establish contact with the Rumanian 1st Panzer Division by means of launching an attack in a northerly direction. The elements of the Sixth Army which arrive in the area around Kalatsch will attack in a northwesterly direction. The following units are approaching: the 6th and 11th Panzer Divisions, 3rd Mountain Division from the west and, the 294th Infantry Division, hitherto employed in the area behind the Italian Eighth Army, and the 62nd Infantry Division*. The bulk of the 22nd (Airborne) Division has arrived on the Isle of Crete.

22 November 1942

Situation Report:

The Fuehrer appointed General Von KLEIST, hitherto Commander in

---

* I do not remember where this division came from.

Chief of the First Panzer Army, to the post of Commander in Chief of Army Group A, and General der Kavallerie Von MACKENSEN to the post of Commander in Chief of the First Panzer Army. Alarm units are employed for the protection of the important railroad junction of Tichorezk. The two spearheads of the great Russian offensive in the Don-Volga area have joined forces at Kalatsch. As a result, the Sixth Army is pocketed between the Volga and the Don. This Army is holding approximately the following line: Stalingrad-Rynok-Orlowka - a point north of the Konnaja railroad station (west of Orlowka) - a point south of the Kotluban railroad station - southwest to the heights extending from Kotluban to Dmitrijewka - a point west of Marinowka. From this point the Army's southern front extends to Stalingrad via Zybenko.

Toward noon the Armed Forces Operations Staff receives the order from the Berghof to depart for "Wolfsschanze." The Fuehrer and his closest advisers, General KEITEL and General JODL, will leave tonight on HITLER'S special train, probably for Leipzig, where they will board a plane for "Wolfsschanze." An advance party of the Armed Forces Operations Staff will leave Salzburg tonight on a courier coach attached to the scheduled express train for Berlin. From Berlin it will proceed to "Wolfsschanze" by plane. The first echelon (Colonel Von BUTTLAR with several Army and Air Force General Staff officers) will leave for "Wolfsschanze" tomorrow morning at 0800 hours by direct plane from Einring airdrome near Salzburg. In the afternoon of 23 November the bulk of the Armed Forces Operations Staff will leave the Jaeger-Kaserne in Strupp to board the special train "Atlas" which is waiting at the Bischofswiesen railroad station (at the line Berchtesgaden-Reichenhall) and is scheduled to depart at 2000 hours. The train will go via Freilassing-Munich-Nuremberg-Halle-Kottbus-Posen-Allenstein to "Wolfsschanze" (Goerlitz station east of Rastenburg) where the "Atlas" is scheduled to arrive shortly after 0100 hours on 25 November. The Armed Forces Operations Staff will return to its bunkers and barracks in Second Sperrkreis* during the forenoon hours.

25 November 1942

Situation Report:

East: The Fuehrer is confident with regard to the situation of the Sixth Army. The 294th and 62nd Infantry Divisions arrived quickly and have joined forces with the 22nd Panzer Division. In addition, the 336th Infantry Division is being moved up from the west. There is reason to expect that the 6th and 11th Panzer Divisions will also arrive soon. The Chief of Staff of the Rumanian Fourth Army, German Colonel I.G. WENCK, is organizing a defensive front along the Tschir. The first reserves have arrived at the Fourth Panzer Army in Kotelnikowo. General HAUFFE, Chief of the German Military Mission in Rumania, has urged Marshal ANTONESCU to make additional Rumanian forces available. General Von MANSTEIN will assume the command over Army Group Don tomorrow. The pocketed Sixth Army has been able to hold all its fronts. However, its supply situation is critical and, in view of adverse winter weather and the enemy superiority in fighter planes, it appears doubtful whether it will be possible to

---

* Second security ring around HITLER'S headquarters. (Translator)

supply the army by air with necessary food rations, ammunition, and fuel, which total 700 tons daily. The Fourth Air Force has only 298 transport planes available, but approximately 500 planes are needed. Therefore, General Freiherr Von RICHTHOFEN, Commanding General of VIII Air Force Corps committed in the Stalingrad area, suggested to the Fuehrer that the Sixth Army should first conduct a withdrawal toward the west and resume the attack at a later time. However, the Fuehrer bluntly rejected this suggestion. In the sector opposite the Ninth Army, the enemy launched an attack with strong forces at Subzoff this morning. General MODEL is not worried about his eastern front, but fears for the western front, especially for the sector east of Belyj. For two days the enemy has also been launching fierce attacks against Welikije Luki.

In the Ukraine, according to a report by the liaison officer of the Economy and Armament Office attached to the Armed Forces Operations Staff, we utilized 23 percent of the arable area this year, while 35 percent had been utilized under the Russians. However, the Fuehrer received a report to the effect that we had utilized 36 percent.

West: Reports received from various sources deal with the increasing unreliability of the French Navy. The Fuehrer, therefore, decided to carry out Operation LILA (seizure of the French naval units lying in Toulon harbor) as speedily as possible. OB West reports that the operation can be carried out tomorrow if he receives advance notice before 1600 hours. In answer to an inquiry, OB West reports that the forces of the three reserve divisions which will carry out the operation have been moved into their assembly areas.

Four U-boats can be in position off Toulon at dawn and seven of them by noon. The Armed Forces Operations Staff will prepare a brief containing the charges and the evidence on the basis of which the Fuehrer will prove to the French Minister President that the measures against the French Navy were unavoidable. Reference will be made in this brief to the discovery of the arms depot in Nimes. The question of the seizure of the French merchantmen lying in the harbor of Marseille is closely connected with Operation LILA. The Fuehrer has made it absolutely clear that these ships have to be taken over by German crews with the utmost speed. There must be no jurisdictional disputes between the German Navy and Reich Commissioner KAUFMANN.

26 November 1942

Situation Report:

East: In the area of Army Group B, (General Von MANSTEIN will assume the command over Army Group Don tomorrow), the first four trains carrying elements of the 6th Panzer Division arrive via Rostow-Salsk on the line to Kotelnikowo today. According to prisoner of war statements, the enemy himself is surprised at his great successes south of Stalingrad. Reportedly, he had intended only to reach the railroad line Rostow-Stalingrad and is now undecided whether to continue his operations south of the Don. Now he seems to have committed a tank corps in an attack toward the southwest. The Sixth Army intends to abandon the Don bridgehead* tonight (it is possible however that the night of 25 - 26 November is meant) and to

---

* At Peskowatka and Wertjatschij, however, it seems that this bridgehead was already evacuated on 26 November.

withdraw to a northeast-southwest line, i.e. the line Kotluban-Marinowka, in order to free forces for a thrust toward the southwest. The enemy is moving up reserves into the area of Swoboda (south of Woronesh), a fact which indicates that he intends to attack there. The evacuation of the Woronesh bridgehead in order to free one division is contemplated.

In the area of Army Group Center, the enemy continues his attacks against the eastern and western front of the Ninth Army in the east, particularly at Ssytschewka, in order to reach the railroad line Wjasma-Rshew. In the west, the Stalin Corps has been committed at Belyj, and it is safe to assume that the enemy main effort is concentrated there.

The 28th Jaeger Division (Eighteenth Army) is transferred to the Twentieth Mountain Army in Finland.

West: The Fuehrer does not approve the time set by OB West for the start of Operation LILA, at 0400 hours tomorrow, because he regards this hour as too early for the Air Force. However, the hour is not changed. In a letter to the Duce, the Fuehrer informed the latter that the Italians should take over the French Navy and that the German Navy would claim only some minor vessels as a loan for the duration of the war. In his letter to Marshal PETAIN of 11 November, HITLER stated, inter alia, that he considered it his task to reconquer the French colonial empire in joint action with the French. North Africa: British-American motorized forces yesterday advanced as far as Medjez-el-Bab (45 kilometers southwest of Tunis). The Fuehrer approves General JODL'S suggestion to commit the German air forces in the area of the German-Italian Panzer Army against the rear of

British Eight Army's approach zone in the same manner as the British Air Force had been committed at the start of the offensive.

27 November 1942

Situation Report:

East: Army Group Don took over its sector this morning at 0800 hours. The distribution of the enemy forces in the Stalingrad area seems to favor the Sixth Army's intentions considerably. The Sixth Army's food situation is better than had been assumed hitherto. Only 27 Ju 52 Model planes flew to the Stalingrad area yesterday. There are 298 of these planes available, capable of carrying 600 tons of supplies to Stalingrad daily. At present, 700 tons are required daily, and this requirement will increase to 1,500 tons daily once the stockpiled supplies are exhausted. In the area of Army Group Center, the situation at Belyj remains obscure. On HITLER'S orders, the sector of Welikije Luki will be added to the sector of Army Group Center. The fuel consumption at the eastern front is very low. At present, it amounts to 3,100 cubicmeters daily: the Fuehrer has authorized the amount of 3,500 cubicmeters daily only for Army Groups A and B.

West: This morning, Operation LILA was started and carried out in Toulon proper without encountering much resistance. The French Navy scuttled most of its own units, and the battleship Strasbourg was beached. Simultaneously with the execution of this operation, the French Army was disarmed. The Fuehrer is pleased over the fact that this danger in the rear of the German troops has now been eliminated. He expects LAVAL to stay in office and wants to meet him. HITLER is not very much in favor of establishing a military administration in the newly occupied French territory, as he believes that the French civil administration and police will suffice. OB West is of the same opinion. Therefore, only static agencies will be established for the German troops and the apparatus of the military administration in the originally occupied French territory will be reduced as far as possible. The so-called blocked depots, which had been established in unoccupied France in terms of the armistice, in which the surrendered arms and equipment of the French Armed Forces were stored, are to be taken over as speedily as possible. On a suggestion made by the Air Force, the Fuehrer decided that personnel of the disbanded units of the French Armed Forces can be immediately taken into German service, especially the Air Warning Service, the anti-aircraft artillery, and coast batteries. Such personnel will be compensated on the basis of existing French conditions and will be subject to German military law. In addition, the French real estate and shipyards will be taken over. The Armed Forces Operations Staff will formulate these orders in writing. According to an order by HITLER, the German Air Force will take over the air defense in Toulon for the time being. The Fuehrer definitely has no objections to the transfer of French arms and equipment to Italy, and he has also authorized the production of Tiger panzers by the Italians under license.

General FOERTSCH, Chief of Staff of the Southeast Commander Military District, acting on orders received from General LOEHR, suggested the retransfer of the Croatian regiment which is being trained in Stockerau (north of Vienna) to Croatia. However, Generaloberst FROMM, Chief of Army Equipment and Commander in Chief of the Replacement Training Army, requested that the regiment be left in Stockerau at least until 1 January 1943 because it is not yet ready for action. General Von GLAISE, German General in Croatia, has been advised accordingly. The demolition of the railroad bridge at Thermopylae in Greece by partisans has resulted in an 8-day interruption of traffic on the line Salonika-Athens.

28 November 1942

Situation Report:

East: The Army General Staff has received reports to the effect that the Russians intend to establish themselves on the Crimea. The Fuehrer approves General ZEITZLER'S suggestion to transfer SS and alarm units of the Military District Commander Ukraine to the threatened area. In the sector of Army Group A, additional alarm units are employed for the protection of the Manytsch line. In the sector of Army Group Don, only thirty Ju 52 Model planes flew to the Stalingrad area yesterday. The estimated strength of the German and Rumanian forces pocketed there is approximately 400,000 men (actually, twenty-two German divisions and several Rumanian units totaling about 330,000 men were in the pocket). In the sector opposite the Italian Eighth Army and the Hungarian Second Army, strong enemy forces are concentrated, apparently for an attack against the railroad line Millerowo-Swoboda running in the area behind the front line in that sector. On General

ZEITZLER'S request, one division will be transferred to this sector from the west.

In the area of Army Group Center, enemy tank forces penetrated as far as the railroad line Wjasma-Rshew early this morning. Welikije-Luki is practically encircled by the enemy. The Fuehrer assumes that this strong point is adequately provided with supplies. In the area of Army Group North, the enemy resumed his attacks against the corridor connecting II Infantry Corps with the bulk of Army Group's forces (the Demiansk pocket) from the south and north this morning. General ZEITZLER, reporting to the Fuehrer, voices his objection against the transfer of the 28th Jaeger Division on the ground that this division cannot be spared in the sector of the Eighteenth Army. However, HITLER insists upon the Division's transfer to the Twentieth Mountain Army in Finland. The Twentieth Mountain Army intends to employ the Division in the area behind the center of its front. According to an estimate by Division Foreign Armies East of the Army General Staff, it must be assumed that 5,000 - 6,000 tanks are available to the Russians. Thirty-two Russian tank brigades are employed at Stalingrad, and twelve are committed in the sector opposite the eastern front of the Ninth Army.

West: The Fuehrer declares that the Armistice Pact has to be regarded as void. The Armed Forces Operations Staff will order the Armistice Commission in Wiesbaden to transfer personnel that can be spared there. On HITLER'S orders, no measures aiming at re-establishing the French Armed Forces will be taken in the near future. However, the police and the Garde Mobile* will be reinforced. No French crews are left on the French naval

---

* mobile police unit

MS # C-065a   -138-

units at Toulon. A number of French mine sweepers are taken over by the German Navy to serve as escort vessels.

Mediterranean area: The French forces in Tunisia have given a loyalty pledge. Therefore no compulsory measures are imposed, at least upon the French naval units stationed there. General ROMMEL will arrive at HITLER'S headquarters this afternoon at 1630 hours in order to report to the Fuehrer on the situation in Lybia. He will fly back to Rome with the Reichsmarschall tonight. The strength of the German troops employed on Crete is 36 - 38,000 men. The employment of the 10th Air Force Ground Division on the Peloponnesus rather than on Crete is contemplated. A suggestion to transfer this division to the Isle of Rhodes, which also is regarded as threatened, is rejected by the Fuehrer, who does not wish to interfere with Italian sovereignty.

29 November 1942

Distribution of the Flying Formations of the Air Force along the Eastern Front

	bomber groups	Dive bomber groups	fighter groups	long-range fighter groups	close-support groups
Fourth Air Force:	9	5	8	2	2 2/3
Don Air Forces Headquarters	1 "	0 "	2 "		
Eastern Air Forces Headquarters	7 "	3 "	4 1/3"		
First Air Force	3 "	0 "	3 "		

MS # C-065a

| Northern Air Force Command and Fifth Air Force: | 1 bomber group | 1 Dive bomber group | 2 2/3 fighter groups | 1 1/3 aerial torpedo groups |

Total: 21 bomber groups, 9 Dive bomber groups, 20 fighter groups, 2 long-range fighter groups, 2 2/3 close-support groups and 1 1/3 aerial torpedo groups, each group comprising an average of 20 planes ready to take off, totaling 56 groups, comprising about 1,120 planes.

Situation Report:

East: A Russian submarine carrying out a reconnaissance mission was observed near the coast of the Crimea yesterday. In the area of the Commander of the Ukraine Military District the following troops are available for reinforcement of the forces employed on the Crimea:

(1) Nine alarm battalions comprising 600 men each without heavy weapons, their personnel procured, not from the field forces, but from the administrative services, such as delousing stations, railroad depot commanders, etc.

(2) The Slovakian division.

In the area of Army Group A, the enemy is being reinforced in the sector opposite the Seventeenth Army. The Sixth Army has withdrawn its northwestern front according to plan. The Sixth Army still has available, inter alia, an ammunition dump with 30,000 rounds for light field howitzers. At the newly organized Hollidt Group, committed at the Tschir, the German and Rumanian forces will be consolidated. In the area of Army Group Center, the situation at Belyj is still obscure; the situation at Welikije Luki no longer is regarded as alarming. The Fuehrer rejected General Von KLUGE'S suggestion to withdraw the front there as far as the railroad at Novo Sokolniki. The strong point of Welikije Luki is supplied with food rations for fourteen days, but the Fuehrer deems this inadequate. Ten thousand tons of supplies have been brought up by rail and on motor trucks to the area of Demiansk yesterday.

West: The Third Air Force reported to the Air Force Operations Staff this morning that the speed with which the discharge of personnel of the French Air Force is being carried out makes its transfer into German service impossible. General of the Infantry Von STUELPNAGEL, Military Commander in France, reported that some of the orders issued by HITLER on 27 November conflicted with French sovereignty. The Fuehrer takes an entirely different position. He desires that the newly occupied French territory be utilized for the purpose of the German Wehrmacht to the greatest possible extent. The adherents of General de GAULLE will be shipped to the Eastern Front to shovel snow there. The deputy Chief of Armed Forces Operations Staff instructs General Von STUELPNAGEL accordingly. The monthly fat ration in the newly occupied French territory has been reduced from 410 to 350 grams.

Mediterranean area: Last night the British Air Force carried out another heavy air attack on Turin; approximately 180 planes took part in the attack. The Italians have requested us to dispatch a German commission to Italy to advise them on coast defense. Upon a suggestion made by

General JODL, OB South will be instructed to procure ample supplies of maps of Italy because it may soon be necessary to assist the Italians in the defense of their coasts. In Tunisia, British and American forces occupied the Djedeida airdrome and reached Pont du Fahs yesterday. American parachutists were dropped in the area of Sbeitla and Gafsa. In his report yesterday, General ROMMEL stated that the ration strength of the German-Italian Panzer Army at present is about 60 - 70,000 men*. Casualties since the start of the British offensive amount to a total of approximately nine thousand men. On General ROMMEL'S suggestion, HITLER requested the Duce by telegram to intensify the supply traffic to North Africa.

Greece: As a result of the destruction of the railroad bridge at Thermopylae, the reconstruction of which will take six to eight weeks, the daily traffic of eight trains on the Salonika-Athens line had to be reduced by 2 1/2 trains.

Balkans: The Russian successes at Stalingrad have prompted the Rumanians and Hungarians to seek an understanding. If the Balkans should appear threatened, the Hungarian and Bulgarian forces will be employed in the defense of the peninsula. The Fuehrer does not wish to hinder the Croatians in their action against the Serbs, motivated by the vendetta which is customary in these parts.

30 November 1942

Situation Report:

East: The Sixth Army intends to withdraw its northwestern front again.

---

* Against 82,000 men prior to the offensive launched by the British Eighth Army.

Out of 38 Ju 52 Model planes which took off yesterday, only 12 were able to reach the Stalingrad area. The enemy is expected to launch strong attacks against the sectors held by the Italian Eighth Army and the Hungarian Second Army respectively. The Fuehrer blames the Army for the utterly inadequate equipment of Italian and Rumanian forces with antitank guns. He orders the immediate transfer of guns from the depots of the French Armed Forces and from the blocked depots for conversion into antitank guns. He also sharply criticizes the Army for its failure to adequately equip the support units employed in the area behind the two armies with heavy weapons. Additional units will be transferred to the threatened fronts.

West: Referring to the situation in France, the Fuehrer states that, in his opinion, the French Mediterranean coast is not threatened at all. Only the coastal sectors which are occupied by the Italians could perhaps be regarded as endangered. Therefore, the three reserve divisions employed in the coastal area can be withdrawn and assembled for Operation GISELA (march into Spain and Portugal in case of a British landing there). The Fuehrer, in this connection, states that German interests are best served by a neutral Spain. The delivery of German arms to Spain could only jeopardize that country's neutrality. In case of a British landing attempt on the Iberian Peninsula, the Spanish could be induced to put up vigorous resistance only by our own launching of offensive operations into Spain. As far as France is concerned, the Fuehrer trusts that the SD (Security Service) will uncover the secret arms depots which undoubtedly still exist. Promises made by French officers to the effect that they will no longer fight against Germany will not be accepted in the future.

Mediterranean area: Last night another air attack was carried out on

Turin by approximately fifty planes of the British Air Force. The transfer of a hundred 88 mm. anti-aircraft batteries with German crews to northern Italy will be carried out gradually beginning today. The batteries will eventually be taken over by the Italians. In addition, the Fuehrer orders the transfer of ten Flak battalions, each of them comprising four 88 mm. batteries, to Tunis and Bizerte respectively. These 88 mm. anti-aircraft guns, totaling 560 pieces, represent the production of an entire month. The Fuehrer instructed OB South by telegram to disarm the French forces and naval units stationed in Tunisia. The battery and ship crews will be made up of personnel of the German Navy. In addition, OB South was authorized to commit the 47th Infantry in Tunisia. An additional regiment will be transported to Italy by air for commitment in Tunisia.

(Signed) Helmuth GREINER

15 June 1949

MS # C-065a

1 December 1942

Situation Report:

East: Thirty Ju 52 and thirty-five He 111 Model planes flew to the Stalingrad area yesterday. The Sixth Army's food supplies are sufficient to last until 5 December, and its ammunition for heavier calibers will last until 12 December. According to an estimate by the Army General Staff, the following quantities of war materiel of every kind have been shipped from Great Britain and the United States respectively to Soviet Russia during the period from May to November: 250,000 tons via Murmansk, 100,000 tons a month via Iran, 100,000 tons a month via Vladivostok and other ports of the Far East, totaling 1,650,000 tons. According to General ZEITZLER'S estimate, the number of tanks delivered to the Soviet Union amounts to 400 a month. During the winter, the deliveries will be carried out principally via Murmansk and Archangelsk. (sic)

According to an order by HITLER, the coast batteries in Tunis will be taken over by the German naval coast artillery, and the French warships stationed there, by Italian crews.

The Reichsmarschall reported to the Fuehrer from Rome that he had failed in his efforts to convince the Duce that, in Lybia, the Mersa-el-Brega position (see under 16 November) has to be held. The Duce insisted that the position should be held only as long as it were possible to do so without sustaining major casualties, and that the forces then should be withdrawn to the el-Buerat position. The Mersa-el-Brega position could not be held indefinitely because, owing to the deep arid waste in its rear, it could not be provided with supplies.

A study dealing with the American military objectives in the war prepared by General Von BOETTICHER, former German Military Attache in Washington D. C. (who, since his return from the United States, has been assigned to the OKW for special assignments), prompted General JODL to order General WARLIMONT on 29 November to prepare a new estimate of the over-all situation. For this estimate, which should not comprise more than three pages, General JODL yesterday gave the following directives: being Europe's outpost area, North Africa has to be held under all circumstances. As a prerequisite, sea transportation must be accelerated. (The Reichsmarschall discussed this problem with the Duce yesterday.) If North Africa should be lost, an Anglo-American attack against southeastern Europe via the Dodecanese, Crete, and the Peloponnesus is to be expected. It is therefore necessary to pacify and secure the Balkans. In the west, no major enemy offensive appears to be imminent next spring. In the northern area, the enemy is likely to limit his activities to minor operations. In the east, finally, stable fronts have to be established to make it possible for the German forces to launch a spring offensive at least at one point. General JODL is of the opinion that the Russians are stronger now than at the beginning of last winter.

Therefore the manpower available in the occupied territories must be mobilized.

2 December 1942

Situation Report:

East: On its request, the First Panzer Army is authorized by the Fuehrer to withdraw its attack wedge east of Mosdok in order to free forces for the conduct of mobile operations. The Fourth Panzer Army is reinforced by transferring the 6th Panzer Division, one infantry division from the west, and one Air Force ground division to the Kotelnikowo area. It is not yet decided at what point the 11th and 17th Panzer Divisions will be committed. General Von MANSTEIN will launch the attack in the direction of Stalingrad on 9 December. Only fifteen Ju 52 and twenty-five He 111 Model planes flew to the Stalingrad area on 1 December. Russian pressure against the security line at the Tschir has increased during the last few days. The first antitank guns will arrive in the sectors of the Italian Eighth Army and the Hungarian Second Army respectively on 4 December. These guns are being transferred from Second Army. Area of Army Group Center: On orders of the Fuehrer, the 1st, 12th, 19th and 20th Panzer Divisions will now launch the counterattack (notes disclosing details of this intended operation are not available). Contact with the isolated strong point of Welikije Luki will be re-established. The enemy has renewed his fierce attacks against the corridor connecting II Infantry Corps with the bulk of the forces of Army Group North. Army Group therefore suggested the relief of the 223rd Infantry Division in the sector of the Eighteenth Army by an Air Force ground division and its commitment in the corridor.

The Fuehrer agrees, and also wants Tiger tanks, taken from those destined for shipment to Tunisia, to be moved up into the corridor.

West: Following his report on the situation in the west, General JODL broaches the subject of the assignment of the coast artillery. The Fuehrer declares that the most important task in coast defense is firing upon targets at sea and that therefore all suitable army batteries will be assigned to the naval doast artillery command headquarters.

Mediterranean: Last night two groups of light enemy naval units were observed northeast of the Balearic Islands. At 2240 hours, an additional group of enemy naval units appeared north of Bizerte, and attacked a German-Italian convoy shortly after midnight, sinking or dispersing it. Apparently the convoy's cargo did not include any tanks. A second convoy with a cargo of sixty tanks arrived at an Italian port. The Fuehrer is very angry over the mounting losses of transports in the Mediterranean. Apparently the situation in Tunisia is not yet sufficiently clear to permit a decision on the chain of command there. General NEHRING has been removed from his post. In the northern sector, the commander of the 10th Panzer Division has assumed command.

3 December 1942

Situation Report:

The ration strength of the pocketed elements of the Sixth Army is not 400,000 men as had been assumed hitherto, but only about 300,000.

Seventy-three planes, half of them bombers, flew to the Stalingrad area yesterday, carrying 115 tons of food supplies, ammunition, and fuel. In the newly occupied French territory, the following demarcation line has been established between the German and Italian zones of occupation: St Julien (six kilometers southwest of Geneva)-Lyon (German)-Avignon (German-coast between Marseille and Toulon (Bai de la Ciotat). The shipyard of Toulon, with 18,000 tons of fuel oil, is in German hands.

4 December 1942

Situation Report:

Owing to unfavorable weather conditions, fog and ice formations at temperatures around zero degrees centigrade, no supply planes could fly to the Stalingrad area. The Fuehrer again contemplates the evacuation of the Woronesh bridgehead. However, the Second Army reported that its present positions around Woronesh are better than any support positions that could be occupied. In Tunisia a new army headquarters has been established, namely headquarters of the Fifth Panzer Army. General Von ARNIM, hitherto Commanding General of XXXIX Panzer Corps, who was promoted to the rank of Generaloberst for this very purpose, has been appointed to the post of commander in chief of the new army. The Fuehrer gave the order to ship all Tiger tanks which had arrived in Italy to Tunisia rather than to the German-Italian Panzer Army. This morning, German-Italian forces took Tebourba, 30 kilometers west of Tunis.

MS # C-065a   -149-

5 December 1942

Situation Report:

Sector of the First Panzer Army: Last night, the Fuehrer gave his approval for the withdrawal of those elements of III Panzer Corps which have been holding positions far advanced to the south. However, the "Ossetische Highway" leading from Alagir to Kutais will remain blocked. Forty-nine Ju 52 and seventeen He 111 Model planes flew to the Stalingrad area yesterday. On HITLER'S orders, the 7th Panzer Division will be transferred from the west to Army Group Don and, for this purpose, be included in the west-east transportation schedule. (One armored division requires 108 railroad trains; an infantry division with its complete authorized equipment, 73 trains.)

Area of Army Group Center: The enemy is not expected to achieve any major successes in his attacks at Subzoff which recently have spread southward. The situation at Welikije Luki is regarded as critical!

Area of the Baltic Sea: The ice begins to form in the inner part of the Gulf of Finland. The SS Menes, which was sunk north of Bizerte on the night of 2 December, carried a cargo of 58-ton tanks and ammunition. The Fuehrer is very angry over the composition of the cargo, but thus far only the shipment of ammunition and fuel together with personnel has been prohibited.

6 December 1942

Situation Report:

OB West reports that the 7th Panzer Division will not be ready for shipment until 26 December. On 4 December American four-motor-bombers carried out a very heavy air attack on Naples. The Italian Air Warning Service failed completely. Following a report received from General ROMMEL to the effect that the withdrawal of the German-Italian Panzer Army from the Mersa-el-Brega position is not yet possible, the Supreme Command has not taken any action thus far (see under 1 December). In Greece, another railroad bridge was blown up by partisans on 5 December. OB Southeast reports that, in addition to one Landesschuetzen (regional defense) battalion, he will employ other forces in combatting the partisans.

7 December 1942

Situation Report:

The Fuehrer made the following statement on the development of the situation: He assumes that, in addition to the operations in North Africa, the Anglo-Americans plan to carry out another operation in the Mediterranean area, the objective of which will be the Balkans. Appropriate counter-measures must be taken. After the transfer of the 10th Air Force Ground Division to Crete, that isle can be regarded as safe; however, the Island of Rhodes and the Peloponnesus are still threatened. In addition, the possibility of a thrust by enemy naval forces through the Strait of

Otranto exists. Moreover, Turkey's attitude has become uncertain. Against her, Bulgarian forces must be kept in readiness. It is not advisable to transfer Hungarian troops to Croatia because such measure would serve to strengthen Hungarian expansionism toward the Adriatic Sea. Above all, a German reserve group will be organized in the Balkans as speedily as possible; this group will be composed of Jaeger and Mountain divisions, the cadres of which will be divisions of Army Group North and the SS Division "Prinz Eugen." The ultimate objective is the establishment of a combined operational reserve with strong German forces as its nucleus.

North Africa: On HITLER'S orders, the Air Force will, apart from its local support of ground forces, direct its attacks exclusively against the enemy ports. At present, there are about five hundred saboteurs working for Germany in North Africa. Admiral CANARIS and the Grand Mufti of Jerusalem intend to go to Tunisia to start additional sabotage activities.

Lybia: It seems that a considerable part of the British Eighth Army fails to pursue the German-Italian Panzer Army. The Fuehrer therefore is of the opinion that it would be a serious mistake to abandon the Mersa-el-Brega position as long as such measure can be avoided. The Panzer Army is strong enough to cope with the British forces now opposing it. On the other hand, it would be nearly impossible for the nonmotorized divisions to disengage themselves from the enemy at the end of fierce fighting. Therefore, the position must be held as long as the enemy is not reinforced. At present, the Fuehrer considers it an advantage that the Panzer Army lacks the fuel necessary for the conduct of a further withdrawal. The Supreme Command will not be officially advised of HITLER'S position, but his opinion on the matter will serve to guide the German General attached to the Italian Armed Forces High Command in his discussions with the Supreme Command.

8 December 1942

Last night the Chief of Army General Staff obtained the Fuehrer's approval for severe measures against the dissipation of forces which has become habitual at the Eastern Front. The Fuehrer declared in this connection that through such dissipation which has assumed inconceivable proportions, not a single man would be spared. The dissipation of the forces, HITLER added, is due to the failure to withdraw entire units from quiet front sectors in time.

Situation Report:

East: The impression prevails at Army Group Don that the enemy is concentrating a powerful force between Stalingrad and Kotelnikowo and is also assembling strong forces opposite the Tschir bridgehead. General Von MANSTEIN considers it necessary to defeat the latter forces first, before launching the attack toward Stalingrad aiming at the relief of the Sixth Army. The Romanian Third Army seems to be endangered again because the enemy is moving up forces against its sector. The 17th Panzer Division, therefore, will remain in the sector of this army. The 7th Panzer Division will be shipped from the west to Army Group Don as speedily as possible.

In the area of Army Group Center, XXX Infantry Corps, employed at the Ninth Army's western front, took Dubrawka yesterday and pocketed approximately 40,000 Russians. The Corps is being reinforced by the transfer of two thirds of the 52nd Infantry Division from the Second Army and by the moving up of reserves from the Smolensk area. The Fuehrer wishes that the advance strong points in the Welikije Luki area be held, while General Von KLUGE would prefer a withdrawal to a rearward position. The capacity of the field railroad leading to the Demjansk area is 500 tons a day against a required 1,000 tons.

West: Referring to the question of the re-establishment of the French Armed Forces, HITLER once more declares that, primarily, the police and the Garde Mobile will be reinforced and that the antiaircraft defense will be left to the French. OB West will make his suggestions after a discussion of the matter with his subordinate commands within the next few days. A decision will then be made on the occasion of the next discussion between the Fuehrer and the Duce.

Mediterranean: In Tunisia, the demobilization of the French land, sea, and air forces is being carried out today under the supervision of General GAUSE. The Fuehrer is currently informed on the progress of the action. He approves General ROMMEL'S intention to hold the Mersa-el-Brega position with the motorized units of the German-Italian Panzer Army as long as possible. It is intended to have the 28th Jaeger Division relieved in the sector of the Eighteenth Army by an Air Force ground division,

MS # C-065a   -154-

beginning on 18 December, and to ship the former to Salonika.

While studying the estimate of the over-all situation prepared by the Armed Forces Operations Staff (see under 1 December), General JODL contemplates the employment of the Italian Alpini Corps and the two Romanian mountain divisions stationed in the Crimea in the Caucasus operation.

9 December 1942

On HITLER'S orders, a teletype letter was dispatched to OB South last night in which reference is made to the great disparity between the volume of the enemy seaborne supplies and those of the Axis. Precise information is requested about the possibilities of forwarding supplies to the forces in North Africa. Depending on the answer, the High Command, if necessary, will make very far-reaching decisions.

Situation Report:

East: Weather permitting, General Von MANSTEIN will launch the attack aimed at the relief of the Sixth Army on 11 or 12 December, and expects to carry through the attack until 17 December. The Fuehrer is very confident; he wants to regain the old position at the Don. He is of the opinion that the first phase of the great Russian winter offensive has ended without resulting in decisive successes for the enemy.

Mediterranean: On HITLER'S orders, the air forces under OB South (Air Force 2) will be reinforced and committed principally against the Algerian ports. Therefore, fuel will be stored in Sardinia for the purpose of increasing the range of the bomber formations of Air Force 2 through intermediate landings. The combat power of the enemy forces which reportedly are advancing south of Tunis toward the coast is regarded as rather limited. For the time being, the enemy is not expected to employ strong forces against the Tunisian basis area. The speedy transfer of additional forces to Tunisia appears therefore even more important. The Fuehrer wishes that particular attention be paid to the southeastern area. Developments in Turkey must be watched with the utmost suspicion. This country's uncertain attitude necessitates an acceleration of Bulgaria's armament.

10 December 1942

Situation Report:

East: In the sector of the First Panzer Army, XXXX Panzer Corps will be made available for commitment at the Army's unprotected eastern flank. General Von MANSTEIN will launch the attack from Kotelnikowo in a northeasterly direction on 12 December. The attack from the Tschir bridgehead will be the second phase and the break-through of the Sixth Army toward the southwest will constitute the third phase. The 27th Panzer Division and 306th Infantry Division are transferred to the Kotelnikowo area. The Fuehrer wants to organize an additional attack group, made up of the 7th and 17th Panzer Divisions, for commitment with the Hollidt Group in an attack to be launched from the Tschir aimed at regaining the Don line. According to a report by the Chief of Army General Staff, rear units in

MS # C-065a

the strength of 260,000 men are stationed in the Ukraine.

West: Generalfeldmarschall Von RUNDSTEDT, Commander in Chief of OB West, went to Vichy to see Marshal PETAIN today. According to a report received by telephone from General BLUMENTRITT, Chief of Staff of OB West, it was intended to withdraw General NEUBRONN, Authorized General in Vichy, from that post. However, the Fuehrer gave the order that the general will remain in Vichy for the time being and that he will not be recalled without the approval of the OKW. The Fuehrer approved the release from captivity of all French railroad officials and employees.

Mediterranean: On orders of the Fuehrer, the so-called 999th African Brigade, which is made up entirely of penal prisoners, will not be transferred to Crete as originally intended, but to Tunisia. In Tunisia, an important pass southwest of Tebourba was occupied and an enemy bridgehead south of the Medjerda taken yesterday. In view of representations made by the Italians, it has now been decided that the French destroyers stationed in Tunis will be taken over by the Italian Navy.

11 December 1942

Situation Report:

East: Prisoner of war statements as well as intercepted radio messages show that, due to the bad weather, the Russian forces opposing the Seventeenth Army are encountering the same difficulties in bringing up supplies as Ruoff Army. The 11th Panzer Division will be made available for Army Group Don's attack scheduled to be launched on 12 December, and, for this purpose,

MS # C-065a
-157-

be withdrawn from its position in the Tschir bridgehead. The expected Russian attack against the positions held by the Italian Eighth Army was launched this morning. The Fourth Air Force therefore transferred forces to the Don Air Forces Headquarters. At the Ninth Army's western front, XXX Infantry Corps is engaged in fierce fighting with the pocketed enemy forces.

According to an estimate by the Air Force, the elements of the Royal Air Force based in Britain have approximately one thousand three hundred bombers available for commitment against the continent. Of these, about three hundred bombers are currently employed in operations against northern Italy. Apparently the British Air Force has postponed the launching of concentrated air attacks on western Germany until such time as more favorable weather sets in. On orders of the Fuehrer, naval barges will be built as speedily as possible in Toulon and other ports of the French Mediterranean coast. The Reichsmarschall returned from Italy yesterday, and will report to the Fuehrer today on his discussions with the Duce.

12 December 1942

Situation Report:

East: The Fuehrer orders the withdrawal of "Viking" SS Division from its position in the sector of the First Panzer Army for the purpose of organizing a strong motorized reserve group made up of "Viking" SS Division and the 3rd Panzer Division. In the area of the Don Army Group, the Hoth

Panzer Group launched the attack this morning and good progress was made up to 0900 hours. Army Group is very confident as to the further progress of the attack because the strength of the opposing armored units has considerably decreased. The 11th Panzer Division will be assigned to the Hoth Panzer Group. The Fuehrer rejects General Von MANSTEIN'S suggestion to commit the 16th Motorized Division and 3rd Mountain Division (perhaps the Rumanian 3rd Mountain Division) in the task of covering the eastern flank of the Panzer Group. The shipment of the 7th Panzer Division from the west to the Eastern Front will start on 18 December.

Mediterranean: The British Air Force carried out a very heavy attack on Naples yesterday afternoon, causing heavy casualties among the civilian population. Turin too was attacked again last night, but only ten or fifteen planes took part in this attack. The German anti-aircraft batteries employed there comprise eleven heavy, two light, and two searchlight batteries. Off Bone, the vanguard of a major convoy has arrived. In Lybia the British Eighth Army resumed the attack yesterday. The security detachments of the German-Italian Panzer Army withdrew to the MLR.

The Fuehrer wants to see General Munoz GRANDE, commander of the Spanish 250th Infantry Division, on 14 December. He wishes to see the Duce from 17 - 19 December and Marshal ANTONESCU on 20 and 21 December in order to establish the political basis for further military decisions. In the discussions with Spain, her requests for arms will be granted if she will guarantee serious resistance against enemy landings. Germany, in such case,

MS # C-065a

can only defend the Pyrenees; an advance into Spain cannot be undertaken until such time as adequate motorized forces are available. Then however, the German forces will thrust forward as far as the Ebro. A further subject to be discussed with the Spanish will be their attitude in case of a British landing in Portugal. Following the discussions with the Duce and Marshal ANTONESCU, discussions will be held also with the Bulgars, who will be summoned to HITLER'S headquarters. The Operations Division (Army) of the Armed Forces Operations Staff will work out plans regarding the assembly of Bulgarian troops for the occupation of the Chalcidice Peninsula and the advance into Turkey. All requests made to the Bulgars must be channelled through the Commander of the Southeast Military District because no German general is attached to the Bulgarian Armed Forces. The German Military Attache in Sofia is the authorized representative of the Military District Commander Southeast in the Bulgarian area.

13 December 1942

Situation Report:

East: In view of the situation in the area of the Don Army Group, the Fuehrer contemplates the withdrawal of the First Panzer Army from the Caucasus. In the sector of the Hoth Panzer Group, the 6th Panzer Division has advanced as far as the Aksai. General Von MANSTEIN reported that he is unable to achieve decisive successes with the two armored divisions committed in the attack and that, in view of the extending flanks, the forces at his disposal are no longer adequate. The Fuehrer decided to leave the 11th Panzer Division in its present position in the Tschir bridgehead because fierce enemy attacks are directed against this bridgehead, and to transfer the 17th Panzer Division instead to the Hoth Group. The impression prevails at Army Group B that the enemy may be simulating attack preparations in the sector opposite the Italian Eighth Army in order to tie down forces there.

According to a report by the Chief of Army General Staff, the situation at Welikije Luki is very unsatisfactory.

On 9 December the Fuehrer had expressed the desire to go to the Berghof for an extended stay to clear his mind for new decisions, and thus far he has not abandoned this idea. General ZEITZLER now tries to persuade him to stay at "Wolfsschanze" because of the critical situation in the southern section of the Eastern Front. The Fuehrer has not yet made a final decision.

15 December 1942*

Situation Report:

East: The Hoth Panzer Group has not made any further progress. The 15th Air Force Ground Division, which arrived in Panzergroup's sector and is composed of four battalions only, is still being assembled at a point far in the rear area. The enemy still has not launched the expected major attack against the sector held by the Italian Eighth Army. It appears that the enemy, through constant probing, is merely trying to tie down

---
* 14 December: No notes available.

reserves. The Fuehrer has not drawn any conclusions thus far.

The quantity of grain turned in at the grain-collecting points of the Ukraine this year is ten times as large as last year's amounting to 8.1 million tons.

The Fuehrer finally abandoned his plan to go to the Berghof.

18 December 1942*

Situation Report:

East: Yesterday morning the Russians launched the major attack against the positions held by the Italian Eighth Army and achieved a deep penetration in the center. The enemy also achieved penetrations in the sector of the Hollidt Group at the Tschir. The Fuehrer orders the withdrawal of the front to a tendon position at both points because, here, his principle of holding the foremost line under all circumstances cannot be adhered to owing to the rout of the Italians.

Mediterranean: The German-Italian Panzer Army, which had been attacked by the far superior British Eighth Army in the Mersa-el-Brega position since 11 December, disengaged itself from the enemy in a westerly direction yesterday.

In order to improve the replacement situation which has grown difficult, the Fuehrer orders Reich Minister SPEER to immediately release 50,000 men from the economy in three waves, to exchange 150,000 younger men engaged

---
* 16 and 17 December: No notes available.

in the economy for older soldiers, and to release 100,000 indispensable armament workers hitherto deferred, for service in the Wehrmacht.

At noon Italian Foreign Minister Count CIANO and Marshal Count CAVALLERO, Chief of the Supreme Command, arrive at HITLER'S headquarters "Wolfsschanze" for discussions. The Italians are accompanied by General DEICHMANN, Chief of Staff of OB South, and Colonel Von WALDENBURG, deputy for the German General attached to the Italian Armed Forces High Command (General Von RINTELEN met with an airplane accident).

19 December 1942

Distribution of the Flying Formations of the Air Force along the Eastern Front

Fourth Air Force:	8 bomber groups	3 dive bomber groups	8 fighter groups	1 2/3 close-support groups	2 1/3 long-range fighter groups
Don Air Forces Headquarters:	3 "	2 "	1 1/3 "	2/3 "	
Eastern Air Forces Headquarters:	5 1/3 "	1 "	5 "		
First Air Force:	3 1/3 "	0 "	2 "		
Northern Air Force Command:	1 "	1 "	2 2/3 "	1/3 aerial torpedo group	

Total: 20 2/3 bomber groups, 7 dive bomber groups, 19 fighter groups, 2 1/3 close-support groups, 2 1/3 long-range fighter groups and 1/3 aerial torpedo group, each group comprising an average of 20 planes ready to take off, totaling 51 2/3 groups, comprising about 1,035 planes.

Situation Report:

The enemy deepened the penetration achieved in the sector of the Italian Eighth Army. On orders of the Fuehrer, three additional divisions will be transferred from the west to the Eastern Front, among them the 327th and 335th Infantry Divisions. The 1st Panzer Division, however, will be shifted from the Eastern Front to the west for rehabilitation.

Discussion of the Fuehrer and the Chief of OKW with Count CIANO and Marshal Count CAVALIERO:

In view of the critical situation in the southern section of the Eastern Front and in North Africa, the Italians suggested seeking some kind of an understanding with STALIN. However, the Fuehrer rejected this suggestion at once, because in his opinion, adequate forces can be made available without weakening the Eastern Front. On the basis of the transportation schedule submitted by General DEICHMANN, and an estimate of the enemy situation prepared by him, it has been decided to hold North Africa. The supreme command in Tunisia will be taken over by the Supreme Command. In regard to the chain of command in the southeast, it was agreed to conduct operations on the basis of close co-operation; the Commander of the

MS # C-065a
-164-

Southeast Military District will ensure unity of command. Orders of the Commander of the Southeast Military District affecting the Italian zone of occupation in the Balkans will be submitted to the OKW, then be discussed by the OKW with the Supreme Command and, finally, be issued by the latter. In case of an enemy attack, the Commander of the Southeast Military District will have full command authority. An agreement was also reached on action to be taken against partisans in the Balkans. The Italians decided to call up another 1,000,000 men subject to the draft (age classes 1923 and 1924). Toulon Radio Station will remain at the disposal of the German Navy, but the Italian Navy will remain in control. The German and Italian armistice commissions will remain in Wiesbaden and in Turin respectively, with reduced staffs.

20 December 1942

Situation Report:

East: The Fuehrer is worried about the First Panzer Army's northern wing. The front west of Ordshonikidse will be withdrawn to a tendon position. Thus, the "Viking" SS Division, which will be transferred to the Fourth Panzer Army, will be freed. The Fourth Panzer Army has been very successful, and the Fuehrer has relinquished the idea of abandoning Stalingrad. In view of its present condition, the Sixth Army, in case of a break-through, can advance no more than 30 kilometers and therefore must not jump off prematurely. The Fuehrer, on the other hand,

MS # C-065a   -165-

insists on the re-establishment of contact with the Sixth Army and on maintaining such contact long enough to make the withdrawal of the entire Sixth Army possible. In order to avoid relying exclusively on the Hoth Army, the Sixth Army will be enabled to advance, in case of a breakthrough, at least 50 kilometers. For this purpose, the Sixth Army needs at least 300 tons of supplies daily. The Fuehrer intends to return the Italian Eighth Army to the Duce and to replace it with a German Armeegruppe. The three divisions which will be transferred from the west to the Eastern Front will be assigned to Army Group B, and the 19th Panzer Division and 26th Infantry Division will also be assigned to Army Group B.

21 December 1942

Situation Report:

A report received from General Von MANSTEIN -- that the Fourth Panzer Army is unable to advance beyond the sector already reached (Aksai) and that the Sixth Army cannot possible advance more than 30 kilometers -- gives rise to a lengthy discussion of the situation in the southern section of the Eastern Front between the Fuehrer and the Chiefs of Army and Air Force General Staffs. However, again no definitive decisions are made. It seems as if the Fuehrer is no longer able to make a clear-cut decision. Either SS Division "Viking" or the 7th Panzer Division will be assigned to Panzer Group Hoth. In the concentration area of the 306th Infantry Division, the line Naumow (55 kilometers east of Millerowo)-Millerowo-

Kantemirowka will be occupied by German troops as a rearward covering position for the retreating Italians. On HITLER'S orders, furthermore, 30 - 60 assault brigades in the strength of one reinforced battalion each will be organized as a mobile defense force.

Because of Christmas leave, no notes are available for the period from 22 to 28 December 1942.

29 December 1942

Last night the Fuehrer decided to conduct a far-reaching withdrawal of Army Groups A and Don and to place both army groups under the command of Generalfeldmarschall Von MANSTEIN. The pertinent orders are issued during the forenoon. General der Panzer HUBE, Commanding General of XIV Panzer Corps, who has arrived at HITLER'S headquarters, reports on the situation in the Stalingrad area. The absolutely necessary volume of supplies for the Sixth Army is 300 tons daily. The Sixth Army wants to stay in its organized positions. The Fuehrer orders the Quartermaster General of the Army to allocate rations of concentrated food to the Sixth Army because the available meat supplies will be consumed by the end of January at the latest. OB West was instructed last night to immediately ship three SS divisions under the SS Corps headquarters to the east, to be committed at some point of the front in an effort to relieve the Sixth Army. As a result of the transfer of these divisions, the Reichsfuehrer-SS has to abandon his plans to activate two new SS divisions.

To make up for the loss of the SS divisions, three Air Force ground divisions will be transferred to the troop training grounds in the occupied western territories.

Situation Report:

The Fuehrer points to the importance of blocking Kertsch Strait as a means of preventing Russian naval forces from entering the Sea of Azov, and again demanded that effective measures be taken against the heavy enemy traffic across frozen Lake Ladoga to Leningrad. He also demands the use of heavy mortars in the Leningrad area.

The Duce ordered General ROMMEL gradually to withdraw the German-Italian Panzer Army, which is still holding the Buerat-el-Sun position, gradually to the Gabes position in Tunisia. The flank of the Gabes position is unprotected because even the Schotts (the large salt marshes west of Gabes on both sides of Kebili) are passable. The German-Italian forces in Tunisia are employed along the general line: Mateur -- a point northeast of Medjez-el-Bab -- Pont du Fahs-Djebibina-Djebel bou-Dabous -- a point north of Pichon. The front is divided into four sectors; Sector A (Mateur) is occupied by Group Von Broich, Sector B (Madjez-el-Bab) by the 10th Panzer Division, Sector C by (Italian) Division "Superga," and Sector D by (Italian) Division "Imperiali."

1 January 1943*

Situation Report:

East: The First Panzer Army starts disengaging itself from the enemy today. The 3rd and 13th Panzer Divisions will be committed at the northern wing to cover the Army's deep flank. Together with the 16th Motorized Division, these divisions also will cover the deep southern flank of Army Group Don. The suggestion, made by the Chief of Army General Staff, to transfer the 97th Jaeger Division from the Seventeenth Army to the area of Ssalsk for the purpose of establishing a defensive front against the enemy forces advancing on both sides of the railroad is rejected by the Fuehrer. HITLER considers the Russian thrust from the north toward Rostov to be more dangerous and orders the commitment of the 7th Panzer Division, which is being shipped from the west to the Eastern Front, in that area with its front facing the north. The Fourth Panzer Army's right wing has evacuated Elista and occupied a new position 15 kilometers southwest of that locality. The enemy has penetrated into the gap between the 17th Panzer Division, committed at LVII Panzer Corps' northern wing, and the Don, and his spearheads, advancing on both sides of the Don, have reached the area of Zymljanskaja. Hollidt's** Armee-Abteilung right wing has withdrawn behind the Zymja, its left wing is fighting along the line Tschernyschkowskij (27 kilometers east of Morosowskij)-Skasyrskaja

---
* 30 and 31 December 1942: No notes available.
** One step below an army. More than a corps, but not a full army (reviewer).

(41 kilometers west of Morosowskij). The Fretter - Pico Armee-Abteilung is engaged in fighting at the central and upper part of the Kalitwa. The attack aiming at the relief of Welikije Luki will be launched only after adequate forces have been made available for that task. On HITLER'S orders, the assault-gun battalion of the 10th Panzer Division will be placed at the disposal of the Army General Staff for the Eastern Front and be replaced in the 10th Panzer Division by a newly activated unit.

Last night the Commander in Chief of the Air Force ordered the transfer of sixteen heavy anti-aircraft batteries, eight light anti-aircraft batteries, and three searchlight batteries with five battalion headquarters, two air defense battalions, and one fire extinguisher battalion to the Rumanian oil district.

2 January 1943

Situation Report:

East: The assumption that the enemy intends to effect landings in the Crimea has been verified by prisoner of war statements. The First Panzer Army's disengagement movements are progressing according to plan. The group under General AULEB has withdrawn behind the Lanytsch. In the sector of the Fourth Panzer Army, LVII Panzer Corps starts disengaging itself from the enemy. Armee-Abteilung Hollidt has stopped the enemy at the Zymlja.

The Supreme Command agrees with General ROMMEL in his opinion that the Buerat position cannot be held as a rigid line. According to an order given to General ROMMEL and Marschall BASTICO by the Duce on 1 January the German-Italian Panzer Army will disengage itself from the enemy at the Buerat Position in such manner that the Homs positions will be reached after three weeks and the eastern front of Tripolis by the end of an additional three weeks. General KESSELRING, Commander in Chief of OB South, who had spent several days in Tunisia and had also discussed the situation with General ROMMEL, regards the positions at Homs and Gabes as very strong.

3 January 1943

Situation Report:

The First and Fourth Panzer Armies, the Hollidt Armeegruppe, and the Fretter-Pico Armee-Abteilung continued their withdrawal movements. On HITLER'S orders, Corps for Special Assignments (General FELMY) and elements of the "Brandenburg" Special Unit will be withdrawn from the Eastern Front and transferred to Tunisia. In Lybia, the withdrawal of the nonmotorized units of the German-Italian Panzer Army to a position southwest of Tauorga was started.

4 January 1943

Situation Report:

East: The withdrawal movements of the "A" and Don Army Groups were continued with occasional heavy fighting taking place while these movements were being carried out. The enemy situation in the southern section of the Eastern Front is not clear. Strong enemy forces seem to follow up the First Panzer Army, and apparently no focal points have been formed in the sectors opposite Don and B Army Groups. The enemy obviously is encountering difficulties in supplying his forces owing to the fact that the Germans are still holding the Stalingrad area. In the Black Sea the enemy has approximately 12,000 tons of shipping space available for landing operations, and U-boats and E-boats will be committed against this force. In the sector of Army Group Center, Group Woehler launched the attack aiming at the relief of Welikije Luki.

In Tunisia the Fifth Panzer Army resumed the attack on 1 January, and made some progress.

The Fuehrer gave the order last night that the anti-aircraft artillery which will now be transferred to Rumania be taken over by the Rumanians as soon as possible.

5 January 1943

Situation Report:

The Fuehrer again discusses the measures to be taken against intended enemy landings in the Black Sea area and gives the order to station U-boats at Sevastopol and E-boats at Feodosia. HITLER approves the suggestion, made by the Chief of Army General Staff, to slow down the withdrawal movement north of the Don so as not to create the impression of a retreat under enemy pressure. The Fuehrer states in this connection that there should be no doubt as to the fact that the Rumanians will have to be written off sooner or later.

Regarding tank production, HITLER gives the following order: instead of the Mark III, the production of which is coming to a close, the Mark IV will be produced, and instead of the Mark IV, the Panther will be produced at a later time; the first 160 - 200 Panthers will be delivered in February. In future, the basic principle will be increased armor at the expense of the speed.

General MICHOFF, Bulgarian War Minister, accompanied by Colonel POPOFF, Chief of the Operations Division of the Bulgarian General Staff, arrived at HITLER'S headquarters yesterday afternoon to discuss joint measures to be taken if Turkey should grant the Anglo-Americans permission to march through Asia Minor. General MICHOFF was received by the Fuehrer this afternoon, and had discussions with the Chief of the OKW and the Chief of the Armed Forces Operations Staff. On this occasion he disclosed that, for the time being, Bulgaria contemplates only a defensive concentration of ten divisions in Thrace with the focal point in the area northwest of Adrianople.

6 January 1943

Situation Report:

East: In the Stalingrad area, the food supply situation and the actual strength status of the Sixth Army has deteriorated, and the fuel and ammunition situation has become critical. On 4 January, the Air Force carried approximately 250 tons of supplies to the Stalingrad area. Today forty-five tons reached Stalingrad by air. Unfavorable weather prevented all flights to the Stalingrad area yesterday. The Fourth Panzer Army had to discontinue an attack across the Ssal after some initial success because superior enemy forces were encountered. Armeegruppe Hollidt will continue its withdrawal only until the next sector is reached (probably the Kagalnik sector), and that sector will be held under all circumstances. The Fuehrer expects a strong enemy attack against the Hungarian Second Army with the focal point at Swoboda to be launched in the near future. He, therefore, orders the immediate reinforcement of the Hungarian Second Army by the assignment of 250 75 mm. antitank guns. The 7th Air Force Division will be withdrawn from the front sector north of Smolensk and committed in the south.

The Deputy Chief of the Armed Forces Operations Staff discussed further details of the current problems with Colonel POPOFF, Chief of the Operations Division of the Bulgarian General Staff. It has been agreed to equip the Bulgarian Army as speedily as possible in such manner that it will be able to resist a modernly equipped opponent; at first, it is intended to reorganize ten infantry divisions and one cavalry division into fully efficient attack units and to build up the Bulgarian tank brigade to the strength of a tank division.

In the evening, the Commander in Chief of the Navy reports to the

Fuehrer on the naval situation. The Fuehrer, on this occasion, discloses that he is contemplating scrapping the heavy surface units in order to free personnel for the U-boats, heavy guns for the coast defense, and steel. The question remains undecided for the time being.

7 January 1943

Situation Report:

East: The Fuehrer is of the opinion that the withdrawal movements of the First Panzer Army are being carried out too swiftly; he also believes that the situation does not warrant the extent of the withdrawal. Army Group A, therefore, is instructed by the Chief of Army General Staff to conduct no further withdrawal movements without the OKH's approval. Elements of the 16th Motorized Division and of the 503d Panzer Battalion will be committed in an attack at the Fourth Panzer Army's northern wing tomorrow. The 302nd Infantry Division is transferred to Armee-Abteilung Hollidt*, and the 320th Infantry Division to the southern wing of Army Group B. Progress is being made in reinforcing the Hungarian Second Army with heavy antitank guns. The Chief of Army General Staff intends to have the 7th Air Force Division relieved from its front sector by a division arriving from the west and to commit it together with the "Grossdeutschland" Division in an attack to be launched in the south.

---

* In various parts of the manuscript, writer seems to have confused the term Armee-Abteilung, a temporary-type unit between corps and army level with the term Armee gruppe, a unit between army and army group level. (Translator)

The busy Russian traffic across frozen Lake Ladoga will be impeded through the employment of star shells which will be furnished by the Navy.

OB West is instructed to make three divisions available for shipment to the Eastern Front in exchange for three Air Force ground divisions. Along the Atlantic Wall, 4 - 5,000 armor-protected gun positions will be completed by spring, after which time 800 of them will be built each month.

OB South requested the transfer of at least two additional units to Tunisia. The Fuehrer approves the speedy return of the 164th Light Division, currently employed with the German-Italian Panzer Army, to Tunisia, where it will be reorganized into a motorized division and the 47th Infantry and 190th Panzer Battalion will be assigned to it. However, the Fuehrer was not able to make up his mind to transfer any further units to Tunisia in addition to 999th African Brigade, which will be built up to division strength, and Corps for Special Assignments (General WILLY). The French Prisoners of War in Tunisia will be released to their homeland at once.

8 January 1943

Situation Report:

East: The following quantities of supplies were flown to the Sixth Army: 150 tons on 5 January, 45 tons on 6 January, 75 tons during the night of 6 - 7 January, and 40 tons on 7 January. The Fourth Panzer Army gained ground in the area ahead of the upper Manytsch. In the sector of Armee-Abteilung Hollidt, the withdrawal to the Kagalnik position was carried out without incident. The Eastern Foreign Armies Division of the

Army General Staff received reports to the effect that the enemy reserves are increasing in numbers; however, no new units, but only units withdrawn from the front for rehabilitation have been identified.

Mediterranean: The 10th Air Force Ground Division will not be transferred to Crete as originally planned, but to the Peloponnesus. In the German occupied zone of Greece, the surrender of all radio sets has been ordered. At the same time, thousands of radio sets are being delivered from Germany to Greece in order to improve the financial clearing between the two countries.

9 January 1943

Situation Report:

East: In the sector of the Fourth Panzer Army, the 17th Panzer Division advanced as far as a point due south of the Ssal and a point southwest of Potapowskij (35 kilometers northwest of Kuberle). Armee-Abteilung Hollidt repelled enemy forces which had advanced beyond the Kagalnik. XXXXVIII Panzer Corps is engaged in successful fighting in the Bystraja Valley. The enemy has launched fierce attacks at Millerowo.

Mediterranean: On HITLER'S orders, those elements of the "Hermann Goering" Division which are assembled for shipment to Tunisia are detained until such time as the bulk of the units can be shipped. Meanwhile, the 10th Panzer Division, 164th Light Division, and 334th Infantry Division will be rehabilitated. The 47th Grenadier Regiment is being reorganized into a reinforced motorized regiment.

10 January 1943

Situation Report:

East: The following quantities of supplies were flown to the Stalingrad area: 125 tons on 7 January, 99 tons (including 61 tons of food supplies) on 8 January, and 196.5 tons (including 101.1 tons of food supplies) on 9 January. Eight hundred wounded were flown back from the Stalingrad area on 9 January. At present, the daily food rations for the personnel of the Sixth Army consists of: 75 grams of bread, 200 grams of horse meat including bones, 12 grams of fat, 11 grams of sugar, and one cigarette. By 20 January all horses will be slaughtered.

During the forenoon, Marshal ANTONESCU arrives at HITLER'S headquarters for discussions with the Fuehrer.

11 January 1943

Situation Report:

East: On 10 January, 209.4 tons of supplies including 146 tons of food supplies, were flown to the Sixth Army. Eight hundred and sixty wounded were flown back from the Stalingrad area. The Seventeenth Army has withdrawn its forces from the mountain passes. At the Manytsch canal, Group Auleb withdrew in the face of superior enemy forces. In the sector of the Fourth Panzer Army, LVII Panzer Corps was retired. The 16th Motorized Division was able to establish a bridgehead on the northern bank of the Ssal at Martynowka.

12 January 1943

Situation Report:

East: In the sector of Armee-Abteilung Hollidt, an enemy force which had advanced beyond the Kagalnik was annihilated at Krjukowskij; a defense position was established between Bystraja and Kalitwa. Armee-Abteilung Fretter-Pico repelled enemy attacks at Millerowo. Today, the Russians launched very heavy attacks at Stalingrad as well as at the Seventeenth Army's western wing, and particularly against the positions of the Hungarian Second Army, where the enemy, advancing from the Dawydowka bridgehead, achieved a deep penetration. This morning the Fuehrer was inclined to regard this attack as a diversion; he expects the main attack to be launched at Swoboda.

Mediterranean: In Tunisia, the position held by the 10th Panzer Division now runs as follows: a point east of Goubellat - a point northeast of Bou Arada-defile between the lakes northwest of Pont du Fahs.

Lybia: According to an agent report, the British Eighth Army will have completed its preparations for the attack against the Buerat Position between 11 and 15 January. General ROMMEL suggested the transfer of the 21st Panzer Division, instead of the 16th Light Division, back to southern Tunisia to serve as operational reserve. The Duce agrees under the condition that the period of two months set for the withdrawal to the Gabes position is adhered to.

The discussions between the Fuehrer and Marshal ANTONESCU, which took place yesterday and today, had the following result: the Rumanian Army will be reorganized in such way that at first the eight divisions employed at the front (beginning with the six Caucasus divisions), then the four divisions employed in coast defense in the Black Sea area, and finally, the remaining six divisions will be equipped in the same manner as the corresponding German units. Furthermore, the Rumanian tank division will be re-established. The remnants of the former Rumanian Third and Fourth Armies will be utilized for the organization of GHQ reserves.

General KESSELRING, Commander in Chief of OB South, arrived at HITLER'S headquarters today to report to the Fuehrer on the situation. He begins with a report on the sea transportation situation. With the newly allocated shipping space, it will be possible to meet the transportation schedule calling for a monthly shipment of 60,000 tons to Tunisia. The capacity of the ports of Tunis and Bizerte is also adequate.

The port of Sousse will be placed at the disposal of the German-Italian Panzer Army.

Difficulties are encountered in providing the necessary convoy protection, but the traffic in the Strait of Sicily can be regarded as sufficiently protected by the air forces. General KESSELRING considers the employment of large numbers of small naval craft advisable. The Fuehrer replies that the Army should transfer long-barreled 50 mm. guns which were mounted on motor carriages to the Navy to arm small naval craft. General KESSELRING goes on to state that strong anti-aircraft protection is needed in Naples, Palermo, and Tunis. Good progress has been made throughout the Mediterranean area toward the organization of the aircraft warning service. The number of U-boats ready for commitment in action is considered too small; the E-boats, on the other hand, have been very successful in their operations. The enemy situation is utterly obscure. It cannot be ascertained whether the enemy lacks personnel or supplies. Apparently he is encountering difficulties in the communications zone. The defensive position which is being organized in southern Tunisia does not run through the Gabes area, but through Mareth, 35 kilometers farther to the South; its western flank is based on the mountains. No more than four divisions are needed for the occupation of this position. A second position is being organized at Gabes. At present, vehicles can cross the Schotts west of Gabes only on trails. Due to unfavorable weather, the Fifth Panzer Army has thus far been unable to conduct major operations. The Fifth Panzer Army is able to hold the Tunisian basis area alone without the aid of General-ROMMEL'S Army. ROMMEL, therefore, should not transfer the 164th Light Division to Tunisia, especially in view of the fact that, inclined to withdraw anyway, he would use such transfer as an excuse for his further withdrawal. The Fuehrer approves General KESSELRING'S suggestion of transferring the "Hermann Goering" Division to Tunisia to serve there as operational reserve together with the 10th Panzer Division which will be withdrawn from the front. The 999th African Brigade will also be shifted to Tunisia as speedily as possible, but no unit of ROMMEL'S army will be transferred to the Fifth Panzer Army. General ROMMEL, according to General KESSELRING'S report, requests only fuel and mobile antitank weapons. In organizational matters, the two armies in Africa will both be controlled by an organizational staff which will see to it that the arms available in Italy and the artillery personnel not needed by ROMMEL'S army are consolidated into units fit for commitment with the Fifth Panzer Army.

The Fuehrer advised General KESSELRING that a committee of three men has been appointed in Spain to prepare the country for defense. General Munoz GRANDE and General ASCENCIO (?) are members of the committee. The Fuehrer, therefore, considers the delivery of arms to Spain necessary and contemplates the establishment of training schools for Spanish volunteers in southern France.

13 January 1943

Situation Report:

East: On 11 January, 185.5 tons of supplies, including 114.3 tons of food supplies, were flown to the Sixth Army (no notes are available on deliveries on 12 January). In the sector of the First Panzer Army, LII Infantry Corps reached the line Nagutskoje-Alexandrowskoje; XXXX Panzer Corps evacuated Shurawskoje at its southern wing. In the sector of the Hungarian Second Army, the enemy was able to deepen the penetration achieved by him even further. In the sector of the Eighteenth Army, the Russians have been attacking the eastern front of the "bottleneck" with strong forces since yesterday. During the situation report, the Chief of the Army Supply and Administration reports to the Fuehrer that the enemy is able to supply his forces throughout the Stalingrad area even without the use of the railroads blocked by the Sixth Army, especially since the volume of the daily supply of a Russian division is only 100 tons against the 150 tons required by a German division and since the Russians are expending only small quantities of ammunition in their present offensive. General of Cavalry BREHMER, Ostland Military District Commander (eastern territories), has arrived at HITLER'S headquarters to discuss with the Deputy Chief of the Armed Forces Operations Staff the employment of Lithuanians, Latvians, and Estonians with the Army and the police.

14 January 1943

Situation Report:

East: On 13 January 119.1 tons of supplies, including 61.2 tons of food supplies, were flown to the Sixth Army. In the sector of the Hungarian Second Army, the enemy advanced as far as a point 20 kilometers west of Storechewoje (10 kilometers northwest of Dawydowka).

Mediterranean: OB South was instructed yesterday to advise the Italian Supreme Command and the German-Italian Panzer Army that the Fuehrer wholeheartedly agrees with the Duce's decision to withdraw the 21st Panzer Division to Sfax and suggests that the 21st Panzer Division transfers all its tanks, antitank guns, and other guns to the 15th Panzer Division. The 21st Panzer Division will then be re-equipped in Tunisia as speedily as possible. The original plan to withdraw the 164th Light Division is abandoned.

In a memorandum submitted to the Fuehrer by the Chief of the Navy Command dealing with the significance of the scrapping of the nucleus of the German Navy, dated 10 January 1943, (1 Skl I b 154/43 top secret), the following conclusions are drawn:

By scrapping the nucleus of the Navy, we would relinquish an arm which, far from having become obsolete and thus superfluous, as a result of the progress made in the technique of warfare, is most vitally influencing the over-all war situation, particularly, however, the all-important war at sea. The enemy is utterly afraid of our reinforcing this arm. He knows his own weakness best and is aware of the potentialities which the German battle fleet has. The German battle fleet will be able to take advantage of these potentialities if it can operate and fight with the support of air forces without which no navy can achieve successes today.

Moreover, nobody is able to foresee today where and how soon war developments might demand the commitment of sea power in decisive operations. If we should lack the large naval units at the moment when they are needed, then it will be too late as a result of our own action.

I firmly believe that the insignificant gains in personnel and materiel are out of proportion to the grave military and political disadvantages which the loss of the German battle fleet would entail. I am convinced that, without the battle fleet, the Navy will be unable to fulfill the offensive and defensive tasks assigned to it in the battle for the freedom of Greater Germany.

Signed: READER

MS # C-065a

15 January 1943

Distribution of the Flying Formations of the Air Force along the Eastern Front

	bomber groups	dive bomber groups	fighter groups	long-range fighter groups	close-support groups
Fourth Air Force:	10 1/3	3	8	2 1/3	1 1/3
Don Air Forces Headquarters:	4	1 2/3	3 1/3		1/3
Eastern Air Forces Headquarters:	3 2/3	1 1/3	4 2/3		1/3 night fighter group
First Air Force:	1	0	1 2/3		
Northern Air Forces Command:	1	1	2 2/3		1/3 aerial torpedo group

Total: 20 bomber groups, 7 dive bomber groups, 20 1/3 fighter groups, 2 1/3 long-range fighter groups, 1 2/3 close-support groups, 1/3 night fighter group and 1/3 aerial torpedo group, each group comprising an average of 20 planes ready to take off, totaling 52 groups comprising about 1,040 planes.

Situation Report:

East: The Sixth Army last night withdrew its western front to the line Bolschaja Rassoschka - a point 5 kilometers southeast of Nowo Rogatschik. On 14 January, 120 tons of supplies were flown to the Sixth

Army. The Fuehrer ordered Generalfeldmarschall MILCH to ensure the supplying of the Sixth Army with all means at his disposal. In the sector of Armee-Abteilung Hollidt, the enemy advanced at some points as far as the Donets. In the sector of Armee-Abteilung Fretter-Pico, he reached the road Kamensk-Millerowo at Glubokij (22 kilometers north of Kamensk). In the sector of the Hungarian Second Army, the enemy launched the expected major attack from the Swoboda bridgehead and achieved deep penetrations. In the sector of the Eighteenth Army, the enemy achieved a deep penetration into the "bottleneck" and thus succeeded for the first time in piercing the enveloping ring around Leningrad.

Mediterranean: The German-Italian Panzer Army expects the enemy to attack at any time after tomorrow. The enemy has seven or eight divisions with approximately seven hundred tanks available for the attack. Only the following forces are left in the Bueret position: the 15th Panzer Division, 90th Light Division, and 164th Light Division, 1st Air Force Jaeger Brigade I, and six Italian battalions with strong artillery, the total of tanks amounting to 34 German tanks and 57 Italian tanks. Since it is impossible, at present, to ship other forces to Tunisia, the Fuehrer gave the order to ship at first those elements of the "Hermann Goering" Division which had arrived in Italy to the Tunisian area, but to commit them at the front only when the entire division is assembled.

(For the following period, until the middle of March 1943, the notes which I took at that time contain few references to the military situation

MS # C-065a   -186-

at the Eastern Front and in North Africa. This is due to the fact that, on the suggestion of the Chief of the Army General Staff, the noonday discussions of the situation with the Fuehrer had been steadily restricted.

General ZEITZLER and General JODL usually discussed only matters which were dealt with in the situation report which the Armed Forces Operations Staff prepared for the Fuehrer every morning. Since these reports were available to me for the keeping of the War Diary, it was unnecessary to take notes on the situation and, generally from that time on, I restricted myself to the recording of HITLER'S directives, which now were given almost exclusively during individual discussions between himself and the two generals in the afternoon or evening, and to the recording of other discussions.)

18 January 1943

The following quantities of supplies reached the Sixth Army by air: 92 tons on 15 January, 72 tons on 16 January, and, owing to the danger of ice formations, only 27 tons on 18 January. In carrying out flights to the Stalingrad area, nine planes crashed or were shot down today. On HITLER'S orders, the defeated and routed Rumanian units will be halted and employed in coast defense. Furthermore, all motor trucks available in the ZI will be collected and sent to the area of Kijew in order to intensify the supply shipments to the front. The Fuehrer finally ordered cancellation of all leaves at the entire Eastern Front. Personnel now on leave in the ZI will be gathered at troop training grounds because of the cancellation of the leave trains.

In the course of the British air attack on Berlin during the night of 16 - 17 January, 88 persons were killed, 170 wounded, and 11 are missing. As a retaliatory measure, London was attacked by 118 bombers during the night of 17 - 18 January. The Fuehrer ordered the Reichsmarschall to reinforce the antiaircraft defense of a number of German cities, among them Leipzig, Dresden, Weimar, and Kassel, and approved the request of the Air Force for the reinforcement of the night fighter force.

23 January 1943

The following quantities of supplies were carried to the Sixth Army by air: 60 tons on 19 January, 55.4 tons on 20 January, and 97.3 tons on 21 January; 390 wounded were flown back on 21 January. At present, 495 tanks fit for commitment are available at the entire Eastern Front, and are distributed among the sectors of the various army groups as follows: Army Group A, 34, Army Group Don and Army Group B, 291; Army Group Center, 167; and Army Group North, 3. On orders of the Fuehrer, the divisions employed in the First Panzer Army's northern sector will withdraw first toward Tischorezk and then toward Rostov. The divisions employed in the First Panzer Army's southern sector, together with the Seventeenth Army, will withdraw toward the bridgehead on Taman-peninsula, which will be limited to as small an area as possible. In the sector of the Fourth Panzer Army, the attack launched by the 11th and 17th Panzer Divisions and the 16th Motorized Division southeast of Rostov is progressing well. The question put by General ZEITZLER last night as to whether the Sixth Army could now be authorized to surrender drew a negative reply from the Fuehrer. The Sixth Army will continue to fight to the last in order to gain time. A radio message by the Fuehrer to that effect was transmitted to Generaloberst PAULUS, Commander in Chief of the Sixth Army, who answered, "Your orders will be carried out, long live Germany!" The Supreme Command and the Hungarian Army High Command were requested by teletype letter last night to withdraw their armies from the Eastern Front. The southern wing of the Second Army will withdraw toward Kem. According to an account of the Russian losses prepared by the commander of the Russian replacement training army, which has fallen into German hands, the Russians have lost 11.2 million men, either killed, captured, or wounded and unable to return to the front. Reportedly, the Russian manpower potential is almost exhausted and large numbers of women are being employed at the front.

The OKW has received reports to the effect that the British intend to effect landings in northern Norway and Jutland. In view of the heavy enemy convoy traffic in the western Mediterranean, the Fuehrer fears an Anglo-American landing on Sardinia.

28 January 1943

The Fuehrer urged the Reichsmarschall and the Chief of the Air Force General Staff to commit strong forces of the Air Force on both sides of the Kertsch Strait.

The main subject discussed during today's situation report was the re-establishment of the Sixth Army, which the Fuehrer wants to be effected as speedily as possible. Although the threat to Rostov from the Manytsch area has not yet been removed, the Fuehrer ordered the transfer of the 11th Panzer Division to the northern wing of Armee-Abteilung Hollidt. The Fuehrer is looking forward to the commitment of the SS Panzer Corps comprising the "Reich" and "Adolf Hitler" SS Divisions, which has been shipped from the west to Stalino and which is to be moved up to the area around Kharkov. The situation at the northern wing of the Second Army is critical, as no forces are available to close the wide gap which has been created there as a result of an enemy penetration.

In view of constant attacks by low-flying planes on moving locomotives in France, the Fuehrer wants the French to take over the antiaircraft protection of their own railroad trains and desires that armored locomotives be employed.

Lorient and Brest will be developed into strong bases.

29 January 1943

Situation Report:

The Fuehrer requested a report on the amount of supplies available in the Demiansk area to enable him to make a decision on the evacuation of this pocket. He declared in this connection that he would be reluctant to order the evacuation, since thus far he has not abandoned the plan to close the wide gap between Demiansk and Rshew by launching an attack toward Ostaschkow. On the other hand, he considered the capture of Leningrad more important.

For the period from 30 January to 15 February 1943, only the following brief notes are available:

31 January 1943

In the morning the last radio message is received from the southern group of the Sixth Army from Stalingrad. Army Group A, which is retiring toward the bridgehead on the Taman-peninsula, will be supplied across the Kertsch Strait and will also receive seaborne supplies via Feodosia-Anapa. It is anticipated that Army Group A thus can be supplied with 1,500 tons daily.

2 February 1943

In the morning the last radio message is received from the northern group of the Sixth Army from Stalingrad. Division of the Eastern Foreign Armies of Army General Staff estimates that a total of 107 Russian units plus 13 GHQ tank regiments are freed as a result of the annihilation of the Sixth Army. The plan to commit the 7th Air Force Division in offensive action (see under 7 January 1943) is abandoned, and the Division will remain in its present sector north of Smolensk. The Commander in Chief of the Air Force plans the activation of a second parachute division and the expansion of the "Hermann Goering" Division to the strength of a corps.

3 February 1943

In the evening, General WARLIMONT, Deputy Chief of the Armed Forces Operations Staff, leaves for Tunisia to obtain first-hand information on the situation there.

4 February 1943

Reich Minister SPEER and PLEIGER, Managing Director for the Donets Basin, report to the Fuehrer on the situation in the armament industry. Without the Donets Basin, the annual production of which amounts to 6 - 7 million tons, an increase in armament is impossible. The Fuehrer declares that the Donets Basin must not be abandoned because, without it, he would be unable to continue the war.

6 February 1943

General Von MANSTEIN and General Von KLUGE, who have arrived at HITLER'S headquarters to report on the situation, suggest to the Fuehrer an extensive withdrawal at the Eastern Front. The Fuehrer does not make a decision at this time.

8 February 1943

In the sector of the Second Army, the enemy took Kursk. Agent reports have been received to the effect that an Anglo-American landing in Portugal is imminent. Consequently the forces assembled in southern France for the march into Spain will be moved up closer to the Spanish border.

15 February 1943

In the afternoon the Deputy Chief of the Armed Forces Operations Staff returns from his trip to Tunisia and Italy.

16 February 1943

General WARLIMONT, Deputy Chief of the Armed Forces Operations Staff, reports to the Fuehrer on his journey to Tunisia and Italy.

(1) Summary: Following preliminary discussions in Rome with the Commander in Chief of OB South and with General Ambrosio, newly appointed Chief of the Supreme Command, General WARLIMONT arrived at Tunis on 7 February and discussed the situation with General Von ARNIM and General ZIEGLER. On 8 February, he visited the Von Manteuffel Division (formerly Von Broich) in Pont du Fahs and the "Superga" Division in the sector adjacent to the south. Continuing his journey to Kairouan, he saw the 10th Panzer Division and, in Kairouan itself, the 47th Grenadier Regiment. On 9 February, after spending the night in Sfax, he visited the 21st Panzer Division (commander, General HILLEBRANDT) in the area east of

Sidi bou Zid and went from there to Gabes where he saw the G-4 of the German-Italian Panzer Army. On 10 February he visited General ROMMEL at the Mareth position, and on the following day, after an inspection of the positions at Gabes, he flew to Sicily and from there back to Rome.

(2) <u>Result of the orientation and the discussions</u>: The North African zones of operations constitute one single theater of war. The Fifth Panzer Army, thus far, has not found an explanation for the unusual lack of activity on the part of the opposing enemy forces. The enemy is building a road leading from Bou Arada to Madjez el Bab. He seems to concentrate strong forces in the area opposite the northern sector of the Fifth Panzer Army. Batteries up to 330 mm. caliber are also emplaced in that area. Reconnaissance in the enemy rear area is not possible because the Air Force is unable to penetrate the enemy defense and because the terrain renders observation very difficult. In the southern sector, the enemy is evacuating his forward positions. American forces are employed there, and their personnel is of excellent fighting caliber, but utterly inexperienced. The British and French call them "their Italians." The French units prove very courageous in combat. The French Legion of the Fifth Panzer Army comprises only five officers and 150 men. Many Arabs, who obviously are treated very ineptly by the Americans, join the German-Arabian instruction battalion under Major Meyer-RICKS which has already arrived in Tunis. The instruction battalion belongs to General FELMY'S Corps for Special Assignments which is being shipped to Tunisia.

The British Eighth Army has committed about eight divisions at the front. The powerful armored reconnaissance cars employed by the British shoot down their German and Italian counterparts at a distance of 2 kilometers. The enemy furthermore employs a new 57 mm. antitank gun, the projectile of which even pierces the armor of the Tiger tank. General ROMMEL declared that he cannot leave his rear guards in the Mareth position if he has to release forces for a thrust toward Gafsa. He expects the enemy to launch a general offensive toward the middle of March, but also considers it possible that the enemy will attack only in the Tunis-Bizerte sector. He compares the situation of the German forces to a house of cards; adequate forces to resist a serious attack are not available anywhere. The width of the battalion sectors had to be extended to cover 10 - 12 kilometers, and a critical shortage exists in reserves, artillery, ammunition, supplies of every kind, and transportation space. Thus far, only the 21st Panzer Division has been rehabilitated. The 21st and 10th Panzer Divisions constitute the operational reserve. The combat strength of the 90th Light Division has been reduced to only 2,400 men. In view of these conditions, the conduct of any offensive action by the German forces must be regarded as extremely hazardous and utterly audacious.

The question of whether or not Tunisia can be held will be determined by the supply situation. Stocks of supplies are practically nonexistent. General Von ARNIM, prospective commander in chief of the army group, calculates that for the current supplying of the two armies and for the piling up of stocks he would need 150,000 tons monthly for the next four months. According to the calculation by OB South, the minimum required by the army group would be 69,000 tons; including a safety margin, the required volume of supplies would amount to 90,000 tons. The Italian Supreme Command has stated that, anticipating a sinking quota of 20,000 tons, no more than 80,000 tons of supplies can be shipped via the Strait of Sicily. If sinkings continue at the present rate, the shipping space now available will suffice only until June or July. Thereafter the volume of the seaborne supplies would drop below the very minimum required by the forces in North Africa. Moreover, the needed naval units for the protection of the convoys are lacking. For all these reasons, the increased employment of small vessels is imperative. It is necessary to build Air Force Siebel ferries*, naval barges, sailing boats with auxiliary motors, and other military transport vessels in large numbers. OB South estimates that he would need a total of 400 naval barges and Air Force Siebel ferries. However, OB South shares the opinion that, through the employment of all these measures, only a minimum of supplies can be shipped to North Africa. The tactical and operational requirements have to be adapted to this supply situation, something that has not been done yet by any means.

As far as the chain of command is concerned, the forward echelon of OB South under Colonel WESTPHAL has been incorporated into the Italian

---

* A type of flat-bottom landing craft.

Supreme Command, which objected to its high numerical strength. Only one liaison officer of the forward echelon is attached to headquarters of OB South. In Tunisia an army group is organized under the command of General Von ARNIM with General ZIEGLER as his chief of staff. Assigned to the newly organized army group are: the Fifth Panzer Army under General VAERST (chief of staff: Colonel Von QUAST) and the Italian First Army under General MESSE (chief of staff: Colonel BAYERLEIN, former chief of staff of the German-Italian Panzer Army). The time for the employment of the new army group headquarters has not been set yet. It depends on the preceding assignment of new duties to General ROMMEL which can be made only upon the conclusion of the current operations. The task of preparing Sicily and the Italian mainland for defense has been assigned by OB South to Colonel BADE and General GAUSE respectively. The Italians intend to leave their II Infantry Corps with two divisions at the Eastern Front, but the Fuehrer plans to employ this corps in security missions only.

With regard to the present situation in Tunisia, General WARLIMONT reports: the Fifth Panzer Army originally planned to launch a major offensive toward Tebessa. However, the opinion finally prevailed at Army headquarters that, with the forces available, only an operation with limited objective could be carried out. Therefore, the thrust toward Sidi bou Zid was launched on 15 January. At the same time, the combat group of Colonel LIEBENSTEIN, which is composed of the Ramcke Air Force-Jaeger-Brigade and a tank battalion of the German-Italian Panzer Army, advanced into Gafsa, where no enemy forces were found.

17 February 1943

In the morning the Fuehrer, accompanied by General JODL and General ZEITZLER, takes off by plane for Saporoshe to direct the operations in the southern section of the Eastern Front. General KEITEL remains at HITLER'S headquarters.

18 February 1943

General Von KLEIST, Commander in Chief of Army Group A, has been ordered to report to the Fuehrer at Dnjepropetrowsk today. The plan of the Chief of Army General Staff to ship the Seventeenth Army to the ports of Genitschesk, Berdiansk, and Mariupol via the Sea of Azov for commitment at the Dnjepr cannot be carried out for the time being because of ice conditions.

19 February 1943

Kharkov had to be abandoned yesterday. Since the enemy is advancing toward the south and Saporoshe is also threatened, the Fuehrer and his staff will fly to Winniza and take up quarters at HITLER'S former headquarters, "Wehrwolf."

The Fuehrer and the Chief of Army General Staff are of the opinion that the muddy season has already begun in the southern section of the Eastern Front and that troop movements can be carried out there only on the highways and railroads.

MS # C-065a   -198-

In Tunisia, General ROMMEL temporarily takes over the command of an attack force composed of the 10th and 21st Panzer Divisions and a combat group of the German Africa Corps.

20 February 1943

The chain of command in Tunisia has become very complex. In the Mareth position, General MESSE, Commander in Chief of the Italian First Army, is in command. However, on the request of the Italian Supreme Command, General ROMMEL, who leads the attack force and is 200 kilometers away from the Mareth position, will remain responsible for holding that position. OB South will discuss the matter with General ROMMEL today. In view of the heavy losses in ships on the route from Naples and Taranto to Tunisia, the Chief of OKW urgently requests that the supplies for North Africa be brought up as far as Sicily. Fourteen railroad trains can be ferried via the Strait of Messina daily. In the evening, the Deputy Chief of the Armed Forces Operations Staff leaves for Rome for discussions with the Italian Supreme Command and the German General attached to the Italian Armed Forces High Command.

22 February 1943

The Fuehrer ordered General of the Air Force STAHEL to direct the defense of the Saporoshe bridgehead and instructed Army Group A to consider it its foremost task to make the strongest possible forces available to Army Group South. The placing of the entire German and Italian forces in Tunisia under the command of General ROMMEL is being considered.

1 March 1943

In the sector of the Ninth Army, Movement "Bueffel" (i.e. the evacuation of the Rshew salient, which finally was approved by the Fuehrer) was started this morning. A very heavy British air attack on Berlin was carried out during the night of 1 - 2 March.

3 March 1943

The Commander of the Southeast Military District, who arrived at HITLER'S headquarters "Wehrwolf," reports to the Fuehrer on the situation in the Balkans, especially on the planned Operation SCHWARZ against partisan leader MIHAILOVIC in Montenegro. As a preliminary measure, the Fuehrer wants Collasin, MIHAILOVIC'S headquarters in Montenegro, to be subjected to an air attack. Photographic reconnaissance will be followed by a severe day and night attack. A date for the start of the operation has not been set. To carry out the operation, either an additional combat group will be transferred to Croatia or OB South will assign the necessary forces. General LOEHR requests that the forces assigned to carry out Operation SCHWARZ be equipped with boats and mountaineering boots. If possible, the 1st Mountain Division will be committed in the operation, and will be shipped from the Seventeenth Army by water via the Black Sea to Constantza. It is expected that the Division can be withdrawn from its present front sector within approximately four weeks. In that case, Operation SCHWARZ can be carried out during the first half of May. General

LOEHR, furthermore, reports to the Fuehrer on the measures planned by him to establish stable political conditions in Croatia. He submits a memorandum on the subject, which the Fuehrer hands to General JODL for further study. The pacification of Croatia will be accomplished by building up a German administration from the bottom. For this purpose, the Reichsfuehrer SS will first transfer German rural police posts to that country which will be attached to the Wehrmacht. The Armed Forces Operations Staff will prepare a draft of the pertinent order, which will be discussed with headquarters of the Reichsfuehrer SS. The principal topic discussed by the Fuehrer with the Military District Commander Southeast was operational questions concerning the southeast area. If possible the German-Italian demarcation line will no longer be discussed. The Fuehrer orders the motorization of the 11th Air Force Ground Division because he wants to have a mobile reserve available in the Peloponnesus. He also desires that Crete be provided with supplies sufficient to enable the isle to hold out without any additional supplies for six months. General LOEHR points to the weakness of the antiaircraft defenses in Greece and on Crete.

Referring to the situation at the Eastern Front, the Fuehrer points out that the Russians are no longer susceptible to the German strongpoint tactics, but simply bypass those strong points. Therefore it has become useless to supply the strong points for a longer period.

4 March 1943

Toward noon, General WARLIMONT, Deputy Chief of the Armed Forces Operations Staff, returns to HITLER'S headquarters "Wolfsschanze." Following a short leave which he spent at Lake Tegernsee, he had arrived in Rome on 25 February. On 1 March he flew from Rome to Munich, and on 2 March, to Winniza via Vienna, reporting to the Fuehrer at "Wehrwolf" on 3 March. He left Winniza by plane this morning. His report on the result of his journey is as follows:

General WARLIMONT, within the scope of a political mission sent by the Reich Minister for Foreign Affairs, was ordered to prevail upon the Italians to co-operate more actively in antipartisan combat in Croatia. While the Duce, in a joint politico-military discussion, which took place on 26 February, promised the all-out participation of the Italian forces in the planned operations, the discussion of the Deputy Chief of the Armed Forces Operations Staff with General AMBROSIO, which took place on 27 February, revealed that the Italians actually are not prepared to take part in any of the three planned operations:

(1) Operation WEISS II aiming at the annihilation of the Communists (the so-called Yugoslav Army of Liberation under Tito) in Croatia;

(2) disarmament of all Cetnici-formations in Croatia;

(3) action against the center of the Mihailovic Movement in Montenegro.

General AMBROSIO, in this connection, pointed out that the Cetnicis who had been incorporated into the Italian units could not possibly be shifted from the zone of operations to another region as requested by OB Southeast, because they would become a nuisance in the rear of the Italians, while they would expend themselves in the quickest possible manner if they were committed in combat. General AMBROSIO, furthermore, strongly objected to the disarmament of the Cetnicis, although he immediately ordered discontinuance of the deliveries of arms to them and instructed the Italian Second Army to disarm the Cetnicis upon the completion of Operation WEISS II. After receiving General WARLIMONT'S report, the Fuehrer ordered OB Southeast to continue submitting the intercepted radio messages from the Cetnicis to the British to the Armed Forces Operations Staff, which is to send the reports in duplicate to the German General in Rome to be forwarded to the Italian Supreme Command and, via the German Ambassador, to the Duce. During the discussion with the Deputy Chief of the Armed Forces Operations Staff on 28 February, General AMBROSIO also refused to participate in any operation against the Mihailovic Movement in Montenegro. After the Reich Minister for Foreign Affairs had prevailed upon the Duce to intervene, however, General AMBROSIO finally approved of the planned operation.

On the basis of HITLER'S letter, which he handed to the Duce, General WARLIMONT also discussed with the Duce and General AMBROSIO the situation in the Mediterranean. All agreed in the opinion that the central Mediterranean is to be regarded as particularly threatened because free access to Suez is still denied to the Anglo-Americans, who rely principally on the round-about way around the Cape. Among the primarily threatened islands,

Sicily is best prepared for defense, but the preparations made on Sardinia and Corsica are still rather inadequate. The Italians want German weapons and equipment for these islands, and handed a long list of items desired by them to General WARLIMONT. At present, only a few weak German reserve units activated by Colonel BADE are stationed in Sicily. For the time being, only the commitment of one German division and six German Flak batteries which are being moved up is intended. The assault battalions being activated at the Sennelager troop training grounds might also be transferred to Sicily although it was intended originally to employ these units on Sardinia, and thus far the Fuehrer has reserved his decision as to their commitment there. If these units should not be employed in Sardinia, the German anti-aircraft crews stationed there and those employed on the Isle of Rhodes must be reinforced by German motorcycle riflemen and antitank artillery. As far as Rhodes is concerned, this probably would be the only solution, unless a combat group of the 11th Air Force Ground Division were transferred to the isle. The transfer of German units to Corsica is not contemplated for the time being.

As far as the situation in Tunisia is concerned, the Italians too have realized that the transportation problem is the decisive factor. However, it is impossible to comply with General KEITEL'S request that a greater number of trains carrying supplies for Africa should be directed to Sicily via the Strait of Messina. Three-fourths of the 370 railroad cars that can be ferried to Sicily across the Messina Strait are needed to supply the isle itself, which always receives food supplies for three days only. The remaining 25 percent of the railroad cars is available for the supplying of the forces in North Africa.

6 March 1943

Distribution of the Flying Formations of the Air Force along the Eastern Front

Fourth Air Force: (Army Group A and South)	11 bomber groups	5 dive bomber groups	6 fighter groups	1 close-support group	1 1/3 long-range fighter groups
Eastern Air Forces: Headquarters (Army Group Center)	1 2/3 "	1 "	3 2/3 "		1/3 night fighter group
First Air Force: (Army Group North)	3 "	1 "	3 1/3 "		
Northern Air Force Command: (Finland)	1 1/3 "	1/3 "	2 2/3 "		

Total: 17 bomber groups, 7 1/3 dive bomber groups, 15 2/3 fighter groups, 1 close-support group, 1 1/3 long range-fighter groups and 1/3 night fighter group, each group comprising an average of 20 planes ready to take off, totaling 42 2/3 groups, comprising about 855 planes.

General ROMMEL, in an estimate of the situation, suggested the withdrawal of both armies in Tunisia to a narrow basis area. The Fuehrer rejects this suggestion because, in his opinion, such action would spell the beginning of the end. He is of the opinion that the situation in North Africa can be mastered only by a substantial increase of the supply shipments. The enemy preparations for the attack will be smashed by local thrusts. Last night, the British Air Force carried out a heavy attack on Essen.

9 March 1943

Distribution of the Flying Formations of the Air Force in the Mediterranean area

Second Air Force Corps: Sicily	2 reconnaissance squadrons	8 bomber groups	2 1/3 fighter groups	1 2/3 night fighter groups	2 1/3 long-range fighter groups
Air Force Corps: Tunisia	3 "	1 1/3 "	6 2/3 "	2 dive bomber groups	1 2/3 close-support groups
Tenth Air Force Corps: Athens	3 "	3 "	1 "		

Total: 8 reconnaissance squadrons, 12 1/3 bomber groups, 2 dive bomber groups, 10 fighter groups, 1 2/3 night fighter groups, 2 1/3 long-range fighter groups and 1 2/3 close-support groups totaling 30 groups, comprising about 600 planes plus 8 reconnaissance squadrons.

The Fuehrer instructs OB Southeast that the German forces committed in Operation WEISS II will thrust forward as far as Mostar and occupy the bauxite mines located in that area.

Last night, the British Air Force carried out a very heavy attack on Nuremberg.

10 March 1943

The Chief of the OKW, who returned to "Wolfsschanze" yesterday after having stayed in Winniza for several days, reports that the Chief of Army General Staff intends to commit the bulk of the SS Corps in an attack on Kharkov from the north, and simultaneously launch an attack in the area west-northwest of Kharkov to tie down the enemy forces employed there. At present, the Donets front on both sides of Isjum is regarded as the most seriously threatened sector in the south of the Eastern Front. This sector, therefore, will be strongly fortified.

General ROMMEL, who left Tunis by plane yesterday, arrives at "Wehrwolf" today to report to the Fuehrer on the situation in North Africa. By the order of 5 March 1943, the 999th African Brigade has been changed into a division. For the time being, however, it is composed of two regiments only, as the activation of the third one has not yet been completed. An additional penal brigade will be activated for commitment in North Africa, to be made up exclusively of homosexual men. Although the Army High Command is opposed to this plan, the Chief of OKW insists that it be carried out.

The unit in question is the Thierack Brigade. Anglo-American troops in the approximate strength of 85,000 men reportedly have arrived in French North Africa during the last few weeks. The Anglo-Americans are shipping about 500,000 tons of supplies a month to North Africa against a volume of approximately 35,000 tons currently shipped to North Africa by the Axis powers.

Last night, the British Air Force staged a heavy attack on Munich.

11 March 1943

The Fuehrer ordered that four tank battalions, comprising 30-40 of the heaviest panzers of the "Hornisse" type, be newly organized within the scope of the Inspector General of the Panzer Troops. The battalions are to be activated in the west and stationed in Normandy and Brittany.

General FELMY, Commanding General of the Corps for Special Assignments, who is on his way from the Eastern Front to Tunisia, arrives at HITLER'S headquarters "Wolfsschanze" for discussions.

During yesterday's report by General ROMMEL at "Wehrwolf," the Fuehrer again rejected the suggestion to withdraw the two armies in North Africa to a narrow basis area, because such action would further aggravate the existing supply difficulties. HITLER declared that a supreme effort has to be made to increase the volume of supplies for North Africa to 150,000 tons a month. The Fuehrer will discuss the necessary measures with Gross Admiral DOENITZ, Commander in Chief of the Navy, who thereupon will take the necessary steps in Rome.

12 March 1943

The Duce yesterday agreed to an extension of the German operations in Croatia as far as the gates of Mostar, and to the occupation of the bauxite mines located in that area by German troops.

Last night a heavy air attack was carried out on Stuttgart. According to final reports on results of the air attack on Berlin during the night of 1 - 2 March 1943, 649 persons were killed, 1,570 wounded--369 of them seriously--, 62 persons are missing, 35,000 are homeless, 20,000 buildings were destroyed or damaged, and 1,600 major fires, 500 fires of medium dimensions, and thousands of minor fires occurred. During the air attack on Essen on the night of 5 - 6 March, 304 persons were killed, 1,440 wounded, and 93 are missing; 396 mines and heavy demolition bombs, 119,000 incendiary bombs, and 15,000 phosphorus bombs were dropped; 3,016 buildings were destroyed, 2,050 were heavily damaged, substantial damage was inflicted on 3,000 buildings, and 18,000 were slightly damaged.

13 March 1943

On his return flight from Winniza to East Prussia, the Fuehrer stopped at Army Group Center's command post this morning, and spoke to the commanders assembled there. The commanders are pleased about the extensive withdrawal movement of the Fourth and Ninth Armies, the successful execution of which surpassed all expectations. Large-scale destruction was carried out in the course of the movements, which generally were completed without the loss of any materiel. After the Russians, who were ordered by their command at the outset to conduct a vigorous pursuit, had sustained substantial losses, they very hesitantly followed the withdrawing German armies with reconnaissance forces. The captured materiel referred to in the Russian reports actually comprises previously captured Russian equipment which was abandoned after it had been rendered useless. The new positions have been well developed and provided with uninterrupted wire entanglements and antitank ditches, although they have not been developed in depth. The work has been accomplished by the divisions which are to occupy the positions, and to a great extent by the civilian population. During the afternoon, the Fuehrer arrives at his headquarters "Wolfsschanze."

In view of a report received from General Von FALKENHORST, Military District Commander in Norway, on Sweden's attitude, the Fuehrer contemplates a reinforcement of the occupation forces in Norway. The following measures are under consideration: the transfer of two additional fortress battalions and one mountain division, although it is not yet clear where that division will be obtained, and the reinforcement of the 25th Panzer Division or the activation of a second armored division. For a discussion of the necessary measures, Colonel Von LOSSBERG, First General Staff Officer of the Military District Commander in Norway, and General JODL, Chief of Staff of Twentieth Mountain Army in Finland and brother of the Chief of the Armed Forces Operations Staff, are ordered to appear at HITLER'S headquarters.

Last night, another heavy attack was carried out on Essen.

14 March 1943

The Fuehrer issues a directive concerning the further conduct of operations in the east (the directive is not available). General MARRAS, Italian General attached to the German Armed Forces High Command, acting on orders of the Italian Supreme Command, requests that the Italian air forces which had been attached to the Italian Eighth Army be returned to Italy instead of being rehabilitated at Odessa as originally intended.

The Fuehrer discusses the measures to be taken to increase the supply shipments to North Africa with General KESSELRING, Commander in Chief of OB South, and Gross Admiral DOENITZ. Gross Admiral DOENITZ leaves for Rome by plane during the afternoon.

16 March 1943

The Fuehrer anticipates enemy attacks against the sector of the Sixteenth Army south of Lake Ilmen as a diverson aimed at distracting German attention from the major enemy attack which seems to be imminent at Leningrad. The 7th Air Force Division will finally be relieved by an infantry division and assembled as OKW reserve (parachute division).

During today's discussion with the Chief of Staff of Twentieth Mountain Army and the I a of the Military District Commander in Norway, the following decisions were made:

The Military District Commander in Norway will release the 181st Infantry Division as GHQ reserve in exchange for one of the divisions employed at Leningrad, namely the 295th Division, which will be assigned to him as a fortress division. Furthermore, the 25th Panzer Division will be reinforced, and 500 motor trucks will be transferred to Norway. Thus the supply transportation services in the northern area are working at top pressure for the time being, so that at present it is impossible to move up additional troops. In the area of the Twentieth Mountain Army in Finland, a new jaeger division will be activated from troops released by the two divisions of XXXVI Mountain Corps. A further subject of discussion was the defense against a major enemy landing in the northern area and the close co-operation of the Military District Commander in Norway and the Twentieth Mountain Army in such defense. The Military District Commander in Norway complains that a large number of young sailors who are suitable for service at the front are employed in nonessential positions at administrative headquarters of the Navy. The Fuehrer will discuss the matter with the Commander in Chief of the Navy.

On orders of the Fuehrer, all airdromes in the vicinity of Vichy will be rendered unserviceable in order to prevent an abduction of Marshal Petain. The Fuehrer also wishes that the Italian artillery and engineer officers who are employed in the development of positions in the Peloponnesus and on Rhodes acquaint themselves with the West Wall. This pertinent suggestion will be made to the Italian Supreme Command by the German General in Rome.

17 March 1943

With regard to the over-all situation at the Eastern Front, the Fuehrer and the Chief of Army General Staff are of the opinion that the enemy attacks against the front of the Second Panzer Army have come to an end and that the enemy is withdrawing forces from that area. It is believed that these forces are heading partly toward the south in order to halt the German attack in the Kharkov area, and partly toward the north for the major enemy attack which the German command expects at Leningrad. Russian forces apparently are also being transferred to the Leningrad area from the area of Welikije Luki.

In view of the anticipated enemy attack in the Leningrad area, the Fuehrer orders the reinforcement of the First Air Force at the expense of the Fourth Air Force.

The British Eighth Army launched the attack against the Mareth position yesterday morning, achieving some local penetrations. In view of the comparatively weak artillery preparation, General DEICHMANN, Chief of Staff of OB South, calls the attacks opening actions.

Helmuth GREINER

OPERATION BARBAROSSA

FOREWORD

This manuscript is part of a narrative history of events in the German Armed Forces Supreme Command Headquarters during World War II. The writer, Hellmuth GREINER, was charged with writing the War Diary at that headquarters from August 1939 to April 22, 1943. He has based his work on notes taken at various conferences, copies of final drafts for entry in the War Diary, copies of HITLER'S directives, orders and documents he was able to save from destruction at great personal risk.

With the aid of these sources and the trained mind and memory of a professional historian, he has presented a vivid picture of HITLER'S method of command as well as his reaction to reverses and success and the various other factors which influenced decisions in both the military and the political spheres.

In addition to a general description of procedures in the supreme headquarters it includes details of organization and the composition of HITLER'S immediate staff. Brief graphic descriptions are also included of the outstanding characteristics of its chief members who served HITLER in his capacity as Supreme Commander of the Armed Forces and Commander in Chief of the Army.

The completed work to date is divided into a number of manuscripts. For easy reference the manuscripts have been listed chronologically for inclusion in the English copies.

LOUIS M. NAWROCKI
Lt Colonel, Armor
Chief, Foreign Military
Studies Branch

MS # C-065 1

GREINER SERIES

OKW, WORLD WAR II	MS # C-065 b
WAR DIARY WEHRMACHT OPERATIONS STAFF, Aug-Nov 40	MS # C-065 j
SHEETS OF WAR DIARY OF THE DEFENSE BRANCH OF THE WEHRMACHT OPERATIONS STAFF	MS # C-065 m
RECORDS OF SITUATION EVALUATIONS OF THE NATIONAL DEFENSE BRANCH 8 Aug 40 - 25 Jun 41	MS # C-065 l
WAR DIARY WEHRMACHT OPERATIONS STAFF, Dec - Mar 1941	MS # C-065 k
WAR DIARY NOTES 12 Aug 42 - 17 May 1943	MS # C-065 n
POLAND 1939 (I)	MS # C-065 c
WESTERN AND NORTHERN EUROPE 1940 (II)	MS # C-065 d
Operation FELIX (IV)	MS # C-065 h
ITALY, WINTER 1940-41 (V)	MS # C-065 e
AFRICA 1941 (VI)	MS # C-065 f
BALKANS 1941 (VII)	MS # C-065 g
Operation BARBAROSSA (VIII)	MS # C-065 i
Operation SEELÖWE (III)	MS # C-059

MS # C-065 1

Author

Helmuth GREINER
Ministerialrat im OKW*
Born: 30 April 1892
Leipzig, Saxony.

Helmuth GREINER joined the Army in December 1913, entering the 132d Prussian Infantry Regiment as an officer candidate, and in July 1914 was promoted second lieutenant with commission dated 23 June 1913. In World War I he served at the various fronts from the outbreak of war to June 1917, with two brief breaks to recover from wounds. In June 1917 he was detached to serve as military attache on the staff of the German Embassy in Bern, Switzerland, from which he was transferred to the Historical Division of Army General Staff, Berlin, in January 1919, remaining there until discharged from the Army in March 1920, with rank of captain. Less than a month later GREINER was appointed archivist in the Military History Section of the Historical Branch of the Reichs Archives at Potsdam. He remained in this service until 1935, and it was during this period that he continued his studies in national economy and history at the Berlin University from 1921-24. Also during this period he did a great deal of writing on the German official history of World War I and was promoted Archivrat.

On 1 April 1935 GREINER was re-called for service in the Wehrmacht, promoted Regierungsrat (equivalent to major in rank) and attached to the re-organized Historical Division of the Reichs Archives, a branch of the Military History Research Institute of the Army. On 18 August 1939, he was transferred to the National Defense Branch, which later was re-designated

---

* Administrative official attached to Wehrmacht Command, equivalent in rank to a colonel.

Wehrmacht Operations Staff (*Wehrmachtsfuehrungsstab*), in Hitler's headquarters, as Keeper of the War Diary. Promoted Oberregierungsrat on 1 May 1936 and Ministerialrat on 1 October 1940, GREINER was removed from his post on 22 April 1943 because of his known anti-nationalsocialist sentiments. Following this he was detached to the Office of the German General Attached to Italian Armed Forces Headquarters in Rome for a brief spell, 15 June – 31 July 1943.

From that date to the end of the War, GREINER was not employed, being considered politically unreliable. He was captured by US forces at Oberhof, Thuringia on 4 April 1945.

In addition to his career in the civil service and the Wehrmacht, GREINER is a well-known writer on military subjects in the historical vein, his published works including, VETERANS OF WORLD WAR I, a collection of essays by soldiers of that War; THE 1916 CAMPAIGN IN RUMANIA, written for the Swedish General Staff; THE 1916 INVASION OF BELGIUM AND THE FIRST MAJOR BATTLES; THE FRENCH MOBILIZATION IN 1914; THE AMERICAN WAR OF SECESSION; GUERILLA WARFARE IN 1870-71 and FRENCH MOBILIZATION PLANS, 1885-1914, some of which were written specifically as instruction manuals for use in training.

OPERATION BARBAROSSA

On the afternoon of 29 July 1940, General of Artillery JODL, the Chief of Armed Forces Operations Office,* appeared at the special train of the Department for National Defense which was being held at Bad Reichenhall during HITLER's stay at the Berghof. Under the seal of strictest secrecy, he informed Colonel WARLIMONT, the Department Chief, as well as the chiefs of the operations divisions of the Army, Navy, and Air Force, Lieutenant Colonel von LOSZBERG, Lieutenant Commander JUNGE, and Major von FALKENSTEIN, that the Fuehrer had decided to conquer the Soviet Union by force of arms.

This news aroused extreme astonishment and consternation among the above mentioned officers. Indeed, had not HITLER, while addressing his generals at the Berghof on 22 August 1939 and in his Reichstag speech of 1 September, declared emphatically that the nonaggression pact signed by Germany and the U.S.S.R. on 23 August signified a complete reversal of German foreign policy and for all time precluded the possibility of hostilities between the two nations! Furthermore, had not HITLER concluded this pact principally to insure that Germany would not again become involved in a two-front war as it did during World War I! In addition, the Soviet Union thus far had fulfilled the terms of the treaty in every respect, and the German-Russian credit agreement of

---

* Later changed to Armed Forces Operations Staff.

19 August 1939 and the highly important commercial treaty of 11 February 1940 had resulted in remarkable benefits for Germany. Moreover, immediately after the fall of France, HITLER had issued the first instructions for a partial demobilization of the Army, particularly with regard to the discharge of the older age classes and especially technicians, and had ordered that there be a shift of emphasis on armaments in favor of the air force and the navy. These instructions indicated that he no longer anticipated any large-scale ground operations but was concerned only with war against England. Also, on 16 July 1940 he had actually ordered in his "Fuehrer Directive # 16" that preparations be made for landing operations in England. When in spite of this, HITLER suddenly announced his intention to attack Soviet Russia, the reasons which induced him to take this step could only be surmised.

In this connection, it is questionable whether HITLER ever actually intended to adhere to the German-Russian treaty and whether (as he had asserted in his Reichstag speech of 1 September 1939) he really regarded it as a decisive political turning point. It was possible that he had concluded the treaty simply to eliminate the danger in the rear, in preparation for the expected clash with the western powers, and had been convinced from the first that STALIN, too, would abide by the pact only as long as it served his purpose. It will probably be difficult to ever answer this question with absolute certainty. The fact that HITLER had always emphasized our ideological conflict with Communism and had proclaimed his foreign policy aims in his book "Mein Kampf," and his unscrupulousness in connection with the signing and fulfilling of treaties, were definite indications that he did not look upon the German-Russian nonaggression pact as a permanent arrangement but as a stopgap measure serving to postpone the settling of accounts with the U.S.S.R.

An additional reason for the attack on Russia might have been the fact that the Russians were constantly advancing further westward, and endangering our own military operations. In 1939, when the treaty was signed at Moscow, the Soviet Government had declared emphatically that it had no intentions of occupying, bolshevizing, or annexing the states located within their sphere of influence. Yet in spite of that, the Baltic States of Lithuania, Latvia, and Esthonia -- where the U.S.S.R. had maintained military strongpoints since the late fall of 1939 -- were occupied completely in June 1940, immediately bolshevized, and incorporated into the U.S.S.R. several weeks later as federal republics. In addition, the U.S.S.R. issued an ultimatum to Rumania on 26 June, requesting the return of Bessarabia as well as the northern part of Bukovina which had never belonged to Russia. Two days later the Soviets marched into those territories, and they were incorporated into the Soviet Union as Federal Republics of Moldavia and the Ukraine. This move had brought the Soviet Union alarmingly close to the Rumanian oil fields in which Germany was vitally interested. The Russian advance led to Rumania's waiver of the guaranty pledged by England and France on 13 April 1940 and to her closer connection with the Axis powers, while HITLER promised his full support to the Rumanian Government and instructed the Foreign Intelligence and Counter Intelligence Office, headed by Admiral CANARIS, to take measures for the protection of German oil interests in Rumania.

However, no matter how much the fundamental conflict with Communism and the Russian advance to the west might have played a part in HITLER's decision to attack the Soviet Union, I do not believe that they were the determining factors. Above all, they do not adequately explain why HITLER made this decision at a time when preparations for an invasion of England had just been started. For there can be little doubt that HITLER did not reckon at that time with any participation by Russia in the war against Germany. On the contrary, he believed -- as evidenced by repeated statements to this effect -- that for a reasonable length of time he could definitely depend on a friendly attitude on the part of STALIN. He was also of the opinion that the Soviet Union was too weak from a military point of view and too much handicapped by the state of its home politics to be willing to risk a major armed conflict. Consequently, in this connection, he was under no pressure to act hastily and could even postpone the final settlement of accounts with Russia until he had an absolutely free hand. Surely there must have been another important reason which gave rise to his plan to attack Russia in the near future. I believe we can hardly go wrong in assuming that the reason can be found in the following:

From the very beginning of the war, HITLER had looked upon England as his chief enemy. However, he lacked the military strength to conquer her. Since it seemed to be out of the question to come to an understanding with England, at least under the conditions which HITLER desired, it became his principal aim to break England's will to resist by force of arms. When the British Government, contrary to expectations, remained firm in its decision to continue the war even after its fighting forces had been driven from the Continent and after France had fallen, HITLER ordered intensified air and naval warfare against England and preparations for landing operations. However, he undoubtedly took the latter step with some reluctance, because in view of Germany's hopeless inferiority at sea and the lack of naval transports, he probably did not really feel equal to this difficult task. He probably feared a setback which would certainly undermine his prestige considerably and might have very serious political consequences. He even seemed to have been rather skeptical from the outset of the prospects for success of the intensified naval and air warfare. In any event, he was apparently not nearly as optimistic about it as GOERING. This uncertainty induced him to look strategic stopgaps which might enable him to reach his goal with less risk. This then might have led to the plan to conquer Russia quickly -- for he had reckoned with just a brief campaign from the very beginning -- in order to deprive England of the last trump card she might still possess on the Continent and thus force her to come to terms. As I said before, all this is only conjecture, but many statements made subsequently by HITLER, as well as JODL, definitely indicate that these theories come quite close to the truth.

Owing to the fact that no specific data has been furnished by the parties concerned, I cannot say whether and to what extent General JODL offered any reasons for the new plan during his conference with the officers of the National Defense Department. He announced that the following spring would probably be the time when the campaign against Russia would begin. Originally HITLER apparently had planned to attack the Russians as early as the fall of 1940. However, he had given up this idea, evidently because he had been dissuaded by Generalfeldmarschall KEITEL, who probably pointed out that the Russian winter would greatly handicap the German advance and that the strategic concentration of the German Wehrmacht in the newly gained eastern area involved certain requirements which it would not be possible to carry into effect in a few weeks.

In order to fulfil these prerequisites the National Defense Department was assigned the task of compiling a Wehrmacht High Command directive for all the branches of the Wehrmacht, which was to be designated "Aufbau Ost" (Development of the Eastern Territories) and for which General JODL issued specific guiding principles during the conference on 29 July. On 2 August, General WARLIMONT * submitted a first draft of this directive to Generalfeldmarschall KEITEL. In the introduction, the following statement appeared, in order to veil the real purport of the order:

> The Fuehrer has abandoned the idea of establishing an independent Polish rump government and has decided to incorporate the occupied eastern territories into Greater

---

* The Chief of the National Defense Department was promoted to Generalmajor on 1 August 1940.

Germany. Owing to this fact, it also has become necessary for the Wehrmacht to consolidate and develop the newly won eastern territories, in all respects. Besides, during the war, the ever increasing menace of air attacks in the west requires that the protected eastern territories be utilized for military purposes in greater measure.

The directive further stipulated that these actions be governed by the following precepts:

> Any reorganization or training of forces for which a need will arise in the future should be preferably effected in the eastern territories, and for this purpose the necessary facilities for training maneuvers should be set up immediately. If necessary, Wehrmacht supplies of all kinds should be transferred to the east from the western areas which are exposed to air attacks. The Wehrmacht requirements covering the improvement of the railway and road network are to be transmitted to the competent Reich agencies at the earliest possible moment; the signal communication system is to be improved; installations of the armament industry which serve the immediate troop requirements are to be set up in sufficient quantities; furthermore the mapping system for the east should be immediately adapted to the needs of the forces. On the other hand, the measures concerning the development of fortifications in the country, which have been scheduled on the basis of earlier regulations, are to be deferred for the present.

The directive added that these instructions would be sent simultaneously to the top level Reich agencies concerned and the Governor General of the occupied Polish territories.

Referring to these concluding remarks, the Supply Section of the National Defense Department on 7 August, called attention to the fact that, according to reports on hand, the civilian agencies were still uninformed about the pending incorporation of the Gouvernement Général into Greater Germany. It was pointed out that the OKW (Wehrmacht High Command) directive would now apprise the top level Reich agencies and the Governor General of the political decision made by the Fuehrer from which these agencies would draw far-reaching inferences. In order to avoid this, it was proposed that the Fuehrer directive be made public by the Chief of the Reich Chancellery or the Reich Minister of the Interior, acting as central agency for all questions affecting the eastern territories.

As HITLER, contrary to statement made in the introduction to the Wehrmacht High Command directive solely to conceal actual motives, at that time was by no means clear as to what he should do with the Polish rump territory, he specified, as a result of the above mentioned objection, that the aerial warfare in the west should be the only reason offered for the measures scheduled for the east. In this amended form the directive was signed on 9 August by the Chief of Wehrmacht High Command and distributed to the Wehrmacht branches, the top level Reich agencies, and the Governor General.

In all probability, the Commander in Chief of Staff of the Army at that time had already been informed of HITLER's new plan and were therefore familiar with the real purpose of the Wehrmacht High Command directive; but exactly when this orientation took place is not certain. On 3 September 1940, when Generalleutnant PAULUS assumed his duties as Assistant Chief of Staff for Operations, General HALDER handed him an operations plan covering the campaign against Soviet Russia, which was still incomplete and on which Generalmajor MARCKS had been working thus far, and instructed him to finish this plan after investigating all attack possibilities and proceeding on the assumption that 130 - 140 divisions would be available for this purpose. In this connection, he was to take into account from the first the utilization of Rumania as an area for the strategic concentration of the German southern wing. HITLER had set the following strategic objectives: (1) to annihilate the Russian forces stationed in western Russia and to make sure that none of the elements would escape in fit condition to the rear; (2) to capture Leningrad, Moscow, the Ukraine, and the northern part of the Caucasus with its oil wells; (3) to reach a line from which the Russian air force would no longer be able to effectively attack Germany; the final objective was to be the Astrakhan-Volga-Archangel line. *

Independent of the considerations and investigations of the General Staff of the Army, the National Defense Department also had to compile an operations plan for the campaign against Russia. The Department was given its assignment either during the conference on 29 July or soon thereafter ** by General JODL, who obviously tried to arrive at a basis on which to develop his own ideas concerning the planned operations, so as to be adequately prepared for the consultation with Generalfeldmarschall von BRAUCHITSCH, which was expected to take place in the near future, in connection with the results of the Army High Command investigations.

---

* According to testimony given by Generalfeldmarschall PAULUS during the first trial of war criminals held at Nuernberg in February 1946.

** The exact date can no longer be ascertained.

The Commander in Chief of the Air Force also seems to have been informed by HITLER of his new plan early in the game, for it is reasonable to assume that the operations staff of the Air Force already knew of this project when, on 8 August, they requested the OKH (Army High Command) to furnish the necessary data in connection with the development of the ground organization of the Air Force in the east. On the other hand, the Commander in Chief of the Navy was apparently not notified by HITLER until the end of September, which, however, does not preclude the possibility that he had been previously informed of the new scheme by some other means.

For the present, the two plans of operations and the OKW (Wehrmacht High Command) directive were held in abeyance. On 21 August, HITLER merely sent word via General JODL to the Commander in Chief of the Army that "it is urgently necessary to fortify immediately the Baltic Seacoast with batteries," and that, "for political reasons, it is desirable that an armored unit be detached without delay to East Prussia." The reason for the latter measure was undoubtedly the fact that the Soviet Union, through its recent occupation of all of Lithuania, had forged ahead right up to the eastern borders of East Prussia. The OKH (Army High Command) assigned the 1st Panzer Division which arrived in East Prussia at the beginning of September.

At this time, however, other projects were still foremost in importance -- above all Operation SEELOEWE as well as the plan for an attack on Gibraltar and the contemplated commitment of German armored forces in

Libya in support of the Italian campaign against Egypt. At the beginning of August, HITLER began to worry about the fact that, of late, relations between the Soviet Union and Finland had become strained. The Russians charged that the Finnish Government was making things difficult for the communistic "Association for the Advancement of Peace and Friendship with the Soviet Union" which had been founded in Finland at the close of the Russo-Finnish war. According to a report of the Yugoslav ambassador to Moscow published in Berlin, Russian Foreign Commissar MOLOTOV had called the Finnish ambassador to account for this. Furthermore, a whole series of reports submitted by attaches and agents indicated unanimously that the fifteen Russian divisions stationed at the Finnish border were being reinforced by armored elements and that in all likelihood these forces would be alerted beginning 15 August. We recognized as the true reason behind these moves the Soviet Union's designs against the Finnish nickel ore region of Petsamo; it was of the utmost importance for Germany's conduct of the war that this territory remain in Finland's possession. In addition, HITLER, who even then might have contemplated winning over Finland for participation in the campaign against Soviet Russia, was concerned that the latter might invade northern Norway. During the conference, which has been mentioned previously and which was held on 13 August in the Berlin Chancellery * between HITLER, Admiral RAEDER, and the Chief of Staff of the Navy, HITLER therefore instructed Admiral RAEDER to fortify the area of northern Norway more intensely and above all to secure the fjords there,

---

* See Chapter III, page 7 (German original).

particularly at crossroads, to such a degree that Russian attacks would have no chance of success and that a foundation be laid for a subsequent occupation of Petsamo. The commitment of a naval commander in chief in this area was also to be taken into consideration. The next day HITLER discussed increasing the protection of northern Norway by means of GHQ troops with the Commander in Chief of Norway, General von FALKENHORST, who had been summoned for this purpose. On this occasion the latter proposed that the entire mountain corps be transferred to the Narvik-Kirkenes area, which step HITLER approved. Reichsmarschall GOERING was delegated the task of making preparations for the construction of an air base in northern Norway.

Even though the tension between the Soviet Union and Finland soon relaxed and the reports concerning large-scale reinforcement of Russian troops at the Finnish border did not seem to be based on fact, the orders HITLER had issued nevertheless remained in effect. So far the only elements of the mountain corps in northern Norway had been the 3d Mountain Division. During the next weeks the 2d Mountain Division was also transferred to northern Norway from the area of Trondheim, to which region the 196th Infantry Division was moved from Oslo. In addition, the elements of an SS Brigade which was stationed in Oslo were also committed far up north, at Kirkenes, in the immediate vicinity of the Petsamo region. The problems of supplying all these troops via land route through Norway, which in spite of the rapidly progressing construction of the Narvik-Kirkenes road, * entailed great difficulties, and the construction of an air base in northern Norway, were considerably facilitated by reason of the fact that at the end of August the Finnish Government, owing to the GOERING's initiative, placed 50,000 tons of shipping for supply transports at Germany's disposal and granted the right to use the road leading from Kemi over northern Finland to Kirkenes. They also gave permission in mid-September for a German antiaircraft artillery battalion in uniform to march through on its way to Kirkenes, but requested that the Russians be informed about the German transports. These arrangements were set down in a formal agreement which was signed on 23 September by the German and the Finnish Governments. In return, Germany pledged itself to supply Finland with arms on a large scale. Finland's standing army at that time comprised five army corps with sixteen divisions, totaling 140 - 150,000 men, but was rather weak in artillery, while her air force, numbering approximately six hundred planes, was not able to meet the requirements of modern warfare. In conformity with HITLER's order, the post of an "Admiral of the Polar Coast Region" was created at the beginning of September and Admiral BOEHM appointed to fill this position.

Meanwhile, in the southeast, serious political complications had arisen which affected German interests in far greater measure than the passing

---

* This road, which extended 810 kilometers, was completed at the beginning of November.

tension between the Soviet Union and Finland. Owing to the incorporation of Bessarabia and northern Bukovina into the Soviet Union, the territorial problems in the Balkans once again loomed large. Hungary and Bulgaria had requested the Rumanian Government to return their territories of Transylvania and southern Dobrogea, which they had ceded according to stipulations in the peace treaties signed after World War I. While the Rumanian-Bulgarian negotiations, initiated on 19 August at Craiova, had progressed favorably from the start, the Rumanian-Hungarian discussions, which had begun on 16 August at Turnu-Severin, shortly led to serious arguments and were broken off without result on 23 August. The two governments thereupon turned to the Axis powers, requesting them to act as arbitrators in this controversy. In view of the critical tension between Hungary and Rumania which had already led to border incidents and threatened to result in the outbreak of hostilities, the need for German-Italian intervention became all the more urgent. HITLER, bearing in mind the Rumanian oil shipments on which Germany's conduct of war depended to a large degree, as well as his other plans, was vitally interested in the preservation of peace in the Balkans. Moreover, at the Berghof, where HITLER had been staying since 17 August and where on 31 August he had been joined * by the Chiefs of the Wehrmacht High Command and the Wehrmacht Operations Staff,** startling reports were received on 25 and 26 August concerning Russian troop

---

* The Field Echelon of the National Defense Department was detached on 25 August and arrived the next morning in its special train at the Salzburg main station, where it remained.

** The Wehrmacht Operations Office had been changed to Wehrmacht Operations Staff on 8 August 1940.

concentrations at the Pruth River and in northern Bukovina. It was suspected that the reason behind these moves was the plan of the Soviet Union to seize the Rumanian oil field region in case of an armed conflict between Hungary and Rumania, which HITLER was determined to prevent at all costs.

Consequently HITLER, in conjunction with Italy, invited the two governments to a conference to be held at Vienna on 29 August, and at the same time took preventive military measures. On 26 August he ordered the Commander in Chief of the Army to immediately assign about ten divisions to Poland in order to reinforce the elements stationed there, but without seriously interfering with the regular flow of economic transports. In addition, he ordered that two armored divisions, after their equipment had been put in good repair in the Zone of Interior, be transferred to the extreme southeastern part of Gouvernement Général. The commitment of these divisions was to be effected in such a manner as to make sure that, should the need arise, it would be possible to take prompt action to protect the Rumanian oil field region. At the Hungarian-Rumanian border, according to latest reports, no less than 23 out of the regular 24 Hungarian Brigades were said to be massed, whereas of the 35 Rumanian divisions only 8 - 10 were stationed at the Hungarian border and, on the other hand, 22 - 24 were on the Russian border. New incidents at the Hungarian-Rumanian border induced HITLER two days later, on the morning of 28 August, to order the Army and the Air Force to make all necessary preparations without delay for the immediate occupation of the oil field region in case the intervention proceedings, which had been started, were to fail. It was stipulated that for this purpose, they make use primarily of the mobile units of the Army which at the time were stationed in the Zone of Interior. These units consisted of five armored divisions and three motorized divisions, which, with the exception of one armored and one motorized division, were again fit for service beginning 1 September. In addition, they were to make provisions for the commitment of parachute and airborne troops for prompt on-the-spot protection of strategic points in Rumania. If necessary, permission was to be obtained from the Hungarian Government for the passage of our troops and, as far as possible, for railway transportation through Hungary. It was believed that there would be no difficulty in securing Rumania's agreement for the passage of our troops; she was also be charged with the responsibility for supplying the German troops stationed in Rumania. On the evening of 28 August, these instructions were supplemented to the effect that HITLER might order these movements to begin as early as 1 September, and that consequently, provisions might have to be made for some elements to be prepared for operations on that day. However, in this connection, it was ordered that no redistribution of troops was to take place before 1 September, whereas the shifting from west to east, which had been ordered on 26 August, was to be put into effect with the utmost speed.

On the morning of 29 August the Army High Command reported that steps had been taken in preparation for the occupation of the oil field region, that the motorized 13th Infantry Division had started its march to the area around Vienna, and that it was their plan for the present to place this division and the two armored divisions (2d and 9th) already stationed there under the command of the XXXX Corps Headquarters. The operations staff of the Air Force also sent word that they had taken preparatory measures. When a morning communication brought the news that the first British air attack on Berlin had been launched the night before, HITLER decided at noon to return immediately to Berlin in order to discuss reprisal raids against London with GOERING.* HITLER, together with his party and the Field Echelon of the National Defense Department, arrived in the capital on the morning of 30 August. In the afternoon a conference was held at the Chancellery, presided over by General JODL, during which the measures for the protection of the oil field region taken thus far and those contemplated for the future were discussed. This conference was attended by General WARLIMONT accompanied by two officers of the National Defense Department; the Chief of the Foreign Intelligence and Counter-Intelligence Office, Admiral CANARIS; the Chief of Counter-Intelligence Branch II, Lieutenant Colonel von BENTIVEGNI; the First General Staff Officer of the Operations Division of the General Staff of the Army, Colonel HEUSINGER; and the Chief of the Operations Division of the Air Force Operations Staff, Generalmajor HOFFMANN von WALDAU.

General JODL began by stating that should the intervention fail, it would be necessary to protect the German sphere of interests in Rumania against attack by other powers, and that to this end it would be essential that the Wehrmacht occupy Rumania in the quickest way possible. Hungary

---

* See Chapter III, page 19 (German original).

and Rumania would presumably agree to this move. Although the latest reports indicated that the Vienna negotiations would result in a conciliation of the contending parties, preparations should nevertheless be continued for the present.

Admiral CANARIS then reported on measures taken by him for the protection of the oil field region. He stated that the following forces were available for the prevention of sabotage and surprise raids: (1) approximately one hundred and fifty men led by able officers and stationed at Ruscuk on the Danube, about the same number at Bucharest, and around Ploesti; these men, who had uniforms and weapons as well as heavy machine guns, would be able to reach the oil field region within 15 - 20 hours after the alert had been given; (2) about six Danube cutters and two motor boats which were equipped with arms; (3) armed men hidden on oil tankers. The order for the commitment of these defense elements should be issued twenty-four hours in advance, if possible.

General von WALDAU proposed the assignment of one reinforced parachute regiment consisting of three battalions, one antitank company, and one infantry howitzer company, one parachute antiaircraft, and one light battery. He stated that provisions had been made for the assembly of 270 transport planes, that 230 additional planes could be supplied by the training schools within 72 hours, and that the storing of fuel had begun in the area of XVII Air Force Administrative Command. He also reported that six landing sites were under consideration around Ploesti; however, their present condition still had to be investigated. The Rumanians would be able to take over the air defense and, for this purpose, had HEINKEL pursuit planes and German antiaircraft at their disposal. The withdrawal of fighter planes from the west was, in his opinion, undesirable as well as unnecessary. Should additional antiaircraft protection be required, one mixed motorized antiaircraft regiment and, in addition, one aircraft warning battalion for protection against low altitude attacks could then be assigned. Any parachute troops that landed would have to be conducted to the objective they were to protect by guides who were acquainted with the country.

Finally, Colonel HEUSINGER reported that, beginning 1 September, the motorized XXXX Infantry Corps under the command of General of Cavalry STUMME, in conjunction with the 3d and 9th Panzer Divisions and the 13th motorized Infantry Division, would be held in readiness in the area around Vienna. He added, however, that for the present the two armored divisions had at their disposal only one tank battalion each. Unless it encountered enemy resistance, the Corps would be able to reach the Hungarian border within three days and the oil field region around Ploesti within five days. This could be accomplished by wheeled vehicles by road march, using two or three routes, and by shipping track-laying vehicles by rail, using two routes. In addition it would be possible to commit the following: the motorized "Grossdeutschland" Infantry Regiment and the motorized "Adolf HITLER" * SS Leibstandarte both of which were at present stationed

---

* The "Adolf HITLER" SS Leibstandarte, formerly HITLER's body guard, had been enlarged to a brigade as per Fuehrer directive of 12 August 1940 and now consisted of five battalions and one artillery regiment which also had available one light and one medium flak battery.

in Alsace-Lorraine and could be prepared to march within 48 hours, and after an additional 48 hours could be in a position to reach the German-Hungarian border. Besides, two infantry divisions had been earmarked for future relief of the XXXX Infantry Corps. Owing to the slowness of the Hungarian railway system it would be necessary to give one or two days' advance notice on railway transports passing through Hungary.

In conclusion, General JODL stated that these measures were sufficient for the present and that the preparations were to be continued on that basis. During the next few days, the National Defense Department compiled a "directive governing the occupation of the Rumanian oil field region" which, however, was to be signed and distributed only if and when developments necessitated our taking any action.

In the meantime, the conference, which had been called at Vienna for the purpose of settling the Hungarian-Rumanian dispute, had begun on 29 August in the upper Belvedere Castle, the former summer residence of Prince Eugene of Savoy. The negotiations were carried on by German Foreign Minister von RIBBENTROP and Italian Foreign Minister Count CIANO with the Hungarian and Rumanian delegations, which were headed by their Foreign Ministers Count CSAKY and MANOILESCU respectively. The conference ended on 30 August with a decision rendered by the Axis powers, according to which Rumania had to cede to Hungary most of Transylvania, an area comprising roughly 50,000 square kilometers. Consequently, Hungary's new southern border line was set to extend approximately as follows:

From Gyula-Aiud * to Sighisoara ** along the course of the Oltul (Alt) River north of Brasov (Kronstadt), whereby Aiud was given to Hungary while Sighisoara remained in Rumanian hands. In order to make it easier for Rumania to accept this decision which involved such considerable territorial sacrifices on her part, Germany and Italy, on 30 August, undertook to guarantee the integrity and inviolability of the Rumanian sovereignty within its new borders. In spite of this, violent demonstrations took place in Rumania in protest against the decision reached by the arbitrators. In Bucharest these demonstrations developed into riots and led to the resignation of the GIGURTU Cabinet on 4 September. The new Prime Minister General ANTONESCU established, as he called it in his proclamation of 5 September, "a new regime" with marked totalitarian tendencies, forced King CAROL II to abdicate on 6 September in favor of his son MICHAEL, and cultivated the Axis powers in even greater measure than the previous government. Following this, calm prevailed throughout the country. The march of Hungarian troops into the territory accorded to Hungary was also carried out without incidents during the period from 6 - 13 September. The Rumanian-Bulgarian negotiations held at Craiova ended on 7 September with the signing of a treaty according to which Southern Dobrudja including the Danube Fortress Silistria was ceded to Bulgaria; this was put into effect between 21 and 30 September.

---

* Aiud is the Rumanian name for this locality, which is called Nagy Enyed in Hungarian and Strassburg in German.

** Sighisoara, which is a Rumanian name, is called Segesvar in Hungarian and Schaessburg in German.

Although the decision reached in Vienna had made it possible to consider the danger of an armed conflict between Hungary and Rumania dispelled, there still existed the menace of further Russian advances in the Balkans. This was clearly indicated by Moscow's attitude during those days. Foreign Commissar MOLOTOV expressed to the German ambassador, Count von der SCHULENBURG, his astonishment at the fact that Germany had failed to promptly notify the Soviet Union of the decision and stated that Russia would continue to be interested in problems affecting the Balkans. Thereupon HITLER, on 2 September, mentioned to General JODL that after the Hungarian-Rumanian tension had died down, he intended to request Hungary to permit, should the need arise, passage of German troops, the use of its railroads, and permission for German planes to fly over and make intermediate landings in Hungarian territory. HITLER also stated that he planned to ask Rumania's consent to the occupation of its oil field region, which might become necessary in order to protect it against seizure by other nations. He specified that the same goal was to be achieved in the interim by sending a military mission to Rumania which was to consist of army and air force officers and to which German antitank and antiaircraft "instruction forces" were to be attached. The Army High Command and the OKL (Air Force High Command) were asked to submit proposals in this connection.

These measures contemplated by HITLER coincided with the plans of General ANTONESCU who on 7 September told the German military attache in Bucharest, Colonel GERSTENBERG, that the Rumanian army would like to have German officers serve as instructors at the war college and the military schools, and as technical advisors on the Rumanian General Staff. Furthermore they considered desirable the assignment to Rumania of German mechanized troop units and air task forces as well as the transfer of materiel for antitank and active air defense; in addition, he requested that a German general be sent to Bucharest in the near future to carry on discussions concerning the future collaboration between the German Wehrmacht and the Rumanian armed forces. General ANTONESCU furthermore stated that he intended to decrease the army and at the same time organize strong motorized and mechanized units and that he contemplated placing the focal point of defense at the eastern border while exposing the front lines facing Hungary and Bulgaria. He meant to cooperate with Germany to the fullest extent.

Two days later Admiral CANARIS returned from Rumania, where he had personally investigated the status of the temporary measures taken for the protection of the oil field region and where, among other things, he had detached some of the defense elements assembled at Ruscuk. He too considered it highly desirable to detach a German general to Bucharest at an early date for the purpose of concluding a military agreement. He stated that on the whole he had gained the impression that General ANTONESCU was master of the situation and that his regime would be lasting, although this would be true only as long as German forces remained victorious. In view of the fact that things had apparently calmed down, the order for "alert at a moment's notice," which had been issued to the army troops earmarked for Rumania's occupation, was rescinded on 10 September. Two days later this same order, given to the airborne troops and transportation units which had been scheduled for commitment, was also cancelled.

During the night of 13 September however, the German military attache in Bucharest, reported by radio increasing tension between General ANTONESCU and the nationalistic, anti-Semitic "Iron Guard," and that the latter planned to hold large-scale demonstrations throughout the country on 13 September, marking the birthday of their leader CODREANU who was shot in November 1938. In view of the fact that the situation had again become unsettled, he considered the immediate assignment of a German Military Mission an urgent necessity. Since it was not possible to effect the necessary preparations with such speed, HITLER, on 14 September, ordered that as a first step, Generalleutnant von TIPPELSKIRCH, the Assistant Chief of Staff for Intelligence on the General Staff, who until now had been directing the preliminary work in connection with the Military Mission, be sent to Bucharest. The reports received from there that same day indicated that the demonstrations of the Iron Guard had been peaceful and that their leader, Horia SIMA, and General ANTONESCU had reached an understanding. This was evidenced by the fact that the Cabinet was reorganized and a royal decree issued, on 14 September, whereby Rumania was proclaimed a national legion state and the legion movement recognized as the only legal party in the new state. General ANTONESCU became the leader of the national legion state and chief of the legion regime, and in the new Cabinet, assumed the post of Minister of National Defense in addition to that of Prime Minister, while the commander of legionaries, Horia SIMA, was appointed

Vice-President of the cabinet council, and General PATROCICESCU, who had been proposed by the legionaries, was made Minister of the Interior.

General von TIPPELSKIRCH left for Bucharest on the evening of 14 September. On the next evening he had a conference with General ANTONESCU, at which they discussed all details, and on which occasion General ANTONESCU made the following statement:

> Rumania still feels threatened to a marked degree by her neighbors, particularly Soviet Russia. Consequently, it is Rumania's aim to achieve outwardly visible security, and, hence, her desire that the German guarantee of her borders be put into practice. To this end, Rumania requests speedy German aid in the form of planes, antiaircraft, motorized, and armored units which are to be sent to Rumania under cover of the military mission. The units in question are to be sent with complete instructor personnel who are to give the Rumanian troops tactical and technical training in the use of the materiel, which should later on be turned over to Rumania.

In discussing his plans for the reorganization of the Rumanian Army, General ANTONESCU stated that the future army was to consist of roughly 100,000 enlisted men and 5,000 officers and was to be organized similarly to the former German 100,000-man army. It was to be equipped with the latest type of arms, particularly by antitank and antiaircraft weapons, motorized to a large extent, and led by young commanders. The combined arms brigade was to constitute the nucleus, and was to consist of a reinforced motorized brigade with two infantry regiments of two battalions each, one motorized artillery regiment, and one armored regiment, and was to combine a high degree of mobility and intense fire power.

Following General von TIPPELSKIRCH's report on this conference with

General ANTONESCU, which continued for two more days, HITLER, on 19 September, decided that, contrary to the Rumanian proposals, it was above all necessary to send German troops, approximately one division strong, to Rumania, and that this should be done as soon as possible. He disapproved the transfer of German war materiel to Rumania during the war but stipulated that during future negotiations with the Rumanian Government, this question was to remain open for the time being. The Foreign Office was instructed to approach the Hungarian Government concerning the transportation of these troops through Hungary and to duly inform the Soviet Union of the fact that the Military Mission had been sent to Rumania.

Thereupon, the 13th motorized Infantry Division was assigned as an instruction unit and orders were issued that this division be reinforced by the 4th Panzer Regiment, one corps engineer battalion with two bridge columns, and one corps signal battalion with one intercept platoon. Beginning on 10 October, it was to be held in readiness for evacuation in the area north of Vienna. Generalleutnant HANSEN was appointed chief of the Military Mission. He was aided by Colonel HAUFFE acting as Chief of Staff, Lieutenant Colonel SCHWARZ serving as First General Staff Officer, and Major MERK acting as Supply Officer. This higher echelon of the staff was ordered to meet on 30 September, while the rest, together with the officers who had been appointed instructors at the Rumanian war college and service schools, was to convene in Dresden on 10 October. On 30 September General HANSEN reported to HITLER for instructions. HITLER emphasized the necessity for keeping together the forces at his disposal for the protection of the German oil interests in Rumania, and in addition, with respect to Russia, warned him against attracting too much attention.

General SPEIDEL was appointed Chief of the Air Force Mission which was to be sent to Rumania at the same time. It was proposed that for the time being, the so-called "instruction unit" be composed of the following: one reinforced fighter group consisting of four squadrons and two reconnaissance squadron as well as a number of light and medium antiaircraft batteries. Attaching this Air Force Mission to the Military Mission was a difficult task. Since GOERING flatly refused to have the Air Force Mission under the control of General HANSEN and HITLER yielded, as he usually did, to GOERING's demands no matter how unjustified they were, there was no other alternative but to place both missions on an equal footing. In case of disagreements between the two mission chiefs, it was up to the Chief of OKW (Wehrmacht High Command) to settle their dispute, while it was incumbent on the Chief of the Military Mission, as the senior general, to safeguard the interests of the entire Wehrmacht with the Rumanian Government. These stipulations were incorporated in the directive compiled by the OKW (Wehrmacht High Command). However, negotiations with the Foreign Office concerning the assignment of the Military Mission were still pending. This Mission had high political significance by reason of the fact that world opinion was already vitally concerned with it. In order that the arrival of the German troops in Rumania should not unduly undermine the prestige of the Rumanian Government, and strain relations with the Soviet Union, the Foreign Office endeavored to obtain for the German ambassador in Bucharest greater authority in all questions affecting the Military Mission, and, in addition, requested that the first transports be effected only with his approval.

After this had been established and the Hungarian Government had agreed to permit the transportation of German staffs and units through Hungary, the Chiefs of the Military Mission and Air Force Mission, together with their advance parties, left for Bucharest on 10 October. There they were greeted with enthusiasm. The remaining staffs left on 20 October, and, beginning 24 October, were followed by the army troops, air force, and antiaircraft units. By the end of the month, the Air Force Mission had reached its destination in full force, whereas only about one-third of the reinforced 13th motorized Division had arrived; the transportation of the remaining elements dragged on until nearly the middle of November. During the second half of October, one military economic staff and one special OKW (Wehrmacht High Command) agency of the Office of Wehrmacht Communications were also dispatched to Rumania. The enthusiasm first felt by the Rumanian people relative to the arrival of the German troops was somewhat dampened by the high costs of the Military Mission which, according to agreement, had to be borne by the Rumanian Government. These costs comprised almost one-sixth of the entire Rumanian budget, and, before long, this situation led to the presentation of vigorous protests to Berlin by the Rumanian Government. The attitude of the Soviet Union towards the assignment of the German Military Mission is not known. It might be deduced, however, that they viewed German aims on the Balkans with suspicion in view of the fact that, at the end of October, four Russian officers arrived at the Soviet Embassy in Bucharest to act as observers with the German forces. In addition on 26 October, the Russians occupied three islands located in the Danube Delta between Ismail and Chilia Noua. The purpose of this move was not readily evident. In any case, it seemed advisable to observe proceedings at the northern border of Dobrudja with increased vigilance.

On that same day, 26 October, a reorganization of the German field forces was put into effect which might be regarded as the first step in the concentration of forces against Soviet Russia. This had been preceded by the transfer, ordered during the last ten days of August, of the 1st Panzer Division to East Prussia and of ten divisions to Gouvernement General.* Shortly thereafter, on 5 September, instructions were issued to shift Army Group B under the command of Generalfeldmarschall von BOCK, in conjunction with Twelfth, Fourth, and Eighteenth Army Headquarters, from west to east and to effect this transfer by 24 October. In order to make available the necessary quarters in East Prussia for the field forces, the 141st and 151st Divisions which were stationed there and which constituted the replacement troops for the I Corps Area, were shifted to the Protectorate beginning on 14 September. On 17 September, Army Group B Headquarters moved to Berlin for a while and after 6 October, established themselves in their new headquarters at Posen. The Twelfth Army Headquarters (under Generalfeldmarschall LIST) was moved to Crakow, the Fourth

---

* See pages 10 and 14 (German original).

Army Headquarters (under Generalfeldmarschall von KLUGE) was shifted to Warsaw, and the Eighteenth Army Headquarters (under Generaloberst von KUECHLER) moved first to Bromberg and later to Koenigsberg. The headquarters of the reinforced army in Crakow under General of the Artillery ULUX, the Fifth Army Headquarters in Lodz under General of the Infantry LIEBMANN, and the headquarters of the reinforced army in Koenigsberg under General of the Cavalry Freiherr von GIENANTH which, since the fall of 1939, had been in command of the forces stationed in Gouvernement General and in East Prussia, were dissolved. On 30 October, the military command in Gouvernement General, with its attendant special duties and privileges which -- in accordance with Fuehrer directive of 19 October 1939, had been delegated to the OB East, Generaloberst BLASKOWITZ -- was assumed by General von BOCK, the Commander in Chief of Army Group B. He had now at his disposal in the east a total of 34 divisions, of which 30 divisions -- that is, 25 infantry and 3 armored divisions, one motorized infantry and one cavalry division -- were stationed in Gouvernement General and in East Prussia, while the remaining four divisions -- namely the 2d and 9th Panzer Divisions of the XXXX Army Corps, the 11th Panzer Division which had just been formed out of the 11th Rifle Brigade, and the 60th Infantry Division which had become a motorized division -- were committed in Austria.

While this regrouping in the east, which was concluded on 24 October, was taking place, the army forces in the west and in the Zone of Interior were undergoing reorganization. The Commander in Chief of Army Group A,

Generalfeldmarschall von RUNDSTEDT, was appointed OB West on 26 October. He was in command of all army forces stationed in France, Belgium, and Holland, comprising the following: The Ninth Army (under Generaloberst STRAUSS) and the Sixteenth Army (under Generaloberst BUSCH) of Army Group A which remained under his control, and the First Army of which General BLASKOWITZ assumed command, the Sixth Army (under Generalfeldmarschall von REICHENAU) and the Seventh Army (under Generaloberst DOLLMANN) of the newly organized Army Group D which was under the command of Generalfeldmarschall von WITZLEBEN, the former Commander in Chief of the First Army. The Second Army (under Generaloberst Freiherr von WEICHS) of Army Group C, which was under the command of Generalfeldmarschall Ritter von LEEB, was transferred to the Zone of Interior where the newly activated Eleventh Army of Generaloberst Ritter von SCHOBERT was also placed under the command of Army Group C. Finally, on 30 October, the Army High Command moved from Fontainebleau to the Zossen troop training grounds south of Berlin, which was an obvious sign that the strategic emphasis had been shifted from the west to the east and southeast.

In order to adequately prepare the Army for its future major tasks, it was decided that during the winter months the Army was to expand up to 166 divisions, including 20 armored divisions, 4 armored brigades, and 12 motorized divisions and that a fourth motorized SS division should also be activated. This required an increase in Wehrmacht strength which was attained through the induction of the age classes of 1919 (last third) and

1920. The Wehrmacht thus gained additional strength, bringing the total to 6,763,000 men, of which 4,900,000 men (72.5%) were assigned to the Army, 298,000 men (4.4%) to the Navy, 1,485,000 men (22%) to the Air Force and 80,000 men (1.1%) to the Waffen-SS.

Simultaneously with the regrouping of the Army and in accordance with the directive "Aufbau Ost" (Development of Eastern Territories), large drill grounds were constructed such as the Mitte Training Center at Radom, new quarters set up, the railway, road and communication network improved, supply centers established and the air defense organized; in short, all necessary preparations were made for the strategic concentration of forces against Soviet Russia. On the other hand, HITLER rejected a proposal made by the Army High Command as early as the beginning of September, which called for commitment of a special Air Force squadron for the purpose of making aerial photographs of Russian territory, because he feared that such measures might prematurely cause a conflict with the Soviet Union. Furthermore, at the beginning of October, he ordered General of the Infantry

---

* The registration of the last third of the age class of 1919 provided 208,500 men while the registration of the age class of 1920 brought a total of 613,264 men. The registration total of the age class of 1919 was reduced by 16,424 men with indispensability status and 124,300 volunteers already inducted, while 92,525 men with indispensability status and 201,982 volunteers were deducted from the total registration results of the age class of 1920, which left a sum total of 386,633 men. Of these men, 332,061 were assigned to the Army, 14,687 to the Navy, 49,672 to the Air Force, and 113 to the Waffen-SS. The reason for the small number of recruits allotted to the Waffen-SS lies in the fact that the Waffen-SS had already inducted 17,718 volunteers of these 1-1/3 age classes, which was 9,877 men more than their quota of 1.1% called for.

THOMAS, the Chief of the Wehrmacht Hi. Command Office for Economics and Armaments, to give highest production priority to Russian orders which had been placed in accordance with the Russo-German trade agreements of 19 August 1939 and 11 February 1940 respectively. The Russians, from the start, systematically and punctually had been making their deliveries which were of such vital importance for the German war economy, and, therefore, it was HITLER's aim to effect our shipments to them with greater speed than heretofore.

At the end of October HITLER was faced with an entirely new situation because of the Italian attack on Greece. It had been his endeavor from the very beginning to prevent the war from spreading to the Balkans, primarily because of the vital German oil interests in Rumania. Consequently, he was now, in view of the contemplated campaign against Soviet Russia, all the more concerned that peace should prevail in the southeast. Hence his vexation about the highhanded action on the part of Italy, which was apt to have serious political and military consequences and might ruin all his plans. The greatest danger at present was the possibility that the British might gain a foothold on the Greek Mainland and the Aegean Islands, which would imperil the Rumanian oil field region. HITLER was determined to guard against this by having strong German forces push forward from Bulgaria up to the coast of the Aegean Sea. However, this necessitated a great many political measures. Bulgaria had to be induced to join the military and friendship agreement, the so-called Three-Power Pact, which had been concluded on 27 September between Germany, Italy and Japan.

Bulgaria showed little inclination to take this step, especially since it was concerned about Turkey's attitude. In order to relieve them of this anxiety, HITLER intended to make an attempt to come to an understanding with Turkey. It was also necessary to win over Yugoslavia or at least bring about her friendly neutrality, because without such assurance HITLER considered it impossible to risk any operations in the Balkans. We had every reason to be convinced that Hungary and Rumania would shortly join the Three-Power Pact and that Hungary would allow the transportation through its territory of large German units, while Rumania would agree to the concentration of a German Army in its territory in preparation for a subsequent march into Bulgaria. However, it was by no means certain how the U.S.S.R. would react. Russia, time and again, had stressed her special interest in the Balkans and it was therefore highly doubtful whether it would be possible to induce Russia to turn her ambitions to the Orient. In addition, owing to the geographic and climatic conditions in the Balkans, the launching of an attack against Greece was now out of the question until next spring, which interfered with our plans for strategic concentration of forces against Russia. In any case it was necessary to effect this operation against Greece with such speed that by the beginning of May the units employed for this purpose would again be available for other commitments. HITLER looked upon the settling of the situation in the Mediterranean as the prerequisite for the campaign against Greece and therefore considered it the most urgent military task for the coming winter. To this end, it was his aim to convince Spain to enter the war soon so as to be able in joint action to seize Gibraltar and seal off the western exit of the Mediterranean.* He desired, at the same time, that the Italians should continue their offensive against Egypt and endeavor to reach Mersa Matruh, thus gaining an air base from which it would be possible for Italian and German air forces to attack the British Mediterranean Fleet which was stationed in Alexandria, and to mine the Suez Canal.**

In conformity with these plans HITLER, during the conference which has already been mentioned several times and which was held at the Berlin Reich Chancellery on 4 November ***, instructed the Commander in Chief of the Army and the Chief of the General Staff of the Army to make preparations for the attack on Gibraltar and the campaign against Greece. These instructions, together with additional orders covering the tentatively postponed Operation "SEELOEWE" **** and the commitment of German air forces in North Africa, were outlined in the "Fuehrer Directive # 18" which was signed by HITLER on 12 November and distributed to the Wehrmacht branches. The all-important eastern campaign was referred to in this directive with just a few words and the chapter in question reads as follows:

> "Political conferences, which aim at clarifying Russia's position for the near future, have been initiated. Regardless of what the outcome of these discussions may be, all preparations for the eastern campaign, which have already been ordered verbally, are to be continued. Directives in this connection will be issued as soon as the salient points of the operations plan of the Army have been submitted to and approved by me."

---

* See Chapter 4 (German original)
** See Chapter 5 (German original)
*** See Chapter 4, Chapter 5, Chapter 7, page 1 (German original)
**** See Chapter 3 (German original).

The conferences mentioned above began on that same day, 12 November, between the Reich Foreign Minister von RIBBENTROP and the Soviet Foreign Commissar MOLOTOV who, upon our invitation, had come to Berlin accompanied by a large staff. The Wehrmacht Operations Staff was only superficially informed of the result of these discussions. The main topic seemed to have been the relation of the Soviet Union to the partners of the Three-Power Pact and the coordination of mutual interests. Russia's joining the Three-Power Pact was evidently mentioned but it is questionable whether HITLER seriously desired it. He probably attached greatest importance to the "clarification of Russia's position during the coming months" as mentioned in "Fuehrer Directive # 18", namely the winter months up to the start of the eastern campaign, and to his aim, meanwhile, to divert Russia's ambitions towards the Orient. It is definite that the assignment of the Military Mission to Rumania was the subject of discussion and that MOLOTOV was also informed of the contemplated commitment of an aircraft warning company in Bulgaria. * The Soviet Foreign Commissar raised no objections to this and requested only that 200 men should be the maximum number sent and that they should wear civilian clothes only. At the same time, however, he emphasized Russia's special interest in Bulgaria and, with reference to the German Military Mission to Rumania, inquired what HITLER's reaction would be if Russia on her part should undertake to send a military mission to Bulgaria. HITLER replied that there was really no comparison, because the Rumanian Government had expressly requested Germany to send a military

---

* See Chapter 7, page 2 (German original).

mission, whereas the Bulgarian Government had thus far not yet approached Moscow with any proposal of this nature. This did not deter the Soviet Union from proposing to Bulgaria at the end of November that a mutual assistance pact be concluded and a military mission assigned. However, as has been mentioned previously,* this was turned down by the Sofia Government.

It is open to question whether during the Berlin conference MOLOTOV actually requested -- as asserted in the diplomatic note of the Foreign Office to the Soviet Union which was published on 22 June 1941 -- that Germany and Italy, should the need arise, support a proposal to be made by Russia, Turkey give up military bases at the Bosporus and the Dardanelles. This much, however, is certain: the question was broached and RIBBENTROP, or even HITLER himself, on that occasion called MOLOTOV's attention to the Princes Islands located at the southern entrance to the Bosporus. They also seem to have encouraged the Soviet Union's decision to request Turkey to return the Armenian territories of Kars and Ardahan which had been ceded to Turkey in 1917. In precisely this manner an attempt was made to divert Russia's attention from the Balkans and if possible involve her in a conflict with Turkey. Furthermore, Finland was discussed in great detail, at which point MOLOTOV protested against the transportation of German troops and supplies to Kirkenes via Northern Finland and emphasized the fact that the Soviet Union was vitally interested in the Petsamo nickel-ore mines. He also seems to have intimated

---

* See Chapter 7, page 9 (German original)

that Soviet Russia might feel compelled to resume her attack against Finland and would not want Germany to assist Finland in any way. In reply HITLER stressed that he had neither political nor territorial aims in Finland but was only concerned that there should not be any new Russo-Finnish war. With regard to the exploitation of the nickel-ore mines, an agreement was finally reached whereby 60 percent was to be allotted to Germany while Russia's share was to be 40 percent. These discussions were concluded on the evening of 13 November. MOLOTOV and his party left the next morning. It is doubtful whether HITLER was very pleased with the results of this conference, for it had not been possible to arrive at an absolute clarification of Russia's future position and much less still to divert her attention to the Orient. It was still necessary to reckon with the likelihood of Russia's interference in the Balkans, which considerably complicated our own plans, and by the same token there was no protection against unpleasant surprises far up north on the part of the Soviet Union.

On the afternoon of 14 November Admiral RAEDER reported to the Fuehrer on the situation as it appeared to the Navy General Staff. He called HITLER's attention with even greater emphasis than ever before * to the vital significance of the Mediterranean and North Africa for the over-all situation. He pointed out the following:

> Reports on hand clearly indicate that Great Britain is well aware of the dangers threatening there and is therefore determined to counteract this with all possible intensity. The statements made by British statesmen and high-ranking military men concerning England's forthcoming

---

* Particularly in his reports on 6 and 26 September respectively.

offensive operations; the political activity in Washington, Egypt, Palestine and Turkey; the large-scale military preparations being made in Egypt, West Africa and the mother country, England; as well as the current convoy movements are all unmistakable signs. To counteract all this it is of the utmost importance to retain the initiative in the entire Mediterranean area. To this end it seems essential to speed up the attack on Gibraltar and to give greater impetus to the Italian offensive against Egypt through increased German aid. England is and will always remain the chief opponent and all forces should be concentrated for her defeat. The simultaneous clash with Soviet Russia is liable to be too much of a strain on the Wehrmacht which might result in a long-drawn-out war. It would, therefore, be advisable to postpone this conflict until such a time as England should be defeated, all the more so since for the present, and probably also for some time to come there was no reason to fear that the Soviet Union would enter the war on the side of our enemies.

In reply to these statements HITLER merely remarked that it was impossible to expedite the planned operations in the Mediterranean and that these things take time. The Admiral's suggestion to postpone the campaign against Russia until a more propitious moment was apparently ignored altogether. He (HITLER) was at that time already too self-opiniated and too much imbued with his own importance as a statesman and military commander to let himself be influenced by the advice of his closest collaborators, even though it might be well-founded.

On 19 November General JODL had a discussion with General SPEIDEL, the Chief of the German Air Force Mission in Rumania. The latter reported that of late conditions in Rumania had become very critical. He made the following statements:

"General ANTONESCU stands completely alone and the Army as well as the Legionaries are against him. The Legion has ambitious plans, it claims command of the state as its due, but lacks leaders. Consequently, General ANTONESCU awaits further developments with some apprehension but is firmly resolved to maintain peace in the country with all means at his disposal. The attitude of the Soviet Union continues to arouse serious misgivings. Therefore, during his discussions with the two Mission Chiefs -- which are being conducted in an atmosphere of mutual trust -- General ANTONESCU keeps insisting on the speedy fulfilment of the agreements concluded with General von TIPPELSKIRCH in September. It is essential for the Military Mission to know what their line of action should be in case the Russians suddenly were to march into Moldavia."

General JODL promised that instructions covering such a contingency would soon be issued and that the problem of Rumanian arms requirements would be clarified during the forthcoming visit of General ANTONESCU.

The Rumanian Chief of State arrived in Berlin on 22 November and the next day ratified the treaty whereby Rumania joined the Three-Power Pact, which step had been effected by the Hungarian Government at Vienna three days previously. During ANTONESCU's visit, HITLER, as mentioned previously *, confided to ANTONESCU his plans for the Balkans and obtained the latter's consent to the assembly in Rumania of German fighting forces which had been earmarked for the attack on Greece, and to the contemplated increase for this purpose of the Military Mission which was to be enlarged by one armored division and additional air force units **. ANTONESCU, however, asked that Rumania be exempted from bearing the costs resulting from this increase, which request was granted. He also re   his demands

---

* See Chapter 7, page 4 (German original).

** During the middle of November two more fighter squadrons were added to the four fighter squadrons and two reconnaissance squadrons (see page 25 - German original) originally assigned to Rumania.

for allocation of antitank guns, antiaircraft guns, trucks and planes and was promised compliance with his request in the near future. An order issued during the following days in connection with the expansion of the Military Mission on the scale proposed also included guiding principles governing the line of action the German forces were to follow in case of a Russian invasion of Rumania. These instructions stipulated that border incidents were to be disregarded but that steps should be taken to guarantee protection against Russian attacks in the area of the German fighting forces on land and in the air and that major engagements should be put off until instructions had been received from the Fuehrer.

Immediately after General ANTONESCU's return to Bucharest, serious disturbances broke out in Rumania which indicated how unsettled the country's domestic affairs still were. During the night of 27 November, Legionaries, who had disinterred the body of Cornelius CODREANU *, the founder of the Iron Guard, stormed the prison at Jilava (south of Bucharest) and shot about 50 political prisoners. Despite immediate appeals by ANTONESCU and Horia SIMA, in which the Legionaries were beseeched to refrain from all illegal actions, numerous political murders and progroms still took place during the next few days. For all that, owing to severe measures taken by ANTONESCU, it was finally possible to reestablish order, although relations between ANTONESCU and the Legionaries continued to be strained. The German Military Mission was not affected by these developments.

---

* See page 22 (German original).

On 3 December, Admiral RAEDER, while reporting to the Fuehrer on the situation at sea, again urgently stressed the requirements for waging war against the chief opponent, England *, and once more warned him against undertakings which involved too great a risk, as they might lead to loss of prestige which should be avoided at all costs. Moreover, they would prolong the war and, above all, provoke the United States to an unfavorable attitude towards Germany. However, this appeal, too, had no effect, for by that time HITLER was already too unyielding in his determination to carry out his great eastern campaign to be dissuaded by arguments of this nature. HITLER considered it quite unlikely that America would enter the war on the side of the enemies within any measurable space of time. At the beginning of November, just before the American presidential election, he had expressed the opinion that ROOSEVELT's election would be more favorable for Germany than that of his opposing candidate WILKIE, because it seemed likely that the latter would speed up the American armament industry still more than ROOSEVELT. In addition, he had pointed out that both men had spoken against America's entering the war. After ROOSEVELT had been elected and it was reported he had declared that in the future one half of American industry would work for England and that, in addition to the 50 American destroyers sent to Great Britain in September 1940, he planned to supply England with more ships of this type, HITLER, nevertheless, remained convinced that ROOSEVELT would continue his efforts -- in

---

* See Chapter 3, Chapter 4, page 12 (German original).

which he was allegedly supported by the American Ambassador to London, Kennedy, -- to keep the United States out of the war. On 16 September, the Selective Training and Service Act was adopted in the United States, which provided for the registration of all men between the ages of 21 and 36, the yearly induction of up to 900,000 men for one year's training, and the expansion of the Army up to a total of 1,400,000 men.* However, it was the opinion of the German Military Attache in Washington, General von BOETTICHER, that it would not be possible before the beginning of 1942 to make available the major portion of a modern army. However, by then, HITLER believed that the campaign against Soviet Russia would have been victoriously concluded long since and that perhaps even Great Britain would be ready to come to terms.

On the afternoon of 5 December, two days after the above mentioned conversation with Admiral RAEDER, General von BRAUCHITSCH and General HALDER submitted to the Fuehrer in the Berlin Reich Chancellery, in the presence of General KEITEL and General JODL, the plans of the Army High Command for the execution of the Operations FELIX and MARITA respectively, and put before him the conclusions of the operations analysis which had been compiled, in connection with the contemplated campaign against the Soviet Union, in the Operations Division of the General Staff of the Army under

---

* According to a report of the German military attache in Washington, it was planned to bring the Army up to 35 divisions, namely 13 active and 22 reserve (civilian defense) divisions, and to increase the army and the navy air forces up to a total of 4000 planes each.

the direction of General PAULUS *. The operations plans ** which, for the same purpose, had been drawn up by the Department for National Defense had been submitted as early as 19 September to General JODL by Lieutenant Colonel von LOSSBERG, the First General Staff Officer of the Department. However, this plan was apparently not presented to HITLER and certainly did not affect the operations plan of the Army in any way; it can therefore be left out of account here.

The results of HITLER's conference with the two leading men of the Army, during which all questions were discussed in great detail, have been recorded by General JODL in an official memorandum, a kind of protocol, which was incorporated verbatim in the war diary of the Department for National Defense; it reads as follows: ***

"The Commander in Chief of the Army High Command states as follows: As regards Operation FELIX, emphasis until now has been placed on camouflage. On 6 December, the first reconnaissance staff comprising 15 officers in civilian clothes is leaving for Spain. If the operation is to be executed in the beginning of February, it will be necessary, in view of the fact that proper preparations take 38 days, to issue the appropriate instructions in the middle of December. The Commander in Chief of

---

* See page 8 (German original).

** See page 9 (German original).

*** The passages in the official memorandum dealing with Operation FELIX and Operation MARITA as well as the commitment of German air forces in the Mediterranean already have been quoted verbatim or the gist given in the previous chapters (Chapter 4, pages 12 to 17; Chapter 6, pages 2 to 3; Chapter 7, pages 4 to 6). Nevertheless, parts of it are quoted here again verbatim, so as to show clearly the simultaneous planning of these operations and the eastern campaign and how they were connected in regard to the time element.

the Army High Command proposes that General von REICHENAU be charged with the over-all command.

As far as Operation MARITA is concerned, it will not be possible to put it into effect until the beginning of March, when the snow will be melting. In view of the fact that the strategic concentration of forces will take 78 days, orders for this operation too should be issued in the middle of December.

In the east, the Army High Command hopes to be finished with the construction of the roads and railways by spring, provided no more motor vehicles are withdrawn. Preparations for the storing of supplies have been completed to the extent that it will be possible shortly to begin this operation.

As far as the duration of the planned actions is concerned, Operation FELIX will be concluded by the end of February and the troops committed to this end will again be available in the middle of May. The termination of Operation MARITA cannot be assessed with certainty; however, this operation will run at least 3 to 4 weeks, i.e. until the middle of April. The return transportation of the troops will take an additional four weeks and their rehabilitation will then require some extra time. Although these forces cannot be spared for the eastern campaign, it is essential that this operation begins at the earliest possible moment in order to be able to take full advantage of the season which is favorable for such operations.

Complying with the request of the Commander in Chief of Army High Command for a resume of the over-all situation, the Fuehrer makes the following statements: For the time being, German intervention in Libya is out of the question. It is not yet possible to obtain a complete picture of the situation in Albania. In case the Italians are repulsed still further, the danger exists that all of Albania will be lost. Yugoslavia apparently wants to wait until the situation in Albania is clarified before making a decision concerning her position. The most important factor in the Balkans is Russia which is making an attempt to gain control in Bulgaria since Rumania has been sealed off. This makes it evident that every weakness anywhere in Europe helps the Russians to push forward.

At present, the only way to help Italy is through the commitment of German air task forces out of Sicily (two groups of "Junkers 87") and out of Southern Italy (two groups of "Junkers 88") against the British Fleet in the Mediterranean, as well as through the capture of Gibralter. The latter step is also necessary because of other reasons. In consequence of the new developments, France in substance refuses to cede anything to Italy and in this connection uses as an argument the possibility that French-Africa might break away from the PETAIN Government. However, this contingency will cease to exist as soon as a few German divisions are stationed in Morocco or dispatched there promptly. This will make it possible to set a different tone in dealing with the PETAIN Government. Moreover, the psychological effect of the fall of Gibraltar will be considerable and the blocking of the western entrance of the Mediterranean will be an important step.

Our warnings that attacks launched from Greece against German spheres of interest would be followed by reprisals have resulted till now in no such attacks having been effected. In all probability, this will continue to be the case during the next few months. Nevertheless, German action against Greece is essential in order to settle the situation once and for all, -- unless Greece of her own accord would end the conflict with Italy and force the British to abandon her bases in Greece. In that case, our intervention will have become unnecessary, because the issue of European hegemony will not be decided in this territory.

The strategic concentration of forces for Operation MARITA is therefore absolutely essential. Even if its execution becomes superfluous, the assembly of troops can still be turned to advantage, because the forces committed for this purpose are then immediately available for the eastern campaign. There is no doubt that, in case of an eastern campaign, Rumania as well as Finland will side with Germany.

The planned operations will be executed in the following order:

1) The air attack on the British Fleet in the eastern Mediterranean will be launched beginning 15 December;

2) the attack on Gibraltar is to start the beginning of February and end four weeks later;

3) the campaign against Greece is to be launched the beginning of March; if conditions are favorable it will be concluded the end of March, however, it might take until the end of April. In the latter case, however, it will probably not be necessary to employ all forces until the end.

It is desirable to win over Yugoslavia to the side of the Axis powers, for which there seems to be a possibility if the Italian forces at the Albanian front are brought to a standstill.

In answer to the question of the Commander in Chief of the Army High Command whether the Fuehrer considers the German Air Force strong enough to be able to continue the air war against England in addition to the eastern campaign, the Fuehrer states that in the spring of 1941, the British air force will not be stronger than it is today and consequently will not be able to conduct any daytime raids against Germany, whereas the

German Air Force, in view of its present moderate losses, will be stronger in the spring of 1941 than it is now. Thus, the success of the defensive air war against England is assured, even if good-sized portions of the fighter formations and antiaircraft units are committed in the east, and it will be possible to continue large-scale night nuisance raids against England during a short eastern campaign.

The Russian armed forces are inferior to the German Wehrmacht with respect to armament and personnel, particularly as far as the command set-up is concerned. Consequently, the present moment is especially favorable for an eastern campaign. It is to be expected that the Russian Army, once it is weakened, will face an even greater collapse than was the case with the fall of France in 1940. The main thing to bear in mind is that the Russians should not be driven back in a body, but that on the contrary, after the front has been penetrated, large portions of the Russian Army should be encircled. The eastern campaign will come to a conclusion with the establishment of a line approximately on a line with the Volga, from where raids will have to be conducted for the destruction of armament factories which are located further off. Following that, new buffer states (Ukraine, White Russia, Lithuania, Latvia) will be established and Rumania, Gouvernement General and Finland will be enlarged; about 60 divisions have to remain in the east.

In conclusion, the Fuehrer decrees that Operation FELIX is to be executed as soon as possible and that complete preparations are to be made for Operation MARITA as well as the eastern campaign. The divisions on leave * should be recalled, but if at all possible, not before February. The eastern campaign will begin at the earliest in the middle of May, if the winter is a normal one. The Fuehrer no longer considers it possible for Operation SEALOEWE to be carried out.

The Commander in Chief of Army High Command inquires whether lending aid to the Italians in Albania is altogether out of the question, and the Fuehrer replies that he can see no possibility for it. The Commander in Chief of Army High Command also asks how many troops are to be sent to North Africa after Gibraltar has been taken, and in reply the Fuehrer states that one armored unit and one motorized unit are to be earmarked for that purpose."

---

* In a decree dated 28 September 1940, HITLER had ordered that 300,000 metal workers were to be withdrawn from the field forces and the replacement army and given a leave of absence in order to work in the armament industry during the winter months.

Following that, General HALDER presented the plans of the Army High Command for the execution of Operations FELIX and MARITA respectively. His statements as well as HITLER's comments and orders already have been quoted elsewhere *. The official memorandum then continues as follows:

"The Chief of the General Staff of the Army then reports on plans for the eastern campaign. First he enlarges on the geographical aspects. Then he states the following: The most important armament centers are located in the Ukraine, in Moscow and in Leningrad. The Ukraine furthermore has a surplus of agricultural products. The Pripyat Swamps divide the entire zone of operations into one northern and one southern part. In the latter the road network is poor. The best roads and railways are located in the Warsaw-Moscow area. Hence, the northern part of the zone of operations provides more favorable conditions for large-area operations than the southern part.

The area north of the Pripyat Swamps is therefore apparently occupied by a larger number of troops than the southern part of the zone of operations. In addition, the distribution of Russian forces indicates heavy concentration according to the conflicting Russian and German interests. It is reasonable to assume that the supply base of the Russians, which is protected by field fortifications, is located just east of the former Russo-Polish border. The Dnieper and Dvina Rivers constitute the most eastern line where the Russians will have to take a stand. If the Russian forces fall back any further, they will no longer be able to protect their industrial areas. Consequently, it should be our aim to prevent the Russians, by means of armored wedges, from establishing a closed defense line west of these two rivers. One particularly strong assault detachment is to advance from the area around Warsaw for an attack on Moscow. The three Army Groups assigned for operations are to be employed as follows: The one on the north is to be committed for an assault on Leningrad; the one in the center is to advance via Minsk for an attack on Smolensk; while the one on the south is to concentrate her forces for a push on Kiev. Of the last named Army Group, one army is to advance from the area around Lublin, a second army from the area about Lemberg, and a third one should proceed from Rumania. The Volga River and the Archangel area constitute the final objective of the over-all operation. On the whole, 105 infantry divisions and 33 armored and motorized divisions are to be employed, of which a large number (in the strength of two armies) will, in the beginning, follow in a second line.

---

* See Chapter 4, pages 13 to 17, and Chapter 7, pages 5 to 6 (German original).

The Fuehrer expresses his approval of the outlined operations plans and in this connection also states the following: The main object is to prevent the Russians from withdrawing in a body. The advance to the east should be effected to such an extent that the Russian air force will no longer be able to attack the Zone of Interior, while on the other hand, the German Air Force will be in a position to carry out raids for the destruction of the Russian armament industries. By this means we are bound to bring about the defeat of the Russian armed forces and prevent their revival.

The very first attack should be launched in such a manner as to make it possible to annihilate sizable numbers of enemy forces. To this end, the mobile troops should be committed at the inner wings of the two northern Army Groups, on which the chief emphasis of operations will also be placed. In the north, attempts should be made to encircle the enemy forces stationed in the Baltic States. To this end, it is necessary to reinforce the Army Group which is to launch the attack on Moscow to such a degree that considerable portions will be able to pivot to the north. The Army Group advancing south of the Pripyat Swamps should not launch the attack until later, some of its elements possibly advancing from Rumania, and should endeavor to encircle large numbers of enemy forces in the Ukraine by means of an enveloping attack from the north. At this moment, it is not yet possible to decide whether -- after the bulk of the Russian forces encircled in the north and in the south has been annihilated -- we will advance on Moscow or to the region east thereof. What matters most is to prevent the Russians from reestablishing themselves in the rear. The 130 - 140 divisions earmarked for the over-all operations are considered sufficient.

In conclusion, the Chief of the General Staff of the Army reports that eight weeks will be required for the concentration of troops for action, and that from the beginning or the middle of April, it will no longer be possible to keep the operations secret. Finally, 37 divisions will still remain in occupied France and Belgium, while one division each will be left in Holland, Denmark and the Protectorate, and 8 divisions will still be stationed in Norway; some portions of the latter will be utilized for the eastern campaign. In addition, the Instruction Division and the Airborne Division are still available."

On the day following this conference, General JODL gave the Chief of the Department for National Defense instructions for the compiling of directives of the Supreme Command governing the air war in the eastern Mediterranean, the Operations FELIX and MARITA respectively, and the eastern campaign. On this occasion, he also stated the following:

> "The Fuehrer is firmly resolved to carry out the eastern campaign -- which, with respect to the time element and locality is to a certain extent connected with Operation MARITA -- because the Army will never again attain the great strength it has at present. In addition, Russia only recently -- by her attempt to dissuade Bulgaria from joining the Three-Power Pact -- has proven again that she will always try, whenever possible, to stand in Germany's way. We can definitely count on Rumania's and Finland's participation in the eastern campaign."

On 12 December, a first draft of the directive covering Operation FRITZ -- which, at first, was the cover name for the eastern campaign -- was submitted to the Chief of the Wehrmacht Operations Staff. Lieutenant Commander JUNGE, the Naval Staff Officer attached to the Department for National Defense, took advantage of this opportunity to again point out -- in an estimate of the situation presented from the standpoint of the Navy and with a view to a two-front war against England and Russia -- that Germany, in view of the fact that the hampering of naval warfare against England would be the inevitable result, should not engage in a war with the Soviet Union, as long as she was compelled to put forth all her strength to defeat Great Britain. In view of HITLER's determination, it was to be expected that this warning, the same as all previous ones, would have no effect and besides, General JODL did not agree with the ideas of the Navy

General Staff but, on the contrary, was imbued with the conviction that his lord and master in this case too, with the intuition of a genius, had again chosen the only right way; consequently, the situation estimate was not even put before HITLER.

On 17 December, General JODL, after making some slight improvements, submitted the draft for the directive covering Operation FRITZ, and at that occasion, was informed of an important change affecting the mission of the Army Group which was scheduled for commitment north of the Pripyat Marshes. During the conference held on 5 December, the Chief of the General Staff of the Army, commenting on the strategic plans, had expressed himself to the effect that an especially large armored wedge should advance from the area around Warsaw for an attack on Moscow and that of the three assigned Army Groups, the one on the north should be committed against Leningrad, the one in the center should advance via Minsk for an assault on Smolensk, while the one on the south should attack Kiev with concentrated force. HITLER had approved these plans and had merely pointed to the necessity for making an attempt to encircle the enemy forces stationed in the Baltic States and had suggested that for this purpose, it would be necessary to strengthen the Army Group scheduled to attack Moscow to such an extent that large portions of the Army Group would be able to swing to the north. He had added that it was not yet possible to decide whether we would advance on Moscow or the area east thereof, after we had annihilated the bulk of the Russian forces which were encircled in the north and in the south. At the time the directive was compiled, this suggestion had not been set forth as clearly as HITLER wished; instead, it had been based primarily on the operations plan of the Army High Command which HITLER, to be sure, had approved and according to which the Army Group in the center, and particularly one especially strong armored wedge, was to push ahead via Minsk and Smolensk towards Moscow. In the meantime, however, HITLER had become still more convinced that the advance on Moscow should definitely be preceded by the annihilation of the enemy forces stationed in the Baltic States as well as the capture of Leningrad and Kronstadt, in order to eliminate the Russian Fleet the quickest way possible and bring about a speedy resumption of the flow of traffic in the Baltic Sea, particularly the shipments of ore coming from Lulea. Consequently, on 17 December, when the directive was submitted by the Chief of the Wehrmacht Operations Staff, HITLER once again explained to the latter with great emphasis how vitally important it was for large numbers of the mobile troops of the Army Group in the center, after they had penetrated the enemy front in White Russia, to pivot to the north, in order to destroy the enemy forces fighting in the Baltic States and capture Leningrad, in joint operation with the Army Group in the north. Not until this most vital mission had been accomplished should offensive operations against Moscow be continued. In this connection, he pointed out the great advantage of then being able to effect a converging advance from the west and the northwest against the Russian capital. Only in case of an unexpectedly rapid collapse of the Russian armed forces would it be expedient for the Army Group in the center to simultaneously pivot to the north and advance on Moscow. In addition,

HITLER stipulated that the former cover name for the eastern campaign be changed to Operation BARBAROSSA.

"Fuehrer Directive # 21" was revised accordingly, signed by HITLER on 18 December and distributed to the Wehrmacht branches that same day. Unfortunately, the text of the directive is not available in its original form but only in the final version which is contained in a supplement published in March 1941, with which I will deal later. This version differs from the one published by Peter de MENDELSSOHN * which was changed in part. I am quoting it herewith only insofar as it corresponds to the one issued on 18 December:

---

* Peter de MENDELSSOHN: Die Nuernberger Dokumente. Studien zur deutschen Kriegspolitik 1937 - 45.
(The Nuernberg Documents. Analyses of German Military Policy 1937 - 45).
Published by Wolfgang Krueger, Hamburg 1947. Pages 318 - 322.

"The Fuehrer and Supreme Commander of the Wehrmacht

Fuehrer Headquarters
18 December 1940

OKW/Wehrmacht Operations Staff/Department for National Defense (Group I)
No. 33 408/ 40 Top Secret.

Directive No. 21

Operation BARBAROSSA

The German Wehrmacht is to make preparations for <u>conquering Soviet Russia in a rapid campaign</u> (Operation BARBAROSSA), even before the war against England has come to a conclusion.

To this end, the <u>Army</u> will employ all available forces, with the exception of those required to protect the occupied territories against surprise attacks.

The <u>Air Force</u> will have the important task of making available for the support of the Army in the eastern campaign, forces in such strength as to make it possible to count on a speedy conclusion of the ground operations and the task of making sure that enemy air attacks will inflict as little damage as possible on the eastern German area. This concentration of forces in the east will be limited only insofar as it will be necessary to assign sufficient troops to adequately protect the entire combat zone and arms-producing region under our control against enemy air attacks, and to make sure that offensive operations against England, especially her supply shipments, will not come to a halt.

<u>Naval</u> operations definitely will continue to be concentrated against <u>England</u> even during the eastern campaign.

I shall issue the order for the <u>strategic concentration of forces</u> against Soviet Russia, if the occasion arises, eight weeks prior to the contemplated start of operations.

Those preparations which require a longer period to get under way should -- as far as this has not been done already -- be initiated immediately and be concluded by 15 May 1941.

However, it is of decisive importance to make sure that there is no indication of any plan to attack.

The preparations made by the High Commands are to be based on the following elements:

I. OVER-ALL OBJECTIVE:

The bulk of the Soviet Army stationed in western Russia is to be annihilated in bold operations and with far-extending drives of armored spearheads; the withdrawal to the rear of elements at fighting strength is to be prevented.

Thereupon a line will be reached in rapid pursuit, beyond which the Russian air force will no longer be able to attack the Zone of Interior. The final objective of the operation is the establishment of a general line from the Volga to Archangel which will constitute a covering line against Asiatic Russia. In this way, the Air Force, if necessary, will be able to destroy the last remaining Russian industrial areas in the Ural.

As a result of these operations, the Russian Baltic Fleet will be quickly deprived of its bases, which will render it unfit for combat. From the very beginning of the operation, we must, by means of powerful blows, prevent the Russian air force from taking any effective measures.

II. PROSPECTIVE ALLIES AND THEIR MISSIONS:

1. We can count on Rumania's and Finland's active participation in the war against Soviet Russia on the flanks of our operations.

The Wehrmacht High Command (OKW), in accordance with current requirements, will arrange and determine the manner whereby the fighting forces of these two countries will be placed under German command.

2. Rumania's task will consist in pinning down the enemy troops they are facing in joint operation with the German forces stationed there, and on the whole, in rendering assistance in the rear area.

3. Finland's mission will be to cover the strategic concentration of the German northern Army Group (portions of XXI Group) withdrawing from Norway and to carry out joint operations with this Group. In addition, Finland will be assigned the task of depriving the enemy of the use of Hango.

4. We have reason to believe that Swedish railways and roads will be available for the assembly march of the German northern Army Group at the latest beginning with the start of operations.

III. THE CONDUCT OF OPERATIONS:

A. **Army** (approval of the plans submitted to me):

In the zone of operations, which is devided by the Pripyat Marshes into one southern and one northern part, the emphasis will be placed in the north. Two Army Groups will be assigned here.

The Army Group in the southern part -- in the center of the over-all front -- will be charged with the mission to advance with particularly strong armored and motorized units from the area around Warsaw and north thereof and to rout the enemy forces in White Russia. This will perforce make it possible for large portions of the mobile troops to pivot to the north in order to be able to annihilate the enemy forces fighting in the Baltic States, in joint operation with the northern Army Group advancing from East Prussia in the general direction of Leningrad. Only after the success of this most urgent mission has been assured, which should be followed by the occupation of Leningrad and Kronstadt, should offensive operations for the capture of the important communication and armament center Moscow be continued.

A simultaneous attempt to accomplish both objectives could be justified only by a surprisingly rapid collapse of Russian resistance.

The protection of Norway is still the most important mission of the XXI Group, even during the eastern campaign. Those forces which are available beyond these requirements, will be committed in the north (Mountain Corps), first of all for the protection of the Petsamo region and its ore mines and also of the Arctic Sea Route. Following that, they will push forward, in joint operation with Finnish forces, for an attack against the Murmansk Railway and in order to prevent the land shipments of supplies destined for the Murmansk region. Whether or not it will be possible to conduct such an operation with larger numbers of German forces (2 - 3 divisions) advancing from the area of Rovaniemi and south thereof, depends on Sweden's willingness to place her railways at our disposal for such a strategic concentration.

The main body of the Finnish Army will be charged with the mission, in keeping with the progress made by the German northern wing, to tie down as many Russian forces as possible by attacking west of or on both sides of Ladoga Lake, and to take possession of Hango."

The two chapters of the directive quoted below cover the assignments of the southern Army Group and of the combined German-Rumanian Group, which was to be assembled in Moldavia, at the right Army Group wing. These chapters are available only in the wording contained in the supplement published in March 1941, with which I shall deal at the appropriate time. In the absence of their original version, we must content ourselves here with an approximate summary. The Army Group scheduled for commitment south of the Pripyat Marshes was to advance from the area around Lublin and push ahead with concentrated force in the general direction of Kiev, while the combined German-Rumanian Group, which was to be formed at the right wing of the southern Army Group, was charged with the task of protecting the Rumanian area and, following in the course of the northern wing of the Army Group, was to advance from Moldavia and push northeastward. The directive then continues as follows:

" As soon as the battles south and north of the Pripyat Marshes have been fought, the following objectives should be aimed at in the course of pursuit:

> In the _south_, the early capture of the Donetz Basin which is important from the viewpoint of military economics;
>
> in the _north_, the swift capture of Moscow.

The capture of this city means a decisive victory politically and economically and, in addition, spells the elimination of the Russian's most vital railway junction.

B. **Air Force:**

The Air Force will be charged with the responsibility to as far as possible paralyze the activities of the Russian air force and put it out of commission, and to support the operations of the Army at its points of main effort, particularly at the Army Group in the center and the wing which constitutes the focal point of the southern Army Group. The Russian railways -- depending on their relative value for the success of the operations -- are to be suspended or their most important nearby points (such as bridges!) captured in bold operations by parachute and airborne troops. In order to be able to concentrate all elements against the enemy air force and for the direct support of the Army, the armament industry should not be attacked during the major operations. Such attacks, particularly against the Ural region, are advisable only after the mobile operations have been concluded.

C. **Navy**:

In this campaign, the Navy is charged with the mission of preventing the escape of enemy naval forces from the Baltic Sea, besides safeguarding our own coast. In view of the fact that after the capture of Leningrad, the Russian Baltic Fleet will be deprived of its last stronghold and thus be placed in a hopeless position, major naval operations should be avoided prior to that. After the Russian Fleet has been put out of commission, it will be essential to safeguard the total maritime traffic in the Baltic Sea, including the supply shipments for the northern army wing (mine sweeping!).

All measures which will be taken by the Commanders in Chief on the basis of this directive should definitely concur in one point: they are to be referred to as precautionary measures, in case Russia should change her previous attitude towards us. The number of officers, who will be assigned to preliminary duties at an early date, is to be kept as small as possible. Additional participants are to be briefed as late as possible and then only to the extent essential for the functions of each individual. Otherwise the danger exists that if our preparations -- the execution date of which is still altogether indefinite -- become known, very serious political and military complications will be the result.

I await the reports of the Commanders in Chief concerning their future plans based on this directive.

All Wehrmacht branches will report to me via the Wehrmacht High Command (OKW) on the measures they contemplate, including their chronological progress.

signed: Adolf HITLER "

Although the wording of this directive hardly left room for any doubt concerning HITLER's determination to wage war against Soviet Russia, Admiral RAEDER still considered it imperative to make one last attempt to bring about a postponement of the eastern campaign until after England had been defeated. He also might have been encouraged to do so by the concluding statements of the directive to the effect that the execution date of Operation BARBAROSSA was as yet altogether indefinite. On 27 December, while reporting to HITLER, he stressed once more that strict concentration of the entire war apparatus against England as the chief opponent was the urgent necessity of the hour. He also stated the following:

> "On the one hand, Great Britain has gained in strength owing to the ill-fated Italian campaign in the eastern Mediterranean and due to increasing American aid. On the other hand, however, it is possible to deal her a fatal blow through cutting off her maritime traffic, which is already producing results. However, far too little is being done to promote U-boat construction and the development of the naval air arm. Germany's entire war potential should be employed to intensify the campaign against Great Britain, which means to strengthen the Navy and the Air Force. Any dividing of forces prolongs the war and endangers the ultimate success of the campaign. Consequently, the Navy General Staff, now as before, has serious misgivings about effecting this campaign before the defeat of England.

HITLER replied that U-boat construction should be promoted as much as possible and that the previous production of 12 to 18 boats per month should be increased. However, he stated that, in view of the present political developments and Russia's tendency towards interfering in Balkan affairs, it was absolutely necessary to first eliminate the Soviet Union, the last continental enemy, before thinking of the conquest of England. The Army should therefore be brought up to the required strength; only then would it be possible to fully concentrate on the Air Force and the Navy. Thus, as was to be expected, this last attempt of the Chief of Naval Operations to effect a postponement of the eastern campaign was also doomed to failure.

Directive # 21 constituted the basis for additional preparations for Operation BARBAROSSA on the part of the Wehrmacht branches. The Army High Command (OKH) now decided they would not wait until February, as requested by HITLER during the conference of 5 December, but would begin as early as the middle of January to recall to a large extent the field forces which had been placed at the disposal of the armament industry during the winter and the twenty divisions which had been sent to work in the Zone of Interior on a leave of absence, on the basis of the Fuehrer decree of 28 September. However, the Chief of the Wehrmacht High Command (OKW) managed to bring it about that the men were not recalled all at once but only in sections, after being replaced by civilians, and that the so-called "furlough divisions" too were called back only when needed and at certain intervals and for a while minus the armament workers. It was stipulated that those installations which were the most vital for the campaign against England should, for the time being, not be affected at all by this and the troops employed there should be organized to form an OKH reserve.

The task of procuring the necessary fuel for the contemplated operations involved considerable difficulties. On 28 November, General KEITEL

---

* See footnote on page 45 (German original).

had pointed out to the high commands of the Wehrmacht branches that during the last few months, the Wehrmacht's consumption of fuel for motor vehicles had been increasing steadily and to a marked degree -- in October, for instance, to about 100,000 tons of gasoline and 25,000 tons of motor fuel oil -- while on the other hand, the present situation, and particularly the great need for accumulating during the inactive months sufficient supplies for future operations, at the moment only warranted a maximum monthly consumption of 65,000 tons of gasoline and 20,000 tons of motor fuel oil. Therefore, he stressed that, effective immediately, the fuel ration should be adapted to this over-all quota. On 4 December, the Army High Command, which in matters of this kind was the competent authority for the three Wehrmacht branches, reported that the newly established allowance would not be sufficient for the tasks which had to be accomplished, but on the contrary, that the monthly requirements amounted to about 90,000 tons of gasoline and 27,000 tons of motor fuel oil and that even these quantities would be inadequate as soon as Operations FELIX and MARITA should get under way and as soon as the amount of supplies stored in the east should be increased, which probably would be in January. However, on 19 December, the Chief of the Wehrmacht High Command (OKW) was compelled to reply that a decisive curtailment of fuel consumption was an absolute necessity, lest in the Spring of 1941 we be faced with a shortage which would make it impossible to effect the contemplated large-area operations.

In view of these plans, it was absolutely necessary to make sure that there was no disruption of oil shipments from Rumania. Therefore, now as before, it was of the utmost importance to protect the Rumanian oil region against seizure by a third power. In the meantime, on the basis of the Wehrmacht High Command (OKW) directive issued on 26 November *, the Chief of the German Military Mission in Rumania had submitted his plans for the commitment of German instruction elements in case of military measures on the part of the Soviet Union. His report, which was received on 12 December, stated the following:

"The tactical grouping of Russian troops indicates a concentration of forces in Southern Bessarabia and in Bucovina. Consequently, we must reckon with the possibility of a westward thrust via Galati aimed at cutting off the Province of Moldavia and an advance from Bucovina in a southeasterly direction in order to roll up the Pruth River front.

The Rumanian plan of operations provides for the defense of the Pruth River front in a line running from Galati to Jassy and the withdrawal of the forces committed in Northern Moldavia and Southern Bucovina to a fortified field position extending from Jassy via Targu Neamt to the Carpathian Mountains. In case of a Russian break-through this line or the Pruth River front line, and in the event of a thrust via the Eastern Carpathian Mountains on the part of Hungary, the Province of Moldavia should be given up and a line of defense set up in a prearranged support position extending from Braila over Focsani to the Trotusul Valley.

However, instead of the above, the German Military Mission has proposed to the Rumanian General Staff that the eastern and northeastern borders of the Moldavia Province, with the exception of the northeastern corner, be defended to the last, in order to prevent the enemy from breaking through at Galati and to stop enemy troops from pushing forward from Bucovina on both sides of the Sereth River. The German instruction elements would support the Rumanian armed forces in these operations. In case of an impending Russian attack, they are to be massed in the Focsani - Ramnicul Sarat - Buzau - Sereth sector for offensive defense against enemy

---

* See page 38 (German original).

attacks at Galati or a Russian thrust from Bucovina. The assembly of these forces will be concluded within eighteen hours of receipt of marching orders. The units of the German Air Force stationed in Rumania will, in the main, be charged with the mission to protect the Ploesti oil region.

In order to avoid any incidents at the Russo-Rumanian border, the Military Mission has decreed that a zone, 5 kilometers in width, be established along this border, which members of the German Wehrmacht are forbidden to enter. On the other hand, they have issued instructions to the German Wehrmacht to repulse any Russian attack, and in such cases to launch immediate counterattacks with all means at their disposal. The 16th Panzer Division*, which has been on the approach route since 15 December, will for a short while serve as reserve of the Chief of the Military Mission, in order to be ready, if called upon, to be employed either in Northern Moldavia, after crossing the tip of Hungary, or in Southern Moldavia, advancing via Brasov and Buzau."

HITLER expressed his approval with these plans.

At the end of December, there began the transportation to Rumania of the advance echelon of the assembling Twelfth Army. In conformity with a request by Bulgaria, the two armored divisions which arrived first (the 5th and 11th) were billeted in and around Cernevoda, so as to make it possible for these divisions to resist a Russian penetration of Dobrudja and check a push on Varna, which Bulgaria feared might happen.**

On 9 January 1941, a meeting took place at the Berghof which already has been mentioned several times.*** This conference was held by HITLER with General von BRAUCHITSCH, the Deputy Chief of Operations and the Chief of the Operations Division of the General Staff of the Army, the Chief of

---

* See Chapter 7, page 4 (German original).

** See Chapter 7, page 10 etc. (German original).

*** See Chapter 4, page 19; Chapter 5, page 36 etc.; Chapter 6, page 8 etc.; and Chapter 7, page 11 etc. (German original).

the Operations Division of the Navy General Staff and the Chief of the General Staff of the Air Force, and was also attended by General KEITEL and General JODL. The main topics of discussion were the measures to be taken in support of the Italian campaigns in Libya and Albania, the additional preparations for Operation MARITA and the procedure to be followed in conducting Operation ATTILA*. The only thing of interest in this connection is the remark made by the Commander in Chief of the Army High Command to the effect that the units committed for Operation MARITA would not in any case participate in the eastern campaign. In this connection HITLER stated that the forces earmarked for protection against Turkey as well as some of the other units could probably soon be withdrawn for commitment in the eastern campaign.

Supplementing these discussions, HITLER, addressing the members of the conference in the presence of the German Foreign Minister, set forth his views concerning the over-all military/political situation. The gist of his statements was as follows:

At the time, he viewed the chances for success of the campaigns in Poland and in the west with optimism, because cool-headed reflection had

---

* Owing to reports received at the beginning of December, we had become apprehensive that General WEYGAND and the French Colonies in North and West Africa might break away from the PETAIN Government. In that event, HITLER planned to immediately seize unoccupied France and on 11 December had issued Fuehrer Directive # 19, in which he instructed the Wehrmacht branches to take the necessary measures for this purpose. These preparations were referred to by the cover name "Operation ATTILA". See Chapter 10.

convinced him that the claims made by the enemy powers with respect to their gigantic armament program could not possibly be true, owing to economic reasons. For instance, Germany's production of iron has been greater than that of England and France combined. Likewise, Germany has produced far more aluminum than these two nations and, in addition, has had larger numbers of workers at her disposal. Besides, democracies are not in a position to increase their economic power to the extent possible in Germany. He has arrived at the same conclusion after studying the financial expenditures of the enemy nations. In addition to all that, the German Wehrmacht definitely has taken the lead in technical knowledge. Such an analysis of economic, financial and military affairs can be depended on, and should also be applied at this time while evaluating the situation.

Norway is under our firm control and her protection is assured; it is not likely that British forces will make any landings there, and the only possibility to be considered is that of English nuisance raids.

The occupied western territories are threatened only by the British Air Force. The following situation exists in France: She has stumbled into the war and the first disillusionment took place in the Fall of 1939; the crushing defeat she suffered in the Summer of 1940 was utterly beyond anything the French had expected and the result was inevitable. At the present time, a certain change of attitude has set in owing to the Greek victories in Albania. In the occupied territory, the people have only one desire: to end the war as soon as possible. In unoccupied France, some portions of the population and of the Army too still entertained hopes for a change of the situation; these people are still willing to resist Germany. On the whole, there is a growing tendency not to commit oneself. This is true of North Africa to an even greater degree. The entire French nation unanimously opposes the cession to Italy of Nice, Corsica and Tunis. The de GAULLE movement is certainly troublesome for the French VICHY Government, but has also gained many followers in France. Particularly dangerous is General WEYGAND, who undoubtedly has told Marshal PETAIN he would make North Africa independent if the PETAIN Government takes up the fight against England. Consequently, the French Government is in a dilemma. At the moment, opposition to Germany is increasing, although responsible military authorities are quite aware of the fact that France is weak and helpless. The preparations for Operation ATTILA have not remained a secret, which has made the French all the more inclined to await developments. Since LAVAL's dismissal *, Germany is no longer under any obligation, and that is all the better.

Spain's attitude is one of hesitation. Although there is apparently little chance for success, another attempt will be made to convince the Spanish Government to enter the war.

In the Balkans, Rumania shows a friendly attitude; Bulgaria is loyal to the Axis powers. King BORIS' hesitation in joining the Three-Power Pact has been motivated by fear. As a result, he has been under pressure by Russia, whose aim it is to be able to use Bulgaria as a concentration area

---

* Pierre LAVAL, Vice-President of the French Council of Ministers, was dismissed from his post by Marshal PETAIN on 13 December 1940. See Chapter 10.

for action against the Bosporus. Since then Bulgaria is determined to join the Three-Power Pact. Yugoslavia maintains a cautious attitude; she wants to win without any active intervention on her part, and therefore withholds her decision.

In these territories, a change to the detriment of Germany is out of the question. Even the loss of North Africa would, from a military viewpoint, only restore the situation as it existed prior to 25 June 1940. Consequently, Germany's over-all situation is far more favorable than it was on 1 September 1939.

An invasion of England is possible only after complete control of the air has been achieved and she has suffered a definite loss of power; otherwise it would be a crime to undertake it. The British, in fighting the war, ultimately aim at defeating Germany on the Continent; however, their own resources are not sufficient to accomplish this. The British Navy, owing to its commitment on two widely separated theaters of war, is weaker than ever and is not in a position to effect major reinforcements to any decisive degree. The British Air Force has been very adversely affected by the bottlenecks in the supply of British raw materials resulting from the stoppage of imports, especially of aluminum, and also by the effects of the German air and naval attacks on British industries. Their own aircraft industry has been impaired to such an extent that instead of an increase there has been a curtailment of production. These damaging attacks by the German Air Force should be continued even more systematically than heretofore. Finally, as far as the British Army is concerned, there is no chance of its functioning as an invasion army. The main thing which keeps England going is the hope for aid from the United States and Soviet Russia, for the destruction of the English mother country is just a matter of time. However, England hopes to be able to hold out until she succeeds in effecting a large continental block against Germany. The diplomatic steps taken for this purpose are plainly evident.

STALIN, the leader of Russia, is a shrewd person; he will not openly come out against Germany, but we must reckon with the fact that in situations difficult for Germany, he will complicate matters to an increasing degree. It is STALIN's desire to fall heir to an impoverished Europe; besides, he stands in need of victories and is imbued with the drive to the west. He is also definitely aware of the fact that a total victory by Germany would place Soviet Russia in a very difficult position.

The British are sustained by the likelihood that Russia may enter the war. They will be out of the running only when this last hope left on the Continent is crushed. It is not his (HITLER's) belief that the English are "mad fools"; if they realize there is no longer any chance of winning the war, they will stop, for they know that if they lost the war they would be deprived of the power to hold the Empire together. However, if they could succeed in holding out and activating 40 - 50 divisions and should receive aid from the United States and Russia, Germany's situation would be very critical. This must not be allowed to happen.

Until now (HITLER continued), he has been guided by the principle to always smash the enemy's most important positions in order to advance.

Consequently, it is now necessary to defeat Russia. Then the British will either give in or Germany will be able to continue the fight against Great Britain under the most favorable conditions. Russia's defeat would also make it possible for Japan to attack the United States with all means at her disposal, which would prevent the latter from entering the war.

The time element plays a particularly important part in the defeat of Russia. Although the Russian armed forces resemble a giant made of clay and without a head, the nature of their future development cannot be predicted with certainty. Since it is necessary to conquer Russia in any case, it is preferable to do so now when Russia's armed forces lack leaders and are inadequately equipped, and while the Russians are struggling to overcome great difficulties in their armament industry, which has been developed with outside aid. Nevertheless, the Russians should not be underestimated even now, and it is therefore necessary to launch our attack with the greatest possible strength. Under no circumstances should the Russians be driven back in a frontal move. For this reason it is essential to effect the most savage penetrations. The most important task is the rapid cutting off of the Baltic Sea area; to this end it is necessary to especially reinforce the right wing of the German elements advancing north of the Pripyat Marshes. Distances in Russia are great, but not more so than those already being overcome by the German Wehrmacht. The operations are to be aimed at the annihilation of the Russian Army, the seizure of the most important industrial regions, and the destruction of the remaining industrial areas, particularly in the sector of Jekaterinburg; in addition, we should take possession of the district of Baku.

The defeat of the Soviet Union will mean a great relief for Germany. It would then be necessary for only 40 - 50 divisions to remain in the east, while it would be possible to reduce the Army and to devote the entire armament industry to production for the Air Force and the Navy. Then it will be necessary to set up a fully serviceable system of antiaircraft - artillery protection and to transfer the most important industries to regions which are not in danger. Germany will then be unassailable. Russia's immense territory contains boundless riches. Germany should control this area economically and politically, without annexing it. Germany would then command all potentialities to also wage future wars against continents; then it could no longer be defeated by anyone. When the eastern campaign has been carried out, Europe will hold her breath.

The 15th of May had been tentatively designated as the starting date of operations. In the meantime, the railways had begun preparations for the strategic concentration according to plan. On 17 January, General GERCKE, the Chief of the Wehrmacht transportation system, reported to the Wehrmacht Operations Staff that so far, out of the total of 8,500 kilometers of railways in the east, which had to be prepared for most intensive utilization, 40 percent double track and 30 percent single track railways already had been completed. Upon commencement of the assembly march, 36 trains would be running daily on each of the scheduled assembly routes. In view of the fact that Operation BARBAROSSA would considerably aggravate the already existing shortage of engines and railway cars, it was necessary to intensify accordingly the construction program of the Reich Railway.

The preparations for the eastern campaign were quite considerably handicapped because of the fact that they had to be carried out with the most perfect camouflage possible. It was essential to avoid anything which might make the Russians suspicious and prematurely cause strained relations with the Soviet Union. On 10 January, a new trade treaty as well as a boundary and resettlement agreement had been signed in Moscow. HITLER emphatically expressed his desire that the obligations specified in these agreements and undertaken by Germany should be fulfilled promptly. This complicated matters considerably, because the Russian requests submitted to the German industries conflicted with their shipments to the Wehrmacht. Nevertheless, the Russian deliveries were given priority status. Even in questions of a purely political nature HITLER exercised the greatest caution. At the beginning of January, he had issued instructions that the Soviet Union should not be informed of the German troop movements to Rumania until she herself should make inquiries. However, for the sake of maintaining more or less normal relations, he deemed it advisable to anticipate a Russian demarche by an explanation on our part. Consequently, on 12 January, the State Secretary of the Foreign Office, von WEIZSAECKER, notified the Russian Ambassador in Berlin, DEKANOSOW, of the concentration of forces in Rumania, and in this connection the reason specified presumably was the presence of British troops in Greece. Thereupon, the Soviet Union raised vehement objections in Berlin, with the result that HITLER issued orders to stop for the moment all visible preparations for the crossing of the Danube by the Twelfth Army. HITLER did not believe that the Twelfth Army's forthcoming entry into Bulgaria would bring on a war with Russia, but he thought it likely that the Soviet Union would make an attempt to induce Turkey to commit hostile acts against Germany.

As mentioned previously **, the Italian Government and the Wehrmacht Operations Staff were informed about Operation MARITA during conferences which took place between HITLER and MUSSOLINI at the Berghof and which lasted from 18 to 20 January. On the last day, HITLER enlarged upon his ideas and interpretations of the situation before the Duce, Count CIANO and the Italian Generals GUZZONI, GANDIN and MARRAS, in the presence of the Reich Foreign Minister and his party, the Chiefs of the Wehrmacht High Command (OKW) and the Wehrmacht Operations Staff, the authorized German General in Rome and the Chief Adjutant*** of the Wehrmacht; on this occasion, he also hinted at his attitude towards the Soviet Union, without, however, disclosing his true intentions.

HITLER started by pointing out that Finland, owing to its nickel-ore deposits, which were the only such deposits in Europe, was of great importance

---

* See Chapter 7, page 13 etc. (German original).

** See Chapter 7, page 14 etc. (German original).

*** Chief Adjutant to HITLER. The full designation was "Chef Adjutant der Wehrmacht beim Fuehrer." His responsibilities were much wider than is normally the case with an adjutant. They included coordination of the work of the Army, Navy and Air Force adjutants (who were really more or less liaison officers) attached to HITLER's headquarters, and control of the Army Personnel Office.

for Germany. Then he went on to point out that although the Russians have promised to supply Germany with the required quantities of nickel they will do this only as long as they consider it desirable. Therefore, no further interference in Finland must be allowed.

The assembly of German troops in Rumania has resulted in a demarche on the part of the Soviet Government, which will be duly rejected. The Russians always become insolent during those periods when the wheather makes it impossible to attack them. The strategic concentration in Rumania has a threefold purpose: To conduct a campaign against Greece, to protect Bulgaria against attacks on the part of Russia and Turkey, and to fulfill the guaranties given to Rumania. Each of these missions requires a special force; therefore, on the whole, it will be necessary to commit very large numbers of troops and their assembly will take a great deal of time.

It is desirable to effect this strategic concentration without enemy interference. Consequently, our plans should not be revealed prematurely, and it is therefore necessary to delay crossing the Danube as long as possible and then to launch the attack as early as possible. For this reason, it is also inadvisable to transport a German force to Albania at this time. If these troops remain behind the front, it will have an undesirable psychological effect; on the other hand, if they are committed for action, it would also prematurely set off the war in the southeast.

In all probability, Turkey will remain neutral. Things could become very unpleasant for us if Turkey would declare her solidarity with England and place her airfields at England's disposal.

However, (HITLER continued) the over-all situation in the east can be evaluated correctly only by taking as a basis the situation prevailing in the west. The attack on the British Isles is the final aim. Germany's situation in this connection resembles the predicament of a man who has only one shot left in his gun; if he misses, his situation will be much more critical than heretofore. By the same token, it would not be possible to effect another invasion, because a failure would involve too great a loss of materiel. Then it would no longer be necessary for England to worry about an invasion and she would be in a position to concentrate her forces wherever she wished and at any desired point of the perimeter. However, as long as the landings have not yet materialized the British will always have to consider the likelihood of an attack. The invasion, however, can be carried out only under certain conditions with regard to the weather, and these were not prevalent in the Fall.

The mission in the west also includes protection of the front extending from Kirkenes to the Spanish border against attacks from England. In addition, it is necessary to always keep in readiness one force in Southern France which would be able to take action in case England should gain a foothold in Portugal. The blocking of the Strait of Messina by the Air Force is but a poor substitute for the possession of Gibraltar. The plans for the attack on Gibraltar guarantee certain success. With Gibraltar in her possession, Germany would also be in a position to establish herself with strong forces in North Africa and thus put an end to WEYGAND's blackmailing. Therefore, if the Italian Government should succeed in finally convincing Franco to enter the war, it would be a great victory and within a short time would result in a fundamental change of the situation in the Mediterranean.

America, even if she participates in the war, does not represent any great danger. The giant block Russia is much more dangerous. Although Germany has concluded very advantageous political and economic agreements with the Soviet Union, it is better to rely on our power. To be sure, this would tie down a very considerable number of forces at the Russian border, which would make it impossible to provide the armament industry with the sufficient number of workers necessary to increase armament production for the Air Force and the Navy to maximum capacity. As long as STALIN, who is clever and prudent, is alive, there is probably no danger of any Russian attack; however, when he is gone it might be possible for the Jews, who are now keeping in the back ground, to again gain control. On the whole, the Russians are constantly endeavoring to read new claims into the agreements; that is why they also oppose any precise wording of such pacts. It is consequently necessary not to lose sight of the Russian factor and to protect ourselves with power and diplomatic skill. In the past, Russia constituted no danger whatsoever for Germany; however, today, in this age of aviation, it is possible to launch air raids out of Russia and the Mediterranean area on the Rumanian oil field region, which could reduce this territory to a smoking heap of ruins; and these oil fields are of vital importance for the Axis powers.

These statements were followed by HITLER's lengthy and didactic discourses concerning the determining factors in modern warfare, which are not of interest here. It is not known what impression HITLER's recital made on MUSSOLINI and his party. However, it is difficult to imagine that these views, some of which were really completely erroneous and foolhardy, had a very convincing effect.

Toward the end of January, the Eastern Foreign Armies Section of the Army General Staff coordinated the information they had obtained concerning the Red Army in a summary which was submitted to the Wehrmacht Operations Staff on 29 January. In this survey they estimated the peace strength of the Red Army at 100 rifle and 32 cavalry divisions as well as 24 motorized and mechanized brigades, all in all totalling 2 million men, while the war strength of the Russian field forces was calculated at 20 armies, 150 rifle divisions (15 of them motorized), 32 cavalry divisions and 36 motorized and mechanized brigades, with a sum total of roughly 4 million men. It was furthermore assumed that of these formations, 29 rifle and 7 cavalry divisions as well as 5 motorized and mechanized brigades were tied down in Asiatic Russia, so that it was necessary to reckon with 121 rifle and 25 cavalry divisions as well as 31 motorized and mechanized brigades in European Russia, although it was reasonable to assume that of these, 15 rifle divisions would be committed for protection against Finland and that 6 mountain divisions would be kept in the Caucasus. Owing to the absence of Russian figures, it is, for the present, not possible to ascertain to what extent these estimates were correct.

MS # C-065 i   -77-

On 1 February, the Army High Command (OKH) submitted to the Fuehrer the "initial assembly order" for Operation BARBAROSSA which had been compiled by the Operations Division of the General Staff. This order too, the same as "Fuehrer Directive # 21", was not published in its original form but in the later final version *, according to which -- owing to new instructions issued by HITLER in March 1941, which will be discussed later on -- the assignments for Army Group South and the armies under its command were changed through a supplement. The earlier version, with which we are concerned here, is not available. Consequently, as far as Army Group South is concerned, we must confine ourselves to general statements. Those portions of the initial assembly order which sets forth the assignments for the Army Groups and the armies and which deal with the over-all mission, the line of action the enemy is likely to follow, and our own aims, can be omitted here, because we are already familiar with the salient points through "Fuehrer Directive # 21" and records of HITLER's conferences with the Commander in Chief of Army High Command and the Chief of the General Staff.

The directive stipulated the following:

"The reinforced left wing of Army Group South under General von RUNDSTEDT will push forward from the area around Lublin in the direction of Kiev, annihilate the Russian forces in Galicia and in Western Ukraine while still west of the Dnieper River, and take prompt possession of the Dnieper bridges at and below Kiev in order to be able to continue operations on the other side of the Dnieper River.

---

* Peter de MENDELSSOHN, see also pages 332 - 339 (German original).

As part of this mission, the right wing of Army Group South, i.e. the <u>Twelfth Army</u> which is assembling in Moldavia, will safeguard the Rumanian area, which is of vital importance for the German conduct of the war, against a Russian attack and, following in the path of the northern wing of the Army Group, will advance, supported by armored elements, across the Pruth and Dniester Rivers in a northeasterly direction.

The bulk of the armored elements which has been combined to form the <u>First Panzer Army</u> will, in conjunction with the Seventeenth and the Sixth Army, penetrate the enemy defenses between Lemberg and Kowel and, advancing via the Berditschev - Shitomir sector, will speedily reach the Dnieper River at and below Kiev and then push forward along the Dnieper River in a southeasterly direction, in order to prevent the enemy forces, which are fighting in Galicia and Western Ukraine, from escaping across the Dnieper River and to annihilate them through a rear attack.

The <u>Seventeenth Army</u>, by vigorously pushing forward its left flank which is to be reinforced, will drive back the enemy to the southeast and, taking advantage of the assault by the armored elements, will quickly reach the Winniza - Berditschev area and then continue the attack either in a southeasterly or easterly direction, depending on the situation.

The <u>Sixth Army</u>, while covering the northern flank of the Army Group against attacks from the Pripyat Marshes, will send forward the largest possible number of forces to follow the Panzer Army as quickly as possible in the direction of Shitomir, in order to pivot to the southeast west of the Dnieper River and, in collaboration with the Panzer Army, prevent the enemy from escaping across the Dnieper River.

The <u>Army Group Center</u>, under the command of General von BOCK, is charged with the task of routing the enemy forces in White Russia and, by combining its mobile elements, which are to be moved up south and north of Minsk, will speedily reach the Smolensk area, thus making possible the coordinated action of large portions of its mobile elements and the Army Group North for the purpose of crushing the enemy forces fighting in the Baltic States and in the Leningrad region.

In addition, the <u>Second Panzer Army</u>, in combined operation with the Fourth Army, will penetrate the enemy lines at and north of Kobryn and, through a rapid advance towards Sluzk and Minsk together with the Third Panzer Army, which will push forward into the region north of Minsk, will bring about the destruction of the enemy forces stationed in the territory between Bialystok and Minsk. Then the Second Panzer Army, in close collaboration with the Third Panzer Army, will as speedily as possible reach the area of Smolensk and south thereof and prevent the assembling of enemy troops in the Upper Dnieper region, so as to make sure that freedom of action for further missions be retained by the Army Group.

The <u>Third Panzer Army</u>, in joint action with the Ninth Army, will break through the enemy lines north of Grodno, and by rapidly advancing to the region north of Minsk together with the Second Panzer Army, will make possible the annihilation of the enemy elements committed between Bialystok and Minsk. Thereupon, in close contact with the Second Panzer Army, it will reach the area of Witebsk and north thereof as speedily as possible and prevent the concentration of enemy forces in the Upper Dvina region, so as to make sure that the Army Group will retain freedom of action for additional operations.

The <u>Fourth Army</u> is assigned the task of attacking with concentrated effort on both sides of Brest-Litovsk and to force a crossing over the Bug River, thus clearing the way towards Minsk for the Second Panzer Army, enabling the majority of its units to push forward across the Sscrara River at Slonim and south thereof; and, taking advantage of the assault launched by the Panzer Armies, it will destroy the enemy troops stationed in the area between Bialystok and Minsk in cooperation with the Ninth Army. Then, following the Second Panzer Army and covering its southern flank against attacks from the Prinyat Marshes, it will force a crossing over the Beresina River between Bobruisk and Borissov and reach the Dnieper River at Mogilew and north thereof.

The <u>Ninth Army</u>, in joint action with the Third Panzer Army, will concentrate its forces at the northern wing and penetrate the enemy lines west and north of Grodno; it will then press forward in the direction of Lida and Vilna and, exploiting the advance of the Panzer Armies, will rout the enemy elements stationed between Bialystok and Minsk together with the Fourth Army and then, following the Third Panzer Army, will get up to the Dvina River at Polotsk and south thereof.

The <u>Army Group North</u>, under the command of General von LEEB, is charged with the mission of crushing the enemy forces committed in the Baltic States, and of occupying the Baltic harbors as well as capturing Leningrad and Kronstadt, thus depriving the Russian Fleet of its bases. The Army High Command (OKH) will take steps in due time to arrange for the joint action of Army Group North and strong elements of Army Group Center which will advance towards Smolensk. In addition, the Army Group will penetrate the enemy front by attacking with concentrated force in the direction of Dvinaburg and, sending ahead its mobile elements, will drive with its right flank, which is to be reinforced, as rapidly as possible to the region of Opotschka, in order to stop enemy troops at fighting strength from escaping eastward from the Baltic States and to make possible further rapid thrusts in the direction of Leningrad.

The Fourth Panzer Army, in joint action with the Sixteenth and the Eighteenth Army, will penetrate the enemy front line between Lake Wystit (east of Goldap) and the Tilsit-Schaulen road; they will push forward towards the Dvina River at and below Dvinaburg and establish bridgeheads at the northern banks of the river; they will then reach the area northeast of Opotsch as speedily as possible and from there advance either northeastward or northward, depending on the situation.

The Sixteenth Army, in collaboration with the Panzer Army, will attack the enemy they are facing with concentrated force on both sides of the Gumbinnen - Kowno road. While vigorously driving with its right flank, which is to be reinforced, to follow the Panzer Army, they will as speedily as possible reach the northern banks of the Dvina River at and below Dvinaburg and then follow the Panzer Army to the region of Opotschka.

Finally, the Eighteenth Army will pierce the line of the enemy it is facing with concentrated force at the Tilsit - Riga road and east thereof and, by rapidly driving the majority of its elements across the Dvina River at and below Stockmannshof (17 kilometers northwest of Jakobstadt), it will cut off and annihilate the enemy troops stationed southwest of Riga. In addition, it will, by rapidly pushing ahead towards the Ostrov - Pskov line, prevent the enemy troops from escaping south of Lake Peipus and, following the instructions of Army Group North, will -- possibly in conjunction with mobile forces stationed north of Lake Peipus -- clear Estonia of enemy elements. The arrangements for the occupation of the Baltic Islands Oesel (Saaremaa), Dagoe (Hiiumaa) and Moon (Muhu) will be made in such a manner that it will be possible to carry them out suddenly, as soon as the situation warrants it.

At the start of operations, the Army High Command (OKH) will bring up its reserves as follows: One strong group each will be assigned to the region of Reichshof (Rzeszov) and the area east of Warsaw, while one smaller group each will be brought up to the territories of Zamosc, Suwalki and Eydkau (Eydtkuhnen) respectively."

The following instructions were issued to the Army Headquarters Norway which was under direct command of the Wehrmacht High Command (OKW) * :

---

* Peter de MENDELSSOHN. See also pages 337/38 (German original).

"The most important task continues to be the certain protection of the entire Norwegian territory, not only against surprise raids but also against resolute invasion attempts on the part of the British, with which we must reckon during the course of the summer.

This mission requires

a) that first of all, the batteries earmarked for strengthening the coastal defense be set up by the middle of May with all possible energy and with the aid of all transportation facilities.

b) that the formations at present stationed in Norway not be weakened to any large extent through the operations conducted in connection with the BARBAROSSA campaign outside of Norway, but that they even be enlarged in the Kirkenes – Narvik sector which is the most vulnerable. Steps should be taken immediately to effect this reinforcement with the aid of elements already stationed in Norway.

In addition to these defensive functions, the Army Headquarters Norway is charged with the following mission:

a) At the beginning of operations, and if necessary even sooner, they will march into the Petsamo region and, together with Finnish forces, will protect it against attacks launched by land and sea and from the air; in this connection, the nickel mines, which are essential for German armaments, are particularly important. (Operation RENNTIER);

b) they will take action to reduce as far as possible the area of the Murmansk base for use as an installation for offensive operations by enemy land, sea and air forces and, if sufficient troops become available, they will take possession of this strong point. (Operation SILBERFUCHS).

In any case, it is to be expected that Sweden will herself safeguard her northeastern border with sufficiently large numbers of troops."

As far as the cooperation of other countries was concerned, the initial assembly order mentioned that we could rely on the active participation of Rumania and Finland in the campaign against the Soviet Union, and that the method of their collaborating and the placing of their fighting forces under German command would be regulated in due time.

It was stated that <u>Rumania</u> would be charged with the task of keeping occupied the enemy forces they were facing in conjunction with the German elements assembling there, and on the whole would be responsible for rendering assistance in the rear area. Finland, after depriving the enemy of the use of Hango at the earliest possible moment, was to be responsible for covering the assembly march of the German troops in Northern Finland. Her troops were to launch an attack -- at the latest when Army Group North would be crossing the Dvina River -- on the Russian forces committed before the Finnish southeastern front, with their main effort either east or west of Lake Ladoga, depending on the instructions of the Army High Command (OKH), and were to aid the Army Group in routing the enemy troops.

We were informed that we could presumably not count on Sweden's active participation, but that there was a chance that Sweden would permit the utilization of her railways for the assembly and the supply of German elements in Northern Finland.

On 3 February, the Chief of the Army General Staff, on the basis of this initial assembly order, reported to the Fuehrer at the Berghof concerning the contemplated mode of procedure in connection with Operation BARBAROSSA. This conference was also attended by the Commander in Chief of Army High Command, the Chief of the Operations Division of the Army General Staff, Colonel HEUSINGER, as well as General KEITEL and General JODL. The war diary of the Wehrmacht Operations Staff contains the following entry concerning this parley:

"The Chief of the Army General Staff states as follows:
It is to be expected that the enemy has available approximately 100 infantry,

25 cavalry and 30 mechanized divisions *". It is important to note that the Russian infantry divisions too have at their disposal a relatively large number of tanks; however, they are odds and ends of inferior quality. While the Russian Army possesses more mechanized divisions, the German mechanized divisions are superior in quality. The Russians have standard artillery equipment, but here too the materiel is inferior. Among the Russian leaders, only TIMOSCHENKO ** is outstanding. The aims of the Russian command are not plainly evident. Strong forces are committed at the border; a withdrawal is feasible only to a limited degree, because the Baltic States and the Ukraine, for reasons of supply, are of vital importance for the Soviet Union. The Russians are constructing fortifications, especially in the northern and southern part of the Russian western border.

The instructions issued to the three Army Groups are aimed at breaking up the Russian front, splitting it into two parts, and preventing the enemy from escaping across the Dnieper and Dvina Rivers. The armored elements of the Army Groups Center and North, which have been combined into three Armies, are charged with the mission to advance northeastward across the Dvina River towards Smolensk. The Panzer Army farthest to the north has been started off towards Lake Peipus and from there will advance further eastward in conjunction with the two other Panzer Armies which are on the march to Smolensk. Army Group South will push forward south of the Pripyat Marshes towards the Dnieper River, which it will cross. The point of main effort will be north of the Pripyat Marshes; consequently, the majority of the OHQ reserves will also be committed there. The two northern Army Groups all in all have at their disposal 50 infantry, 9 motorized and 13 armored divisions, while the southern Army Group has 30 infantry, 3 motorized and 5 armored divisions; and in addition there are the Army High Command (OKH) reserves. We are in need of the six armored divisions which are part of the forces assigned for Operation MARITA; we particularly require the

---

* In the survey compiled by the Eastern Foreign Armies Division of the Army General Staff (see page 73 - German original), the Russian armored formations were referred to as brigades, which probably was more in keeping with their strength and composition.

** TIMOSCHENKO was descended from Bessarabian small holders, fought in the civil war as a partisan leader and then led a squadron in BUDJONNY's cavalry army. As early as 1918, he was appointed division commander. In 1938, he became Commander in Chief of the Military District of Kiev, and on 8 May 1940, he assumed the post of People's Commissioner in charge of defense, taking the place of Marshal WOROSCHILOV.

two instruction divisions *. Whether or not it will be possible to withdraw all six divisions, will depend on the situation in the Balkans, especially Turkey's position, at the time Operation BARBAROSSA will be launched.

In this connection, the Fuehrer expresses himself to the effect that Turkey will take no action when the die is cast. Consequently, no special protection of the Balkans will be necessary. Danger will arise if all of Libya falls into British hands, because England would then be able to employ all her available forces against and in Syria.

HITLER states that he approves in principle the operations plan drawn up by the Army High Command (OKH) for the BARBAROSSA campaign. He also makes the following comments: The zones of operation involved are immense. We must aim at encircling large portions of the Russian Army; however, this will come off successfully only if we will be able to make an out-and-out effort. We cannot expect the Russians to immediately surrender the Baltic States as well as Leningrad and the Ukraine; however, there is a chance that, after the first reverses and in recognition of the German strategic objectives, the Russians will fall back on a large scale further eastward in order to reassemble for defense behind some barrier or other. In that case it will be necessary to first of all occupy the Baltic States and the Leningrad area regardless of the Russian troops stationed further eastward, because it will thus be possible to gain the best supply base for future operations. The important thing is to annihilate large numbers of enemy forces and not to put them to flight. This can be achieved only if the flanking areas are occupied by the strongest possible forces, while the center halts all action and then, operating from the flanks, by maneuvering the enemy out of the center.

The Chief of the Army General Staff continues as follows: One and a half divisions of the forces stationed in Norway are to advance against Petsamo, while another one and a half divisions, including one SS brigade, will be transported to Northern Finland on Swedish trains, provided we are able to utilize them. These troops will be charged with the mission to protect the industrial area of Northern Finland and to tie down and cut off

---

* This refers to the 2d, 5th, 9th and 11th Panzer Divisions of the Twelfth Army and the two so-called instruction divisions attached to the Military Mission in Rumania, which were the 13th motorized Division, which had been reinforced through the 4th Panzer Regiment, and the 16th Panzer Division.
(See Chapter 7, pages 3 to 8 - German original).

the Russian elements committed in the area of Murmansk. Finland plans to assemble approximately 4 infantry corps in the south; of these, 5 divisions will be committed for an attack on Leningrad, 3 divisions will advance against Lake Onega, and 2 divisions will launch an attack on Hango; however, they are in need of strong support*. At the Russo-Finnish border, 18 Russian divisions are massed, and in the area of Murmansk about one division is committed.

To this, the Fuehrer replies as follows: He assumes that Sweden will be willing to cooperate in return for possession of the Aland Islands. A Swedish-Finnish union is out of the question, because it does not fit into the new European order. Norway must be safeguarded against British attacks and setbacks must not be allowed to happen there; it is therefore absolutely necessary to strengthen her artillery coast defense. In Rumania, the protection of the oil field region is the most important task, which necessitates readiness for rapid advance out of Rumania.

The Chief of the Army General Staff then discusses Hungary's position. He remarks that even if Hungary does not participate in the operation, she should at least agree to the detraining of German troops in her territory. Rumania should be specified as the destination for these forces to march on, and only at the last moment will they pivot towards the Russian border.

The Fuehrer replies the following: Hungary will accede to all German demands in exchange for appropriate political assurances. However, the necessary discussions with the nations concerned should not take place until the last moment, with the exception of Rumania for whom active participation in the operations is of vital importance.

Then the Chief of Army General Staff reports on a number of special problems. He mentions that the question of antiaircraft artillery protection is still undecided; the Air Force intends to provide 30 battalions and the Army will set up 30 new batteries. The Navy should open the supply routes to the Baltic Sea harbors as speedily as possible. The problem of supplies will have to be solved by means of motor transports, since the Russian tracks first have to be adapted to standard European gauge. It is planned to employ long distance trucks which would bring provisions up to the supply bases. We must take steps, in collaboration with the Air Force, to make sure that no transportation elements remain idle. At present, we

---

* On 30 January, General HALDER had a discussion with the Finnish Chief of Staff, Generalleutnant HEINRICH, at which time they covered in great detail the matter of mutual collaboration in case of a war against the Soviet Union, and the above information was received on that occasion.

are engaged in developing advance supply districts in Eastern Poland; Rumania is still being reconnoitered with regard to the establishment of such supply districts.

Finally, the Chief of Army General Staff, with the aid of maps, also submits the plans for the contemplated time schedule of the initial assembly. At present, the transports of the first advance echelon are on the move. The transports of the second advance echelon, which will begin to move in the middle of March, will already transfer large number of reinforcements to the east, although for the time being just to the rear area. From that time forward, it will be possible only with great difficulty, owing to the shipments from the west, to carry out Operation ATTILA. The economic transports too will be considerably restricted by these movements. At the beginning of April, it will be necessary to approach Hungary concerning the passage of our troops through her territory. The transports of the third advance echelon will be set in motion in the middle of April and with that the maximum capacity schedule will go into effect. In view of the fact that the majority of the OHQ artillery will be transferred, it will then no longer be possible to effect Operation FELIX. At that juncture it will also no longer be possible to keep secret the initial assembly. The fourth advance echelon, which will take from 25 April to 16 May, will divert such large numbers of forces from the west, that Operation SEELOEWE too will then no longer be feasible. The strategic concentration in the east will then be plainly evident. It will be a difficult task to accomplish the timely return of the eight divisions earmarked for Operation MARITA *, which will be urgently needed for Operation BARBAROSSA.

The Fuehrer expresses his approval of the Army's plans. The world, he declares, will hold its breath, when Operation BARBAROSSA is executed."

Following this, the discussion, in which the Chief of Staff of the Air Force joined, turned to Italy's situation in the Mediterranean and the aid which would be rendered her by German forces, as has been already related previously **. Immediately after the conference, HITLER also made the following comments to the Chief of the Wehrmacht Operations Staff: Finland, Sweden, Hungary and Slovakia should be approached concerning their

---

* This probably refers to the six Panzer divisions and two infantry divisions which have been mentioned previously.
** See Chapter 6, page 19 etc. (German original).

participation or direct aid only when it will no longer be possible to disguise our objectives. Only the Rumanian Chief of State should be advised earlier that the time has come to reinforce the Rumanian elements in Moldavia. It is of the utmost importance to give the impression as long as possible that the strategic concentration in the east is a large-scale deceptive maneuver to divert attention from Operation SEALOEWE. The execution of Operation ATTILA should always remain feasible, even though to a limited extent. Consequently, the airborne corps should not be assigned in advance to Operation BARBAROSSA but should be held in readiness as reserve for all eventualities or emergencies.

On the day following the conference, Admiral RAEDER, while reporting to the Fuehrer on the situation at sea, submitted the plans of the Navy in connection with its functions during the eastern campaign. On this occasion too, HITLER emphasized how necessary it was, especially during the spring, for the enemy as well as our own Wehrmacht to be under the impression that the preparations for Operation BARBAROSSA merely served as a pretext to divert attention from an imminent invasion of England.

During further studies of the Army's operations plan, HITLER began to wonder whether the contemplated flank protection would be sufficient against attacks from the vast region of the Pripyat Marshes. On 5 February, he therefore requested the Army High Command (OKH) to submit an evaluation of this territory with respect to the likelihood of the establishment of enemy defensive installations and the possible commitment of Russian troops, particularly cavalry units, against the flanks of the Army Groups which would be advancing on both sides of the Pripyat Marshes.

The memorandum forwarded by the Army General Staff on 21 February reported the following findings:

> "Although the Pripyat - Polesien region is not suitable for large-scale military operations, we nevertheless have to consider the probability that some Russian mobile units, particularly cavalry divisions, operating chiefly on the tongues of land projecting into the swamp region west of Pinsk and east of Kowel, in the hilly country of Ovruch and the area southeast of Slutsk, might attack the flanks of the German assault troops which are facing the Pripyat Marshes. Apart from that, it is possible almost anywhere and at any time in Pripyat - Polesien to conduct operations on a small scale, up to regimental level, provided the existing difficulties are taken into account by careful reconnaissance and preparations. The Russians, who are fighting on their own territory, derive advantage from the fact that they are accustomed to difficult terrain and traffic conditions and besides, can rely on the voluntary support of the resident population which is familiar with the country. Constant surveillance from the air will be the best means to ascertain the movement and whereabouts of large enemy forces."

Thereupon, on 8 March, HITLER issued orders that the inside flanks of the Army Groups South and Center, committed at the tongues of land projecting into the Pripyat Marshes, should be protected through the installation of mine obstacles.

HITLER devoted special attention to the problem of Norway's coast defenses, because he, same as the Army High Command (OKH), expected the British to make resolute attempts to invade the Norwegian coast during the execution of the eastern campaign. The Army High Command (OKH) had made arrangements for the immediate transfer to Norway of 15 heavy batteries from captured stock together with the necessary personnel, which were to be under the command of the commanding general in charge of coast defense in Norway and which were to replace the division artillery stationed at the coast at the time. However, HITLER considered these measures insufficient, especially since this plan made no provision to reinforce the defensive equipment, consisting only of 150 mm guns, of Narvik, which was extremely important for the export of Swedish ore to Germany. Therefore, on 15 February, he issued a basic directive which covered the safeguarding of the coast lines from Kirkenes to the Spanish border against British attacks in case of large-scale operations at eastern theaters of war. In this order, the Commander in Chief West, who had been assigned by the Army High Command (OKH), was charged with the responsibility for the firm resistance against enemy attempts at landing on the coasts of the occupied western territories, and he was instructed to reinforce the garrisons at the British Channel Islands to such a degree that it would be possible to hold them even without the support of bomber units of the Air Force. The directive also stipulated the following: The strengthening of Norway's coast defense is foremost in importance. In this connection, it is particularly advisable to concentrate on Narvik, the Arctic Coast, and all those points where it might be possible for enemy naval forces or small landing parties to disrupt the coastal routes. We have to reckon with the fact that the British will also employ battle ships for this purpose. Besides, it is necessary for dive bombers, fighter airplanes and destroyers to be committed in Norway at all times for protection against enemy attacks at sea and from the air. In order to be able to manage with the smallest possible number of forces, it is advisable to organize combined echelons or to set up schools and courses of instruction. When assigning German naval forces, we must in the spring also take into account the fact that enemy operations at sea will not aim at the Bay of Helgoland but at Norway and the coasts of the occupied western territories.

The measures adopted thereupon by the three Wehrmacht branches had been put into effect only in part, and the majority of the coast batteries transported to Norway -- 55 naval batteries in addition to the 15 batteries provided by the Army -- were not yet ready for action, when a naval operation effected by the British confirmed the necessity for stronger protection of the Norwegian coast. On the morning of 4 March, British light naval forces -- reportedly two cruisers and four destroyers -- carried out a successful surprise raid on the harbor of Svolvaer (on the Lofoten Islands, approximately 110 kilometers west of Narvik), inflicted heavy damage on the steamer "Hamburg" which was berthed there, sank a large number of fishing vessels and took with them fifteen German soldiers and ten Quisling followers as well as three hundred Norwegians who voluntarily joined the British seamen who had landed. HITLER was greatly enraged about this event, demanded an investigation of the command setup and ordered the immediate strengthening of the coast defense system, particularly by means of artillery, for which purpose the Army was to provide additional 160 batteries. He also summoned the Wehrmacht Commander in Chief in Norway and the Admiral of the Arctic Coast to make personal reports to him. The conference with Generaloberst von FALKENHORST and Admiral BOEHM took place on 14 March in the Berlin Reich Chancellery. On this occasion, HITLER emphasized the fact that the Wehrmacht Commander in Chief was fully responsible for the internal security of Norway and its defense against enemy attacks from the outside, and issued instructions to commit the forces assigned for coast defense in support of the coast batteries and to distribute them in such a manner that enemy surprise raids would in future be impossible.

Another subject of HITLER's discussion with General von FALKENHORST was the mission which devolved on Norway Army Headquarters in Northern Finland as part of Operation BARBAROSSA. In this connection, HITLER laid particular stress on the well-timed occupation of the Petsamo region which, owing to the great importance of its nickel-ore mines for the German armament industry, at all costs had to be safeguarded against a Russian invasion. HITLER remarked that only recently, the Russo-Finnish negotiations held in Moscow concerning the exploitation of the mines, had again demonstrated Russia's great interest in this territory. They had come to a deadlock almost immediately, because Finland was not inclined to recognize Russia's claim to the control of the mines and to the shareholders' majority. On 8 February, Feldmarschall MANNERHEIM had pointed out to the German Military Attache in Helsinki that compliance with this request would mean that supplies for the German troops in Northern Norway going via the Arctic Sea route would come under Russian control. The Finnish Government, fearing an act of violence on the part of the Russians, had been striving to secure Germany's strengthening of the rear. For a while, they had even contemplated voluntarily ceding the Petsamo corner to the Soviet Union in order to settle things; however, upon Germany's urgent discussion, they had given up this idea. Finally, the German Government had been able, through diplomatic means, to prevent the Russians from gaining too much of a foothold on the nickel mines, and the Soviet Union had again ratified the treaty signed in November *, according to which Germany's share of the output was to amount to 60 percent. However (HITLER continued), there was no doubt that Russian designs on the Petsamo region would continue undiminished and that the Russians would avail themselves of the first opportunity to take possession of this territory. It therefore seemed imperative that this area be occupied by German troops, at the latest with the start of the eastern campaign, but, if need be, even earlier.

In addition, HITLER now requested that the Russian base Murmansk should not only be cut off from its rear communications at land through a thrust against the Murmansk Railway, but that it should be captured in order to deprive the enemy of every chance to operate from there against Northern Finland and Northern Norway and in order to prevent the British from landing at the Murmansk coast. For this purpose he stipulated that the attack echelon, which was to be committed against Petsamo, should be reinforced by a motorized force which was also equipped with heavy tanks. HITLER considered this to be particularly important, because it was his opinion that Murmansk could be attacked only along the roads but not through the Tundra.

---

* See page 35 (German original).

In addition, he ordered that the harbors of Murmansk and Archangel be mined at an early date.

On 17 March, three days after this conference, HITLER had a long conversation with General von BRAUCHITSCH at the Berlin Reich Chancellery, during which, at first, some problems relating to Operation MARITA were discussed. In this connection, HITLER issued instructions, as already mentioned previously *, that the operations against Greece be continued until the British had been driven out of there and that sufficient forces be committed for this purpose. He stated again, as he did during the conference held on 9 January **, that we could reckon with the fact that it would be possible to withdraw the covering forces, committed for protection against attacks from Turkey, shortly after the start of operations, and that these elements would be utilised either for Operation BARBAROSSA -- for which the XIV Panzer Corps (5th and 11th Panzer Division ***) would have to be committed in any case -- or for Operation MARITA itself. However, it now became clear that, owing to the intensification of operations against Greece, the Army High Command (OKH) would be able to utilize for the eastern campaign only a considerably smaller portion of the units of the Twelfth Army than had been contemplated previously and that the Twelfth Army Headquarters too, which originally had been assigned to command the

---

* See Chapter 7, page 31 etc. (German original).

** See page 61 (German original).

*** See Chapter 7, pages 8, 13, 29 and 31 (German original).

Army which was to be assembled in Moldavia, would probably have to remain in Greece. In that case, it was planned to commit in Moldavia an army headquarters which was to be newly organized and to place in command the Chief of the Military Mission in Rumania, General HANSEN, who then was to be replaced by General SPEIDEL, the Chief of the Air Force Mission, who would have to take over the command of the entire Military Mission.

In addition, HITLER requested that the Army's initial assembly order for Operation BARBAROSSA be changed with respect to the assignment for Army Group South. In the meantime, he had become convinced that it was not advisable for the Twelfth Army to advance, as had been originally contemplated, from Moldavia in a northeasterly direction, because the Dniester River constituted too great an obstacle. Therefore, he ordered that in even greater measure than had been envisaged, the main effort should be executed by the Sixth Army, which was scheduled to be assembled in the area around Lublin. He issued instructions to also commit all mobile forces of the Army Group at that point, to push ahead with them towards Kiev, and to breach the Dniester River line from the rear. He specified that at the Pruth River, the number of forces assembling there should not be larger than would be required to tie down the enemy elements they would be facing; they were to pursue those enemy troops who tried to escape. They should, however, be strong enough to be able to resist a Russian invasion of Moldavia. The protection of the Rumanian oil field region, which was of vital importance for Germany, was to be ensured at all costs and was to remain the responsibility of the Chief of the Military Mission. Consequently, it was necessary to reinforce the fighting forces and the antiaircraft artillery units committed there. Hungary should in no way participate in Operation BARBAROSSA; Slovakia, on the other hand, was to be utilized for the assembling of troops and providing of supplies for Army Group South.

These new instructions by HITLER made it necessary to issue supplements for Fuehrer Directive # 21 and for the Army's initial assembly order covering Operation BARBAROSSA. The former now specified the following:

"The main effort of the Army Group committed south of the Pripyat Marshes will be placed in the area of Lublin, in the general direction of Kiev; they will rapidly and with strong armored elements advance against the deep flank and the rear of the Russian forces whom they will then roll up along the Dnieper River.

The combined German-Rumanian forces at the right wing are charged with the mission

    a) to protect the Rumanian area and consequently the southern wing of the over-all operation.

    b) to contain the enemy forces facing them following the attack at the northern wing of Army Group South and, in the course of further operations, to pursue the enemy in conjunction with the Air Force, to prevent enemy troops from making an orderly retreat across the Dniester River."

In the Army's initial assembly order, the changed passage read as follows:

"Army Group South is charged with the task of driving its reinforced left flank -- mobile elements leading the way -- in the direction of Kiev, to annihilate the Russian forces stationed in Galicia and Western Ukraine while still west of the Dnieper River, and to take early possession of the Dnieper bridges at and below Kiev, in order to continue operations on the other side of the Dnieper River. Operations will be conducted in such a manner that the mobile troops advancing from the area of Lublin, will be assembled for a break-through in the direction of Kiev.

As part of this mission, the Armies and Panzer Armies, according to detailed instructions issued by the High Command of Army Group South, are assigned the following tasks:

The Eleventh Army is responsible for the protection of the Rumanian area, which is of vital importance for Germany's conduct of the war, against invasion by Russian forces. Within the scope of the attack of Army Group South, it will, by feigning greater strength of assembled forces, hold the enemy troops facing it, and in the course of further operations, pursue the enemy in conjunction with the Air Force, and will prevent the Russian troops from making an orderly retreat across the Dniester River.

It will be the main objective of the First Panzer Army to penetrate the enemy lines near the border, between Rawa Ruska and Kowel, in joint operation with the Seventeenth and Sixth Armies, and, advancing via the Berditschev - Shitomir sector, to speedily reach the Dnieper River at and below Kiev. From there, they will, without losing any time, continue the attack, according to instructions of the Army Group High Command, in a southeasterly direction along the Dnieper River, with the objective of preventing the enemy forces fighting in Western Ukraine from escaping across the Dnieper River and annihilating them through attacking them in the rear.

The Seventeenth Army will penetrate the enemy border defenses northwest of Lemberg. By vigorously driving with its reinforced left flank, it should endeavor to push the enemy forces in a southeasterly direction and defeat them. In addition, it will be the objective of the Army, by taking advantage of the assault of the Panzer Army, to speedily reach the Winniza - Berditschev area, in order to continue the attack either southeastward or eastward, depending on the situation.

The Sixth Army will penetrate the enemy front in the area on both sides of Lucki, in conjunction with portions of the First Panzer Army and, while covering the northern flank of the Army Group against attacks from the Pripyat Marshes, will assign the largest possible number of forces to follow the Panzer Army towards Shitomir as quickly as possible. It should have ready strong forces which will pivot southeastward west of the Dnieper River, according to instructions of the Army Group High Command, so as to be able, together with the First Panzer Army, to prevent enemy troops fighting in Western Ukraine from escaping across the Dnieper River, and to annihilate them."

Finally, the conference held on 17 March also touched upon the operations to be carried out by Army Headquarters Norway in and out of Northern Finland. In this connection, however, the Commander in Chief of Army High

Command declared that he left all arrangements in this realm to the discretion of the Wehrmacht High Command, which had been in command in Norway from the first. HITLER agreed to this and now delegated General JODL to draw up an Wehrmacht High Command directive to this effect, which was to be based on the following factors:

As has been mentioned previously, the plans call for a thrust from the Arctic region for the purpose of occupying Petsamo and launching an attack on Murmansk as well as pushing forward from Central Finland against the Murmansk Railway and the Bay of Kandalaksha. The forces required for the northern operation, which is referred to by the cover name RENNTIER, are to be made available in Northern Norway; the 2d Mountain Division has been earmarked for this undertaking *. For the southern project, which is referred to as Operation SILBERFUCHS, the Army High Command contemplates assigning the 199th Infantry Division as well as another infantry division from its reserves. Both divisions are to be transferred to Norway and from there shifted via Sweden to Finland. However, if the time element makes it impossible to carry this out, it is planned to transport the 163d Infantry Division, which is stationed around Oslo, via Sweden to Finland and have a division from the GHQ reserves replace it in Norway, while the second division, on the other hand, is to be sent from the Zone of Interior by water to Finland. It is intended to give Stockholm the explanation that the troops to be transported through Sweden are replacements for the mountain corps. However, in case the Swedish Government does not agree to the utilization of its railways, we will procure a division by means of another

---
* See page 11 etc. (German original).

shift to the north * of the forces stationed in Norway. Furthermore, one combined tank battalion of Army Headquarters Norway is to join the southern attack echelon instead of the northern one, which HITLER's order called for just a few days previously. The two German Battle Groups are to be assigned to the Finnish Commander in Chief, General MANNERHEIM, while the northern one is to be led by the commanding general of the Mountain Corps Norway, General of the Infantry DIETL.

In the meantime, the Chief of the Wehrmacht High Command had issued a decree on 13 March, which was entitled "General Directions with Regard to Special Assignments, Supplementing Fuehrer Directive # 21 (Operation BARBAROSSA)", and which regulated the administrative setup of the Russian territories which were to be conquered. On 3 March, HITLER had expressed the following ideas in this connection:

"The forthcoming campaign is more than just a struggle of arms; it is also a clash of two different ideologies. In order to bring it to a conclusion, it is not sufficient, in view of the size of the territory, to defeat the enemy armed forces. The entire captured territory should be broken up into states that would have their own governments and with whom Germany would be able to conclude a peace treaty. The establishment of these governments requires a great deal of political skill and the application of well weighed general principles.

Every major revolution produces effects which are impossible to obliterate. The socialistic idea cannot be separated from the Russia of today, and this idea alone can constitute the basis for home politics when new states and governments are created. The Jewish-Bolshevistic intelligentsia, which has been the oppressor of the people till now, must be eliminated. The former middle-class and aristocrats, as far as they still exist, particularly among emigrants, are likewise out of the picture because they have been rejected by the Russian people and are

---

* As mentioned previously (see page 11), the first shift of this kind took place in the early fall.

on the whole anti-German. This is particularly true also of the former Baltic States. In addition, it must be avoided at all costs that a nationalistic Russia now takes the place of the bolshevistic regime, because history has taught us that such a government would again be opposed to Germany. Instead, it should be Germany's mission to establish as soon as possible, and with a minimum of military forces, socialistic states which will be dependent on the Reich.

This is such a difficult task that the Army cannot be expected to accomplish it. Consequently, the Army's zone of operations as far as possible should be restricted in depth. No military administration should be established in the rear; instead, Reich commissioners should be appointed to certain "Grossraeume" * which are to be determined on the basis of ethnic groups, and these Reich commissioners are to be responsible for the rapid development of new political states. They are to be assisted by military district commanders, who will be under the control of the Commander in Chief of Army High Command only in purely military matters connected with the progress of operations but in all other respects will be under the command of the Wehrmacht High Command. Their staffs should also incorporate the agencies for military economics, communications and defense. The majority of the police forces will be placed at the disposal of the Reich commissioners. The question of whether or not it will be necessary already in the zone of operations to employ, in addition to the Secret Police, agencies of the Reich Fuehrer SS (HIMMLER), will have to be determined in conjunction with the latter. It is an advisable measure, in view of the necessity to immediately render harmless all bolshevistic leaders and commissars. The military courts should have nothing to do with these problems but should devote themselves only to legal matters affecting the forces."

The discussions held thereupon between the Wehrmacht High Command, the Army and the Reich Fuehrer SS resulted in the fact that the Reich Fuehrer SS was charged with special assignments by the Fuehrer, which were to be effected also in the Army zone of operations "in preparation for the political administration", and in connection with which the Reich Fuehrer SS was to act with complete independence and on his own responsibility. These "special assignments", which, as stated in the "general directions", arose

---

Transl. note: * "Grossraeume" - territories which retain their "independence" but which also fall under the "guidance" of the Reich.

from "the clash between two opposed political systems, which had to be fought to the finish", primarily involved political purges, which meant the extermination of whole classes of people, which HITLER's doctrine considered necessary. In conformity with HITLER's additional directives, the "general directions" stipulated that the Russian territory which was to be occupied in back of the zone of operations" should for the time being be subdivided, according to ethnic elements and approximating the dividing lines of the Army Groups, into a northern (Baltic States), central (White Russia) and southern (Ukraine) area.

On the morning of 30 March, HITLER held a meeting at the Berlin Reich Chancellery with the top-level Commanders in Chief of the Army, the Navy and the Air Force who were taking part in Operation BARBAROSSA, as well as their chiefs of staff, in order to personally brief them for the tasks assigned to them. After presenting in minute detail his reasons for waging war against the Soviet Union, he pointed to the following with emphasis:

> "This war should not be fought according to general military rules; it is a clash of two opposed ideologies which requires relentless hard-heartedness. Consequently, the Wehrmacht should discard completely all the traditional conceptions and standards. The thing that matters is the eradication of bolshevism. The political functionaries and the commissars in the armed forces are the exponents of the bolshevistic idea. The latter cannot be regarded as soldiers and consequently, if the occasion arises, also cannot be treated as prisoners of war. These commissars, same as the political functionaries, should be separated from the other prisoners of war immediately upon capture and placed under the control of the special task detachments (Einsatzgruppen) of the SD (Security Service) who, under the command of the Reich Fuehrer SS, will accompany the German troops to Russia. Wherever the combat situation makes it impossible to turn them

over to the SD (Security Service), the functionaries and commissars should be shot by the troops."

HITLER, in explaining his motives for this order, which was entirely in keeping with his views expressed on 5 March, stated that the Soviet Union had not signed the Geneva Convention and would certainly not treat the German prisoners of war in accordance with its stipulations. He pointed to the behavior of the Russian soldiers and particularly the commissars in Poland, during the Finnish winter campaign, in the Baltic States and in Rumania as a warning example. *

After a brief lunch, HITLER discussed in detail the conduct of the eastern campaign with the Commanders in Chief of the Wehrmacht. He set forth the following:

> "At Army Group North, the Fourth Panzer Army under Generaloberst HOEPFNER will be committed north of the Niemen River in order to avoid having to cross it. Whether or not it will be necessary -- in order to cut off the enemy's retreat at the coast -- for them to pivot northward already when advancing against the Bay of Riga or later, along the Peipus Lake, will depend on the situation. It is to be feared, however, that the Russians, according to their customary procedure, will, particularly in the Baltic States, try to avoid a decisive engagement in the border area; we must seek to frustrate this attempt. There is also a chance that the enemy will make a flank attack; however, in that case, the LEEB Army Group will have to be concerned only about its right flank. The frontier guard of the Memel area is to be increased without delay to two divisions. At the Army Group Center, the Ninth Army, in conjunction with the Panzer Army of Generaloberst HOTH, will

---

* In addition to this so-called "Commissar Directive", which played such an important part in the Nuernberg war crimes trials, HITLER on 6 June also issued regulations with regard to the method of procedure, which cannot be discussed here because the text is not available.

be committed at the left, and the Fourth Army, together with the Panzer Army of Generaloberst GUDERIAN, at the right; the main effort of both will be placed at the southern wing. The Osowiec - Grodno fortress front is to be attacked only with one division. The two Panzer Armies should subsequently push ahead in the direction of Leningrad; however, not before they reached Minsk."

In this connection, General GUDERIAN remarked that he hoped to get to the Minsk area in five to six days.

HITLER continued by stating the following:

"The Panzer Armies' push on Leningrad is to be regarded as the ideal solution of the strategic problem. The spring-fed swamps of the Beresina River will probably seriously hamper the movements of the tank units. The air forces are to be controlled as firmly as possible within the attack sector of the Panzer Armies. The bulk of the GHQ reserves should follow north of the Pripyat Marshes. The point of main effort of Army Group South will be placed at the Sixth Army; the latter will have the task to make it possible for the First Panzer Army of Generaloberst von KLEIST, which for the time being is operating in close contact with the Sixth Army, to cross the Bug and the Styr Rivers. Following this, the Panzer Army should advance against Kiev, and in this connection it will be necessary -- owing to the limited number of usable roads -- to reckon with the fact that the march columns will be extended to several 100 kilometers in depth. The Seventeenth Army will advance from the area northwest of Lemberg in a southeasterly direction to the right of the Sixth Army. Hungary will be bypassed.

In Moldavia, the Eleventh Army of General Ritter von SCHOBERT * will carry out its covering operations in three separate groups in order to render the necessary aid to the Rumanian troops."

---

* The Seventeenth and the Eleventh Army Headquarters had just been activated in the Zone of Interior. The plan to appoint the Chief of the Military Mission in Rumania to the post of Commander in Chief of the Army which was to be assembled in Moldavia (see page 92 - German original) had been given up in the meantime, apparently because it was believed that he could not be spared in Rumania.

Finally, the practicability of a German advance from Hungary was also discussed. General von RUNDSTEDT argued that in his opinion it was necessary to attack the six Russian divisions stationed at the Russo-Hungarian border. HITLER did not believe it would be possible to induce Hungary to agree to this step, unless we made certain territorial concessions at the Carpathian border; however, he stated he would continue to study this question.

The following two significant political events took place just prior to HITLER's meeting with the top-level Commanders in Chief of the Wehrmacht; One was the visit to Berlin of the Japanese Foreign Minister Yosuke MATSUOKA, and the other the coup d'etat in Yugoslavia. In order to correctly understand the significance of the former, it seems fit to briefly touch upon the relations between Germany and Japan as they had developed since the conclusion of the Three-Power Pact.

According to article IV of the Three-Power Pact, which was signed on 27 September 1940, three committees were to be organized in Berlin, three in Rome and three in Tokyo, namely, in each of these cities one central committee consisting of the foreign minister of the country in question, who acted as chairman, and the ambassadors of the two other countries who served in the capacity of members; one committee as an economic mission and one as a military mission. The latter was to be composed of the representatives of the various arms of the country in question and the military, naval and air force attaches assigned to the embassies of the two other countries. On 24 December 1940, the Chief of the Bureau for

Economic Warfare, Viceadmiral GROOS, was appointed chairman of the military mission in Berlin. According to an Wehrmacht High Command directive issued on 5 January, the following competent representatives of the various Wehrmacht branches were attached to him: By the Army, Colonel MATZKY, who formerly served as military attache in Tokyo and was now acting as Assistant Chief of Staff for Intelligence of the Army General Staff; Naval Captain STANGE by the Navy and Colonel OLLBRICHT by the Air Force.

Before these commissions had a chance to join forces -- the Japanese especially attached great importance to having this take place soon -- a delegation of the Japanese Army, headed by Generalleutnant YAMASHITA and consisting of 16 members, arrived in Berlin on 9 January. This delegation had been sent to Germany and Italy upon the invitation of the German and Italian Governments in order to study European military methods and experiences on the spot. At the same time, the Japanese Navy too, on its own initiative had sent a delegation of officers to Germany for the purpose of studying and discussing problems of armament. The Chief of this delegation, Viceadmiral NOMURA *, reached Berlin during the middle of January, while the other members of the mission did not arrive until 24 February. Neither of these two delegations had any connection with the Three-Power Pact; however, the Japanese Navy planned to appoint Admiral NOMURA as their chief representative at the military mission to be organized in Tokyo.

During his first conversation with Admiral GROOS, which took place on 18 January, Admiral NOMURA termed the following the most important points

---

* Not to be mistaken for Admiral KICHISABURO NOMURA who, in January, was appointed Japanese Ambassador to Washington.

of negotiation for the military missions of the Three-Power Pact;

1) Steps to be taken by the Axis powers in order to prevent the United States at the present stage from participating in the war, and to forestall the outbreak of a Japanese-American war;

2) Joint operations plans to be drawn up by Germany, Italy and Japan in preparation for the contingency of America's entering the war;

3) Support to be rendered Japan by Germany and Italy in order to strengthen the Japanese war potential.

On 23 January, Admiral GROSS submitted a report concerning this meeting to the Chief of the Wehrmacht High Command, and on 29 January, General JODL, commenting on this summary, expressed himself to HITLER as follows:

> "The proposals made by Admiral NOMURA have raised the issue of Germany's views regarding joint military actions with Japan. The conclusion we can draw from these recommendations is that Japan desires the compilation of joint operations plans of the three powers and intends to approach Germany and Italy with requests for materiel. On the one hand, Operation BARBAROSSA will relieve Great Britain, particularly in view of the fact that only a small portion of her forces is contained in the Mediterranean area; on the other hand, however, it will also lighten Japan's burden. Besides, at the time the eastern campaign will be put into effect, the United States, owing to the inadequacy of its war preparations, will hardly represent a menace to Japan. If Japan, under these circumstances, would be ready to enter the war and launch an attack on Singapore, it would be of decisive importance from a military, economic and psychological point of view. According to information furnished by Oberst MATZKY, the former military attache in Tokyo, the Japanese armed forces have a very affirmative attitude in connection with the attack on Singapore. Consequently, we should contemplate entering into discussions with the Japanese with the aim of assembling forces for such a mission. Prior to that, it will be necessary to sound out the military missions of the Three-Power Pact; then arrangements should be made by the Wehrmacht and the Japanese armed forces to prepare the joint operations."

On 4 February, Admiral RAEDER, in his report on the situation at sea, expressed himself along similar lines. On that occasion, he submitted to the Fuehrer a memorandum of the Navy General Staff concerning Japan's mission in case her neutrality was to be maintained and for the eventuality of America's entering the war. Thereupon HITLER gave his approval that arrangements be made to prepare for military collaboration with Japan, and on 18 February, he instructed the Chief of the Wehrmacht Operations Staff to compile a directive, which should provide the Wehrmacht branches with guiding principles for handling the Japanese requests and safeguarding our own interests in the military missions of the Three-Power Pact. In this connection, HITLER expressed himself as follows:

> "It should be Germany's aim to induce Japan as soon as possible to take active measures in the Far East. The earlier Japan will strike, the easier she will find the military situation. Japan should take possession of Singapore and all regions which are rich in raw materials, which she requires in order to continue the war against Great Britain and especially in the event the United States enters the war. The longer Japan hesitates the stronger will America become and the more difficult their own task. Germany has neither political nor military nor even economic interests in the Far East which might prompt her to restrict Japanese operations. Germany should specify all the military operations which she considers desirable in the interest of her war against England and perhaps even the United States. In exchange, the Japanese should be afforded comprehensive and openhearted insight into Germany's military methods and combat experiences and given permission to reproduce modern weapons and equipment. They can be trusted to keep secrets more than any other nation. It seems out of the question that the Japanese Government might still change sides."

Two days later, Admiral GROSS reported on his recent conversation with Admiral NOMURA who, in the meantime, had been appointed to serve as member of the Tokyo Military Mission of the Three-Power Pact. Admiral NOMURA expressed the following views, which, as he stated, he intended to advocate within the scope of his present mission as well as in Tokyo:

"Since the signing of the Three-Power Pact, the situation in the Far East has slowly become increasingly crucial. America is holding her naval forces in readiness for war in the Pacific and is reinforcing her bases there, while increasing economic pressure on Japan and supporting the Chungking Government * in collaboration with Great Britain. In French Indo-China too, Anglo-American influence makes itself felt and in Netherlands Indies, Anglo-American machinations frustrate Japan's efforts to procure by peaceful means, through negotiations with the local government, the oil which is indispensable for home defense.

Japan really does not desire a war with the United States, but is firmly resolved to make it perfectly clear that she is holding herself in readiness to meet any provocation on the part of America and that little by little, her attitude towards the economic pressure exerted by Great Britain and the United States will undergo a complete change.

These views definitely necessitate joint action by the three Axis powers. Consequently, the Japanese Navy is of the opinion that the commissions envisaged in the Three-Power Pact should join forces at the earliest possible moment. Since the pact has been concluded, the Japanese Navy, in requesting aid, primarily asked for shipments of machine tools and weapons as well as technical advice. The respective requests have been transmitted via diplomatic channels. Furthermore, the Japanese Navy is extremely interested in obtaining an idea concerning the subsequent developments of the military situation, the German air and submarine warfare, the chances for an invasion of England, the Italian operations in the Mediterranean, and the extent of German aid rendered to Italy. Although they are aware of the fact that Germany is hardly in a position to indicate the time when the invasion of England will be effected, they would, however, at least like to know whether or not Germany expects Japan to undertake any operations in the Pacific in conjunction with such landing operations."

---

* This was the Chinese National Government headed by Marshal CHIANG KAI-SHEK, which since 10 December 1937, when the Japanese had captured Nanking, had had its seat in Chungking.

The Wehrmacht Operations Staff expressed the following opinion concerning these statements:

> "It seems to be an established fact that Japan does not want a war with the United States and intends to launch operations against Great Britain only in the event Germany will strike a decisive blow against the latter. In the meantime, Japan will do everything possible to increase her war potential with German aid. It is now necessary to ascertain whether or not the views of the Japanese Navy are in harmony with the general political outlook in Japan, and investigations should be conducted to determine to what extent economic facilities will enable us to comply with Japan's requests."

At the end of February, Foreign Minister von RIBBENTROP discussed these questions with the newly appointed Japanese Ambassador, Generalleutnant HIROSHI OSHIMA who had just arrived in Berlin and who, for a long time, had been a friend of Germany and an advocate of closest possible collaboration of the Three-Power Pact nations. He announced that in May, Japan would be ready to attack Singapore by land route. To be sure, this gave no indication of the date when she would enter the war. It was expected that the forthcoming visit in Berlin of the Japanese Foreign Minister, Yosuke MATSUOKA, would provide additional clarification. On 7 March, the "Fuehrer Directive # 24 Concerning Collaboration with Japan", which, on the basis of the guiding principles and the memorandum issued by the Navy General Staff, had been compiled by the Department for National Defense, was distributed to the Wehrmacht branches, after the Chief of Wehrmacht High Command had signed it. This directive began by stating that the collaboration based on the Three-Power Pact should aim at inducing Japan to take active measures in the Far East as soon as possible, so that the concentrated efforts and interest of the United States would be diverted to the Pacific area. The actual military conferences with Japan were not to be conducted by the German representatives attached to the Military Missions of the Three-Power Pact but by the High Command of the Navy as the Wehrmacht branch which was the most interested.

On 26 March, the Japanese Foreign Minister MATSUOKA arrived in Berlin from Moscow, where he had had brief conferences with STALIN and MOLOTOV. It was his aim to establish personal contact with the German and Italian statesmen and to gain a picture of the situation through personal observation while visiting Berlin and Rome. On 27 March he was received by HITLER and during the next few days had conferences with von RIBBENTROP and GOERING. He then went to Rome where, after an audience with the King, he met with MUSSOLINI and Count CIANO. Upon his return to Berlin, he had another long discussion with HITLER and the Reich Foreign Minister *. During this parley, the question of Japan's action against England through an attack on Singapore was taken first into consideration. MATSUOKA asked that the requests of the Japanese Military Mission be complied with as liberally as

---

* Information concerning this conference has been furnished through the notes of the trial of chief war criminals held before the International Military Tribunal in Nuernberg. During the proceedings on 26 November 1945, the American prosecutor read the major portion of an official "Record of the Conference between the Fuehrer and the Japanese Foreign Minister MATSUOKA, held in Berlin on 4 April 1941 in the presence of the Reich Foreign Minister and the Minister of State MEISSNER", on which the information which follows has been based (official text in German of the minutes of the meeting, published in 1947 by the Secretariat of the Tribunal in Nuernberg, volume II, pages 332 - 336).

possible, because Japan, particularly in the field of submarine warfare, was in need of information about the latest German military methods and technical improvements. He stated that the Japanese Government would do everything in its power to avoid a war with the United States. However, in case they did decide to strike a blow against Singapore, they would also have to make preparations for fighting against the United States, because the latter would then most likely side with Great Britain. Although it was his personal opinion that it might be possible, by means of diplomatic endeavors, to prevent America from entering the war on the side of Great Britain, it was nevertheless necessary to assume the worst and reckon with a war against the United States, and for this purpose the Japanese Navy required information about the latest technical developments.

HITLER promised fulfillment of the Japanese requests and declared that Germany, too, considered a conflict with the United States as undesirable but that he was taking such a contingency into account. He stated that he had made his preparations in such a manner that no Americans would succeed in invading Europe and that, with submarines and the Air Force, he would conduct a vigorous campaign against America and, owing to his greater experience, he would be far superior in this fight. Should Japan become involved in a conflict with the United States, Germany would immediately enter the war on her side, for the strength of the Three-Power Pact nations lies in joint action.

MATSUOKA replied that in his opinion a war between Japan and the United States was inevitable and was likely to happen rather sooner than later.

Consequently, the Japanese Government must take resolute action at the right moment and take upon itself the risk of a conflict with the United States. However, in Japan they hesitated to follow such a train of thought. He related that recently, the United States had also attempted one last stratagem by declaring she would not fight Japan for the sake of China or the South Sea area if Japan would freely allow the exportation from there to America of rubber and tin, but that she would immediately take action against Japan if the latter should enter the war in order to assist in the defeat of Great Britain. In view of the fact that many Japanese had been given a pro-English education, it was only natural that such arguments did not fail to take effect.

To this, HITLER replied that the American maneuvering meant nothing more than that the United States was greatly interested in the preservation of the British Empire, because she hoped to be able one day to take action against Japan together with Great Britain, whereas in case of a collapse of the British Empire, she would have to face Japan completely isolated and would be helpless.

Finally, MATSUOKA pointed out that as Foreign Minister he was not able, not even under present conditions, to express anything in Japan about his plans as he had presented them here and that consequently, he was also not in a position to state how soon he might be able to submit to the Japanese Prime Minister or the Emperor a report concerning the questions which had been discussed. He stated that for the time being he would carefully watch further developments in Japan and then, at a propitious moment, tell the truth about his actual plans to the Emperor and Prince KONOYE. Upon his return, if questioned by the cabinet members and the Emperor, he would state that the issue of Singapore had been discussed in Berlin but only as a hypothetical case.

On the day following this conference, the Japanese Foreign Minister left for Moscow in order to continue his negotiations with STALIN and MOLOTOV. It is doubtful whether he was very satisfied with the result of his Berlin talks, for the questions in which he was particularly interested, namely, whether or not Germany was still planning an invasion of England and information about relations between Germany and Russia, had not been clarified and naturally, much less still was he appraised of the forthcoming attack on the Soviet Union. To be sure, he himself had not made any promises concerning Japan's participation in the war and the attack on Singapore and evidently he did not state definitely how far he might possibly go in Moscow. Consequently, they were greatly surprised in Berlin when, on 13 April, it was reported that MATSUOKA had concluded a neutrality pact with the Soviet Union in Moscow and had signed a proclamation whereby they agreed to mutually honor their territorial integrity and the inviolability of Manchukuo and the Mongolian People's Republic. While Japan thereby gained freedom in the rear in case of an attack against British bases in the Far East, Russia, at the same time, gained the same advantage, in case of a German attack. The latter was definitely forthcoming, whereas the former was still uncertain; consequently, Berlin did not see any direct advantage for Germany in the Russo-Japanese neutrality pact.

MATSUOKA's arrival in the capital on 27 March coincided with the Belgrade military putsch, which necessitated a sweeping change of plans for Operation MARITA, as has been explained elsewhere *. It was now arranged that the campaign against Greece, which was to have started on 1 April, would be combined with a simultaneous attack on Yugoslavia, which it was not possible to put into effect before 6 April. This resulted in a postponement of Operation BARBAROSSA. While previously, it had been doubtful whether those units of the Twelfth Army which were indispensable for the eastern campaign -- this referred above all to the armored divisions -- would be available for new commitments on time, we now had to realize it was out of the question for us to be able by the middle of May -- which hitherto had been the earliest date contemplated for the start of the eastern offensive -- to transport the majority of the divisions of the Second Army under General Freiherr von WEICHS from the Balkans to the area of Warsaw. This Army, according to the operations plan for the BARBAROSSA campaign, had been designated to follow the Army Group Center as the main reserve, but was now assigned to first launch the attack on Yugoslavia together with portions of the Twelfth Army. Even under the most favorable conditions and the speediest execution of the campaign against Yugoslavia and Greece, it seemed necessary to postpone Operation BARBAROSSA for about five weeks, which would be until the second half of June. In all probability, even if the operation lasted only three months, this would still bring us into Russia's rainy season during which all movements, particularly

---

* See Chapter 7, page 36 etc. (German original).

of the mobile forces, would be considerably handicapped due to the fact that the streets would turn into mud; however, it was unavoidable and we had to make the best of it. A new date was not set for the time being. After the Yugoslav Army had capitulated on 17 April and after the surrender of the Greek Epirus Army on 21 April, the Army High Command reported the next day that the transfer to the eastern front of the bulk of the Balkan forces would probably be concluded by 23 June and that consequently, the eastern campaign could begin on 25 June. Finally, since it seemed possible to speed up this transport movement by several days, HITLER on 30 April designated the 22d of June as the so-called B-Day (i.e. the day on which Operation BARBAROSSA was scheduled to begin). However, after operations against Crete had begun (on 20 May), it seemed advisable to again postpone this date by about ten days, because we did not believe we would be able to transfer in time to the area north of Warsaw the participating reinforced VIII Air Force Corps under Air General Freiherr von RICHTHOFEN, which, in the eastern campaign, was to be committed with the Second Air Fleet which was instructed to cooperate with Army Group Center. However, the rapid capture of Crete then nevertheless gave us a chance to effect the transfer of the VIII Air Force Corps from Craiova to Suwalki during the period from 7 to 20 June, which made it possible to adhere to the specified date for B-Day.

After the Belgrade military putsch, Yugoslavia sought closer collaboration with the Soviet Union and on 5 April, concluded a non-aggression and friendship pact with Russia, in which the two nations pledged themselves to maintain their friendly relations even in the event one of them was attacked by a third power. HITLER regarded this as further evidence of Russia's aim to interfere in his Balkan policy. However, during the campaign against Yugoslavia and Greece, the Soviet Union concentrated on observing strict neutrality and seemed to endeavor as much as ever to closely cooperate with Germany in the economic field. As a matter of fact, she even increased her shipments effected on the basis of the trade agreements, although Germany, at this point, was increasingly delaying her reciprocal deliveries under one or the other pretext.

This line of conduct on the part of Russia proved very useful for the German war economy. The constant flow of rubber shipments from East Asia via Russia was particularly important. On 8 February, the Chief of the Office of Economics and Armaments, General THOMAS, had reported to General KEITEL that the rubber reserves on hand and the anticipated quantity of rubber imported during the first quarter of 1941 would make it possible only until the end of March to achieve a volume of production such as was required by the procurement agencies. He pointed out that, if after the first of April no further importation would be possible, we would have at our disposal nothing but a small reserve of natural rubber which would, at the most, allow for a monthly production of 3500 tons of rubber for a period of eight months *. According to this report, Germany would have

---

* In comparison, I wish to point out that in 1940 the consumption of rubber in the United States came to 650,000 tons and during the first half of 1941 amounted to 408,000 tons.

to depend entirely on buna * (without the addition of natural rubber) which, for instance, was not suitable for the production of truck tires.

This report induced the Chief of the Wehrmacht High Command to take additional measures to economize on rubber consumption and to instruct the Chief of the Bureau of Economic Warfare to investigate whether in future it would be possible to import rubber with the aid of blockade runners. The Reich Marshal too, in his capacity as General Deputy for the Four Year Plan, concerned himself with this extremely important question and consulted with economic experts. Plans were made which called for the traffic of blockade runners, consisting at first of four ships running between Brazil and the areas under German control. Furthermore, we hoped that in future we would be able, at least to some extent, to carry on by means of blockade-runners the importation of rubber from the Far East, which at present was still moving via the Trans-Siberian Railway; for this purpose, it was planned to employ primarily motor boats because of their greater radius of action. In order to save rubber, instructions were issued which called for a new decisive curtailment of civilian as well as military truck traffic and the appropriation of the tires of the vehicles which were out of commission. It was highly doubtful whether it would be possible in this way to procure rubber in sufficient quantities for future use. However, in the meantime, owing to the uninterrupted flow from East Asia via Russia, we received rubber in such large quantities that the top-level

---

Transl. note: * buna — a synthetic rubber made from butediene.

Wehrmacht command did not fear any marked obstruction of the eastern operations due to rubber shortages. In March, the daily average of imported rubber amounted to 300 tons, and, according to the status as per 22 March, 5800 tons were being transported from Mandschurija, the Manchuria-Siberia border station, to the Reich border; 3000 tons were on the way from the Manchurian harbor Dairen to Mandschurija; 4000 tons were in Dairen, while 3800 tons were in Japan and 5700 tons on the way there. The largest portion of these quantities still reached Germany in time before the start of the eastern campaign, the last train being received on the eve of B-Day, which can be regarded as additional evidence that the Soviet Union at that time did not entertain any hostile plans against Germany. In May, the importation of rubber on blockade-running ships also began to function, the first of which sailed into a harbor in western France around the 20th of June.

On 6 May, Stalin took over the post of Chairman in the Council of the People's Commissars in place of MOLOTOV who continued to serve as Vice-President and Foreign Commissar. This too HITLER regarded as an indication of Russia's endeavor to maintain and even strengthen friendly relations with Germany. On the other hand, Russia of late was taking measures at the German border which were indubitably of a military nature, which, however, were evidently supposed to be for defense purposes only. This was not surprising in view of the strategic concentration in the east, which it was not possible to conceal from the Russians. Of the 121 rifle divisions, 25 cavalry divisions and 31 mechanized brigades, which the Eastern Foreign Armies Division of the Army General Staff took into account in

European Russia *, we had, during the middle of March, ascertained that 84 rifle divisions and 8 mechanized brigades were along the German and Finnish borders. Since that time, the Russians were constantly bringing additional forces up to the borders. At the beginning of June, photographic reconnaissance and radio interception showed that there were about 4600 planes in the border districts and additional 1100 planes close behind them. During the middle of June, the German Naval Attache in Moscow reported the movement of large-scale railway transports from there to the Baltic States.

The largest concentration of Russian forces seemed to be in the Ukraine which again aroused German apprehensions with respect to the Rumanian oil field region, where the Air Force had committed one fighter group, 16 anti-aircraft batteries and 10 fire-fighting companies. The GHQ troops committed there consisted of the 22d Infantry (Airborne) Division which had been stationed around Ploesti since the end of the Balkan campaign; during the middle of June this Division was to be replaced by another formation and transported to Upper Silesia. At the beginning of June, the Eleventh Army began to assemble in Moldavia; at the same time, the instruction division (the 13th motorized Infantry Division) which, in the meantime, had been changed to an armored division and was coming from Rumania, and the 16th Panzer Division which, during the Balkan campaign, had been guarding the Turkish border, were transported to their assembly areas in Poland. In their place, portions of the 5th Panzer Division, which was still in Southern

---

* See page 73 (German original).

Greece, were attached to the Eleventh Army. A partial mobilization of the Rumanian Army and the intensification of defense measures at the Russian border were effected simultaneously with the strategic concentration in Moldavia. On 11 June, HITLER confided his plans to General ANTONESCU during a meeting held in Munich and discussed with him the mission which devolved upon the Rumanian armed forces within the scope of Operation BARBAROSSA. Beginning with the middle of June, we were, for the present, spared the apprehension concerning a Russian invasion of Moldavia owing to the fact that the Danube and Pruth Rivers were both in flood which, up to Jassy, made a crossing impossible.

Finland's participation in the campaign against the Soviet Union already had been discussed in conferences held at Salzburg from 25 to 29 May between General JODL and General HEINRICH, the Finnish Chief of General Staff. On this occasion, it had been agreed, in keeping with Finnish aims *, that the major forces of the Finnish Army would be committed at the Karelian Isthmus against Leningrad, while smaller forces, consisting of about three divisions, would be employed in East Karelian, advancing in the direction of Petrosavodsk and south thereof, and two divisions would be launching an attack on the Russian naval base Hango. The support of German air forces had been contemplated for all these operations. In addition, the Finns had pledged the early occupation of the Aland Islands in order to block up the Gulf of Bothnia and had agreed that the 163d Infantry Division, as early

---

* See page 83 (German original)

as the first half in June, would be transported via sea-route from Oslo to Turku (Abo) and from there moved via railway to its assembly area east of Rovaniemi *, however, they had expressed the request that the contemplated early shift of the SS Battle Group North from Kirkenes to Rovaniemi be postponed until B-Day. During additional conferences held by Colonel BUSCHENHAGEN, the Chief of the Army Headquarters Norway, with the Finnish General Staff, it was finally also agreed that beginning 10 June, the Finnish frontier guard would be reinforced and that the mobilisation of the V Corps, which was stationed in Northern Finland, would get under way on 15 June. The transportation by water of the 163d Infantry Division began on 5 or 6 June and was concluded by 16 June. Ambassador SCHNURRE, who, at the beginning of June, had been sent to Stockholm in order to sound out the Swedish Government, reported on the 5th it was his impression that after the start of the eastern campaign, Sweden would consent to the railway

---

* The decision to do this had been made recently, because another shift to the right of the forces stationed in Norway, such as was contemplated in case it became necessary to procure one division for Operation SILBERFUCHS (see page 98 - German original), would have been too difficult and time-wasting. In the meantime, the Army High Command, as contemplated, had transferred the 199th Infantry Division to Oslo. The organizational structure of Army Headquarters Norway was now the following: In the Oslo area, the 163d Infantry Division and the 40th Panzer Battalion On Special Assignment were under its direct command. The 69th, the 199th and the 214th Infantry Division were also committed in the Oslo area and assigned to the XXXVI Superior Command. The 181st and 196th Infantry Division, assigned to the XXXIII Superior Command (Trondheim), were stationed at the west coast, while the 2d and 3d Mountain Division and the SS Battle Group North (consisting of two regiments with six battalions and several batteries) of the Mountain Corps (Narvik) in the far north, were stationed in Kirkenes. As replacement for the 163d Infantry Division, the Army High Command also contemplated transferring the 710th Security Division to Norway.

transportation of German troops through her territory. The ambassador was thereupon instructed to approach the Swedish Government on B-Day or shortly thereafter with a request to this effect.

On 2 June, HITLER had met MUSSOLINI at the Brenner Pass; however, on this occasion, too, he again seems to have confined himself to vague allusions to forthcoming events. It was decided not to inform Hungary until the last moment, because HITLER did not trust them. At the end of May, the German Ambassador in Budapest, General HIMER, had discussed with the Hungarian General Staff the protection of the Hungarian area in case of a Russo-German conflict and had been given the information that it would be possible to assemble an army at the Russo-Hungarian border within 12 days if there was danger of a Russian attack. On 15 June, Reich Foreign Minister von RIBBENTROP instructed the German Ambassador in Budapest to inform the Hungarian Government that it should reckon with a rift between Germany and the Soviet Union and that it would therefore be advisable if they would immediately reinforce their frontier defenses against Russia. This was actually done during the next few days; however, no additional measures were taken by Hungary, because to the last, they were in the dark concerning Germany's plans. On the other hand, during the middle of June, arrangements were made with Slovakia concerning the passage of German troops through her territory and the participation of Slovakian forces in the eastern campaign.

Meanwhile, the last preparations were being made in accordance with the "chronological table for Operation BARBAROSSA, which HITLER had approved on 5 June. In endless succession, the transports of the fourth and last assembly echelon were rolling towards their points of destination at the border according to the maximum capacity schedule which had gone into effect on 23 May. Beginning with the 10th of June, the strategic concentration of the bomber units was effected in the east as follows: The assembly of the Fourth Air Force under Generaloberst LOEHR took place in the area of Army Group South, that of the Second Air Force under Generalfeldmarschall KESSELRING was effected in the area of Army Group Center, while the First Air Force under Generaloberst KELLER was assembled in the area of Army Group North. The air force units committed in Finland were subordinated to the Commander in Chief of the Fifth Air Force in Norway, Generaloberst STUMPFF. On 10 June, the planning staffs of the three military district commanders earmarked for assignment in the future Reich Commissariats in the east * were also ordered to report for active duty. In the middle of June, the Navy laid two submarine mine fields in the Gulf of Finland, while five submarines were ordered to take up stand-by positions in the Baltic Sea. A request made by the Navy General Staff for permission to be alerted for action on the eve of B-Day was granted.

On the morning of 12 June, HITLER returned to the capital after a stay of nearly five weeks at the Berghof. Two days later, he summoned the top-level Commanders in Chief of the Wehrmacht and their chiefs of staff to the Reich Chancellery for a last address **. On 17 June, he issued the

---

* See page 98 etc. (German original).
** Records of HITLER's speech held at this occasion are unfortunately no longer available.

final instructions for starting Operation BARBAROSSA on 22 June and ordered that at 0330 A.M., the German-Russian border was to be crossed by land and air, however, with the reservation that as late as 1300 on 21 June, HITLER might still revoke the order at the last moment, for which contingency the code word was "Altona", while "Dortmund" was to be the signal for beginning the attack.

On 18 June, HITLER instructed the Reich Foreign Minister to appeal to him not later than the evening of the next day and, making reference to the reports received by the Wehrmacht High Command, to plead that in view of the danger of the Russian strategic concentration, further delay was no longer justifiable. At the same time, HITLER also stated he would explain the attack on the Soviet Union by asserting that an Anglo-Russian agreement had been in effect for a long time, whereby the Soviet Union was supposed to attack Germany in order to contain her forces in the east and thus relieve Great Britain. In the face of this threadbare pretext, it should again be emphasized that the Soviet Union did everything possible to avoid a conflict with Germany, at least at that juncture.

On the evening of 20 June, HITLER gave the signal "Dortmund" to the Wehrmacht and thus the command to launch the attack at the specified hour. The next day he notified MUSSOLINI of his decision in a personal letter and requested his participation. Finally, during the night of 21 June, RIBBENTROP transmitted to the German Ambassador in Moscow the text of the declaration which Graf von der SCHULENBURG was supposed to hand over early next morning to the Soviet Foreign Commissar. HITLER refrained from calling a session of the Reichstag on 23 June for the purpose of issuing a statement of government policy, because, as he said, 700 Reichstag delegates would end the secret and thus spoil the surprise element. Instead, he issued a proclamation to the German people which on the morning of 22 June the Reich Propaganda Minister announced over the radio.

During his conferences with the Commander in Chief of Army High Command and the Chief of the General Staff held on 9 January and 3 February respectively, HITLER had stated that Europe, and even the world, would hold its breath when Operation BARBAROSSA should be executed. However, in reality it was probably true that the world felt relieved when HITLER, through the attack on the Soviet Union, unnecessarily burdened himself with a new enemy and thus, at the same, with a two-front war, which he had certainly always wanted to avoid. Besides, this was an enemy whose population was more than twice as large as that of Germany and whose country was huge in size and had mineral resources in enormous quantities. This colossus, which had never really been conquered, HITLER seriously believed he would be able to completely defeat and make submissive to his will in a blitz campaign lasting three, or at the utmost, four months. He was so firmly convinced of his success that even before the start of the eastern campaign, he hatched adventurous plans which aimed still higher. As early as the middle of February, HITLER had delegated General JODL to have the Department for National Defense draw up a plan concerning the assembly of troops in Afghanistan for an attack on India. In this respect too, he followed in the footsteps of NAPOLEON I. Strange to say, this time, the responsible men in the Army also seemed to have believed in a rapid and decisive victory. In any case, no warning voices were heard from that quarter at the time. On the contrary, the Army High Command, as early as the beginning of June, suggested that the Wehrmacht Operations Staff at an early date form an idea with regard to the operations which would be conducted after the defeat of the Russian armed forces *, which surely might be construed as an indication of their certain belief in victory. The fact that, up to the present, the campaigns had been conducted rapidly and successfully despite and beyond expectation, and HITLER's predictions had so far always proven true, notwithstanding the scruples and scepticism of the military,

---

* As a result, the Department for National Defense compiled a "Directive # 32" which was subtitled: "Preliminary Arrangements for the Period Following Operation BARBAROSSA", in which the following future Wehrmacht missions were envisaged:
   1) The continuation of the fight against British positions in the Mediterranean and in Asia Minor by means of converging attacks launched from Libya through Egypt, from Bulgaria over Turkey and, if need be, also from Transcaucasia through Iran;
   2) the blocking off of the western entrance to the Mediterranean through the capture of Gibraltar;
   3) the resumption of the "siege of England" by means of naval and air force operations, and finally, the invasion of England in order to deliver the coup de grace to the collapsing enemy.
This directive, which was printed verbatim in Peter de MANDELSSOHN's book "The Nuernberg Documents" (pages 358 - 360) was, according to the latter's statement, signed by HITLER and issued on 11 June. However, in my opinion, this is apparently an error. As far as I remember, this document was nothing but a draft, which was not even submitted to General JODL, much less to HITLER, but which was on 11 June probably transmitted to the Wehrmacht branches for preliminary analysis, which happened frequently, and which was then set aside under pressure of subsequent events.

evidently affected the power of judgement of the army leaders and caused them to underestimate the obstacles, such as the enormous size of the Russian territory, its traffic and climatic conditions, the self-denial, endurance and toughness of the population, and the energy and inflexibility of the bolshevistic regime, which stood in the way of HITLER's extravagant plans.

About the editor . . .

Thomas Fensch has a university degree in History and two graduate degrees, including a doctorate from Syracuse University.

He edited the formerly-unpublished correspondence between novelist John Steinbeck and his editor-publisher Pascal Covici. His book, *Steinbeck and Covici: The Story of a Friendship*, was published in 1979 and has never been out-of-print. It has long been considered one of the seminal books in Steinbeck scholarship.

Fensch has also published the secret correspondence between John Kennedy and Nikita Khrushchev, under the title *The Kennedy-Khrushchev Letters;* the secret files of the U-2 spy airplane program, published under the title *The C.I.A. and the U-2 Program, 1954-1974*, and the formerly secret *FBI Files on the Lindbergh Baby Kidnapping*, all published in 2001.

He has published other secret files books and a variety of nonfiction books, including several biographies. He lives outside Richmond, Virginia.

www.ingramcontent.com/pod-product-compliance
Lightning Source LLC
Chambersburg PA
CBHW060309240426
43661CB00059B/2708